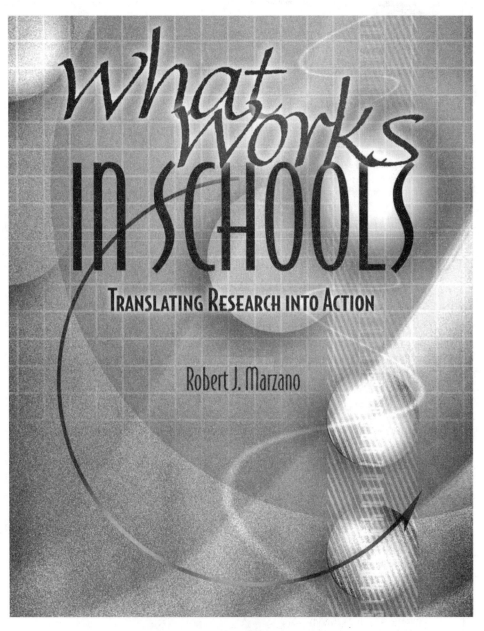

What works IN SCHOOLS

TRANSLATING RESEARCH INTO ACTION

Robert J. Marzano

ASSOCIATION FOR SUPERVISION AND CURRICULUM DEVELOPMENT
ALEXANDRIA, VIRGINIA USA

®

Association for Supervision and Curriculum Development
1703 N. Beauregard St. • Alexandria, VA 22311-1714 USA
Telephone: 800-933-2723 or 703-578-9600 • Fax: 703-575-5400
Web site: http://www.ascd.org • E-mail: member@ascd.org
Author guidelines: www.ascd.org/write

Library of Congress Cataloging-in-Publication Data
Marzano, Robert J.
  What works in schools : translating research into action / Robert J. Marzano.
    p. cm.
Includes bibliographical references and index.
  ISBN 0-87120-717-6 (alk. paper)
 1. School improvement programs. 2. Teaching. 3. Academic achievement. I. Title.

LB2822.82 .M37 2003
371.2'001--dc21
                                        2002015522

what works in schools
Translating Research into Action

List of Figures in Chapter 1

INTRODUCING THE
BEST OF TIMES

Perhaps now more than ever the quotation from Charles Dickens's *A Tale of Two Cities* describes the position of public education: "It was the best of times, it was the worst of times." Actually, given the criticisms of public education, some of those directly involved in K through 12 education might argue that the only relevant part is "it was the worst of times." This book, however, is about *possibility*, specifically the possibility that K–12 education is on the brink of the best of times if we so choose. My premise is that if we follow the guidance offered from 35 years of research, we can enter an era of unprecedented effectiveness for the public practice of education—one in which the vast majority of schools can be highly effective in promoting student learning. As subsequent chapters detail, any school in the United States can operate at advanced levels of effectiveness—if it is willing to implement what is known about effective schooling. Before examining this possibility, let us consider the

criticisms of U.S. education—the argument for the worst of times.

The Case for the Worst of Times

The history of public education, particularly during the 20th century, is rife with criticisms (Tyack, 1974; Tyack & Tobin, 1994). Indeed, the century began with a massive effort to improve K–12 schooling, which was spearheaded by the Carnegie Foundation for the Advancement of Teaching. One significant aspect of that reform effort was the establishment of the "Carnegie unit" as the uniform standard for defining academic achievement.

Criticisms of public education and their accompanying reform efforts flourished for the first five decades of the century. However, it is the criticisms and reform efforts of the second half of the century that most profoundly affect us today. The first of these was spawned by the launching of

Sputnik in 1957. Shocked by this event, the U.S. public began to question the rigor and viability of our schools. Indeed, influential figures such as Admiral Hyman Rickover (1959) forwarded the position that public education was weakening the intellectual capacity of our students. Rickover's book, *Education and Freedom*, made direct links between the security of the nation and the quality of education.

In the 1960s there was no hiatus from the harsh criticisms of public education. In fact, the study that arguably produced the most concrete evidence of the failures or inadequacies of public education was conducted in that decade. It was in the context of President Johnson's "war on poverty" that the Civil Rights Act of 1964, a cornerstone of Johnson's initiative, specified that the Commissioner of Education should conduct a nationwide survey of the availability of educational opportunity. The effort mounted was impressive even by today's standards. More than 640,000 students in grades 1, 3, 6, 9, and 12 took achievement and aptitude tests and were categorized into six ethnic and cultural groups. Sixty thousand teachers in 4,000 schools completed questionnaires about their background and training. The resulting report, *Equality in Educational Opportunity*, was published in July 1966. Although the work of a team of researchers (Coleman, Campbell, Hobson, McPartland, Mood, Weinfield, & York, 1966), it has become known as the "Coleman report" in deference to its senior author, James Coleman. To say the least, the findings did not paint a flattering picture of public education:

Taking all of these results together, one implication stands above all: that schools bring lit-

tle to bear on a child's achievement that is independent of his background and general social context; and that this very lack of an independent effect means that the inequalities imposed on children by their home, neighborhood, and peer environment are carried along to become the inequalities with which they confront life at the end of school. (p. 325)

The report had a profound impact on public perceptions of schooling in the United States (Madaus, Airasian, & Kellaghan, 1980; Madaus, Kellaghan, Rakow, & King, 1979). Specifically, it dealt a veritable deathblow to the belief that schools could overcome students' backgrounds. Perhaps the most publicized finding from the report was that schools account for only about 10 percent of the variance in student achievement—the other 90 percent is accounted for by student background characteristics.

The findings in the Coleman report were corroborated when Christopher Jencks and his colleagues published *Inequality: A Reassessment of the Effects of Family and Schooling in America*, which was based on a reanalysis of Coleman's data (Jencks et al., 1972). Among the findings articulated in the Jencks study were the following:

- Schools do little to lessen the gap between rich students and poor students.
- Schools do little to lessen the gap between more and less able students.
- Student achievement is primarily a function of one factor—the background of the student.
- Little evidence exists that education reform can improve a school's influence on student achievement.

The conclusions stated and implied in the Coleman and Jencks studies painted a sobering picture of U.S. education. If schools have little chance of overcoming the influence of students' background characteristics, why put any energy into school reform?

Although the nation viewed public education poorly in the 1960s and 1970s, the 1980s were even darker times. As Peter Dow (1991) explains in his book *Schoolhouse Politics: Lessons from the Sputnik Era*:

> In 1983 educators and the general public were treated to the largest outpouring of criticism of the nation's schools in history, eclipsing even the complaints of the early 1950s. Nearly fifty reports totaling more than six thousand pages voiced a new wave of national concern about the troubled state of American education. They spoke of the fragmented state of the school curriculum, the failure to define any coherent, accepted body of learning, the excessive emphasis on teaching isolated facts, and the lack of attention to higher order skills and concepts. They called for more individualism of instruction, the development of a closer relationship between teachers and students, and methods that encourage the active participation of the student in the learning process. (p. 243)

Again, a single report laid the foundation for the outpouring of criticism. Without a doubt, *A Nation at Risk: The Imperative for Educational Reform*, issued by the National Commission on Excellence in Education, was considered by some as proof that K–12 education had indeed devolved to a state of irreversible disrepair. The report noted that "the educational foundations of our society are presently being eroded by a rising tide of mediocrity that threatens our very future as a nation and a people" (National Commission on Excellence in Education, 1983, p. 5). To punctuate the importance of the message about public education, the report claimed that "we have, in effect, been committing an act of unthinking, unilateral disarmament" (p. 5).

The effects of the report were profound, due in no small part to the fact that it was perceived as the sanctioned opinion of the White House. As David Berliner and Bruce Biddle note in their book *The Manufactured Crisis: Myths, Frauds, and the Attack on America's Public Schools* (Berliner & Biddle, 1995):

> . . . in 1983, amid much fanfare, the White House released an incendiary document highly critical of American education. Entitled *A Nation at Risk*, this work was prepared by a prestigious committee under the direction of then Secretary of Education Terrell Bell and was endorsed in a speech by President Ronald Reagan. (p. 3)

The effects of *A Nation at Risk* persisted through the 1990s. Indeed, some authors (Bennett, 1992; Finn, 1991) cite the report as one of the primary sources of evidence for public education's decline.

Although *A Nation at Risk* was sufficient to cast a negative shadow on education throughout the 1990s, a newer study, the Third International Mathematics and Science Study (TIMSS), was interpreted as evidence of the ineffectiveness of U.S. education. It involved a large-scale, cross-national comparison of the education systems in 41 countries. TIMSS researchers examined mathematics and science curricula, instructional practices, and school and social factors. In general, U.S. 4th grade students performed moderately well when compared to students of similar ages in other countries; 8th grade students less so; and 12th grade students performed quite poorly. Both technical reports of TIMSS (Schmidt, McKnight, & Raizen, 1996; U.S. Department of Education, National Center for Educational Statistics, 1998) and commentaries on TIMSS (Stevenson & Stigler, 1992; Stigler & Hiebert, 1999) interpret the results as evidence of a dire need for public education reform. Perhaps at the extreme, Chester Finn (1998), in a provocative article in the *Wall Street Journal* entitled "Why America Has the World's Dimmest Bright Kids," described the findings in the following way:

> Today the U.S. Department of Education officially releases the damning data, which come from the Third International Mathematics and Science Study, a set of tests administered to half a million youngsters in 41 countries in 1995. But the results have trickled out. We learned that our fourth-graders do pretty well compared with the rest of the world, and our eighth-graders' performance is middling to poor. Today we learn that our 12th-graders occupy the international cellar. And that's not even counting Asian lands like Singapore, Korea and Japan that trounced our kids in younger grades. They chose not to participate in this study. (p. A22)

Given the criticisms of public education that have flourished over the last half of the last century, it is clear that those who believe that it is the worst of times for public education have plenty of evidence for their position. Indeed, it is hard to imagine an argument for the position that it can be the best of times for public education.

The Case for the Best of Times

My case for the position that public education is at the dawn of the best of times is not necessarily based on refuting the reports mentioned. Such arguments have been made for *A Nation at Risk* and, to some degree, TIMSS. Perhaps the most noteworthy of these arguments are found in David Berliner and Bruce Biddle's (1995) *The Manufactured Crisis: Myths, Frauds, and the Attack on America's Public Schools* and Gerald Bracey's (1997) *Setting the Record Straight: Responses to Misconceptions about Public Education in the United States*. These works take a rather aggressive stance that past research has been either misleading or misinterpreted to paint an unwarranted negative perspective of U.S. education. Although I do not share this view entirely, both works present compelling arguments and provide perspectives with which all educators should be familiar.

My basic position is quite simple: Schools can have a tremendous impact on student achievement if they follow the direction provided by the research. As evidence for this position, I will not use examples of specific schools mainly because other writers have already done so (see Darling-Hammond, 1997a; Reeves, 2002; Schmoker, 1999, 2001). Indeed, perhaps the most compelling evidence for this conclusion is the impressive list of schools that have "beat the odds" compiled by Education Trust (Barth et al., 1999). These high-poverty schools are referred to as "beat the odds" schools because they sport impressive academic achievement from students whose background characteristics would logically preclude it. Rather than present specific examples, I present evidence based on my attempts to synthesize the extant research over the last 35 years, which I assert has provided clear and unprecedented insight into the nature of schooling. I have presented technical and nontechnical descriptions of these efforts in several publications (Marzano, 1998a, 2000a; Marzano, Pickering, & Pollock, 2001). Although my case is made in detail in the chapters to come, it begins with three basic assertions.

Assertion 1: Even those studies that have been interpreted as evidence that schools do not significantly affect student achievement do, in fact, support the potential impact of schools when interpreted properly.

The Coleman report was arguably the first high-visibility study of the second half of the 20th century to advance the position that schools have little impact on student achievement. Recall that its fundamental finding was that schools account for only about 10 percent of the variance in student achievement—a finding that was corroborated later by Jencks and colleagues (1972). Understanding the problems with using percentage of variance as the measure of a school's impact is the key to understanding how these findings could actually support the position that schools do make a difference. (For a technical discussion of issues regarding percentage of variance, see Technical Note 1, pp. 187–188.)

In nonstatistical terms, findings like those from the Coleman report are frequently interpreted in the following way: Assume you are examining the academic achievement of a group of 1,000 8th grade students who attend five different middle schools—200 in each school. Also assume that these students vary in their achievement scores—some have very high scores, some have very low scores, many have scores near the average. Taken at face value, the findings from the Coleman report imply that only about 10 percent of the differences in scores from student to student (more accurately, the squared differences) are a function of the quality of the schools these students attend. In other words, going to the best of the five schools as opposed to the worst of the five schools generates only about 10 percent of the differences in students' scores. What accounts for the other 90 percent of the differences in scores? Coleman and others (1966) concluded it is the background of the students.

How can these findings possibly be interpreted as evidence that schools can have a positive and significant influence on student achievement? Since the Coleman report was published, statisticians have found that using percentage of variance as an indication of a factor's importance is not the most useful way of interpreting research findings on academic achievement. In fact, as is the case with the Coleman report, this technique can paint an unnecessarily gloomy picture of a school's possible effects on student achievement.

Researchers Robert Rosenthal and Donald Rubin (1982) devised a more practical way to interpret research findings reported in terms of percentage of explained variance. Their approach is referred to as the Binomial Effect Size Display or BESD. (For a technical and more detailed explanation of the BESD, see Technical Note 2, pp. 189–190.) To illustrate Rosenthal and Rubin's BESD, consider Figure

FIGURE 1.1		
Reinterpretation of Coleman's Findings Using the BESD		
Group	Outcome	
	Percentage of Students Who Pass the Test	Percentage of Students Who Fail the Test
Effective Schools	65.8%	34.2%
Ineffective Schools	34.2%	65.8%
BESD = Binomial Effect Size Display		

1.1, which is based on Coleman's findings that schools account for only 10 percent of the variance in student achievement.

Although schools would be better described as representing many gradations of effectiveness from highly ineffective to highly effective, Rosenthal and Rubin's approach requires placing schools into one of those two broad categories. That is, a school is classified as being either effective or ineffective. Rosenthal and Rubin's approach also requires assuming that the students in the effective and the ineffective schools are given a test on which you would normally expect half of the students to pass and half to fail. Given these assumptions, we can now interpret Figure 1.1. The columns in Figure 1.1 are labeled "percentage of students who pass the test" and "percentage of students who fail the test." In general, in the effective schools, 65.8 percent of students would pass the test, and only 34.2 percent would fail the test. Conversely, in general, in the ineffective schools only 34.2 percent of the students would pass the test, and 65.8 percent would fail it.

This perspective paints a far different picture of the findings from the Coleman report. In effective schools almost twice the percentage of students would pass the test (on which half are expected to fail and half to pass) than in the ineffective schools. The logical conclusion to draw from the Coleman report, then, is that effective schools **do** make a difference in student achievement.

Assertion 2: The research on the effectiveness of schools *considered as a whole* paints a very positive image of their impact on student achievement.

The Coleman report and the Jencks follow-up study were the first in a series of studies to explore the impact of schools. Scores of similar studies have been conducted since. In a review of some of this research, Charles Teddlie, David Reynolds, and Pam Sammons (2000) indicate that many studies report that schools account for more variance in student achievement than Coleman's meager 10 percent. I have also synthesized much of that research (Marzano, 2000a). I analyzed the findings from 10 high-visibility studies (Bosker, 1992; Byrk & Raudenbush, 1992; Coleman et al., 1966; Creemers, 1994; Jencks et al., 1972; Luyten, 1994; Madaus et al., 1979; Rowe & Hill, 1994; Scheerens & Bosker, 1997; Stringfield & Teddlie, 1989) and discovered that the average finding was that schools account for 20 percent of the variance in student achievement—twice as much as that reported by Coleman. Why were the Coleman findings so low? George Madaus and his colleagues (1979) and Berliner and Biddle (1995) discussed this in detail. In brief, although Coleman and colleagues had access to student scores on standardized academic achievement tests, they chose to use a general measure of verbal ability (focused on vocabulary knowledge) as the primary outcome measure. This created a situation in which student background variables almost by definition were highly correlated with student achievement. Madaus and colleagues (1979) explain

> . . . the construct "verbal ability" in the Coleman study has become equated with "school achievement" and the results have been generalized to the now popular myth that school facilities, resources, personnel, and curricula do not have a strong independent effect on achievement. Coleman's findings have been interpreted in the widest and most damaging sense. . . . To assert that schools bring little influence to bear on a child's general verbal ability that is independent of his background and general social context is not the same as asserting that schools bring little influence to bear on pupils' achievement in a specific college preparatory physics course. . . . The fact that home background variables seem to be vastly more influential in explaining verbal ability should not preclude or cloud any expectations we have that schools should have some independent effect on traditional curriculum areas which are systematically and explicitly treated as part of the instructional process. (p. 210)

The Coleman researchers' use of verbal ability as the primary dependent measure resulted in an underestimate of the effect of schools on student achievement.

How does the picture change if we use the updated estimate of 20 percent? To answer this question, we turn again to Rosenthal and Rubin's BESD approach in Figure 1.2 (p. 8).

As Figure 1.2 illustrates, the updated research indicates that effective schools generally have a fairly substantial impact on student achievement. Specifically, if a test on which you would normally expect half the students to pass and half the students to fail were given to students in effective schools, 72.4 percent of those students would pass the test and the remainder would fail. In the ineffective schools, however, only 27.6 percent of the students would pass the test. In the aggregate, then, the research indicates that schools, when run effectively, make a big difference in student achievement. Again, to quote Madaus and others (1979), the findings from studies that use appropriate student achievement measures "provide strong evidence for the differential effectiveness of schools; differences in school characteristics do contribute to differences in achievement." (p. 223)

Assertion 3: The schools that are highly effective produce results that almost entirely overcome the effects of student background.

Assertions 1 & 2 are based on the convention of classifying schools into two broad and contrived categories—effective schools and ineffective schools. Given that there are about 92,000 public schools in the United

Group	Outcome	
	Percentage of Students Who Pass the Test	Percentage of Students Who Fail the Test
Effective Schools	72.4%	27.6%
Ineffective Schools	27.6%	72.4%

FIGURE 1.2

Effective Versus Ineffective Schools, Assuming 20 Percent of Variance

States (National Center for Educational Statistics, 2002), we can assume that they approximate a normal distribution in terms of effectiveness, as depicted in Figure 1.3.

Let's consider those schools to the far right of the distribution in Figure 1.3—those schools at the 99th percentile in terms of their effectiveness. What effect do these schools have on students' achievement? Using the BESD approach, we find that 84.7 percent of the students in those schools would pass a test on which we would normally expect half the students to pass and half the students to fail. (The explanation for this is presented in Technical Note 3, p. 190). This would be true *regardless of the background of the students who attend the school.* Specifically, these schools provide interventions that are designed to overcome student background characteristics that might impede learning. These interventions are detailed in Section III of this book. For now, it is sufficient to say that this is a remarkable possibility—one that provides great hope for public education.

Research in the last 35 years demonstrates that effective schools can have a profound impact on student achievement. The remaining chapters articulate the guidelines provided by that research. Before articulating and discussing those guidelines, however, we must consider another perspective: Although the research provides clear guidance regarding effective schooling, is the U.S. public education system up to the challenge of following it?

Are Public Schools Up to the Challenge of Research-Based Reform?

In 1990 John Chubb and Terry Moe authored an influential book entitled *Politics, Markets and America's Schools* (Chubb & Moe, 1990). After conducting a study that involved more than 400 high schools and 10,000 high school teachers, Chubb and Moe reached some of the same conclusions that I have:

> All things being equal, a student in an effectively organized school achieves at least a half-year more than a student in an ineffectively organized school over the last two years of high school. If this difference can be extrapolated to the normal four-year high school experience, an effectively organized school may increase the achievement of its students by more than one full year. That is a substantial school effect indeed. (p. 140)

Although this book asserts that public educators are up to the challenge of implementing

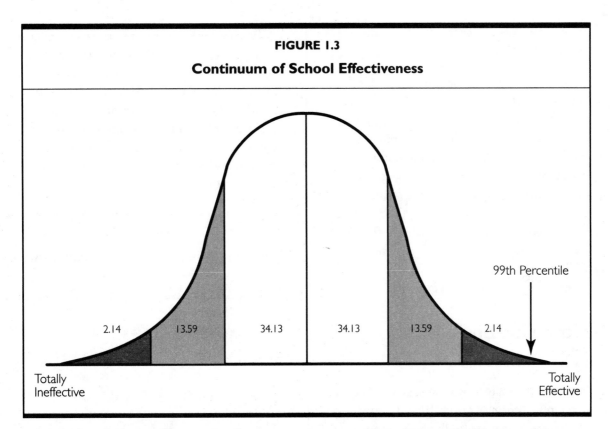

FIGURE 1.3

Continuum of School Effectiveness

99th Percentile

2.14   13.59   34.13   34.13   13.59   2.14

Totally
Ineffective

Totally
Effective

what we know about effective schooling, Chubb and Moe assert that bureaucratic underpinnings of public schools doom to failure any attempts at school reform:

> . . . we can only believe that the current "revolution" in American public education will prove a disappointment. It might have succeeded had it actually been a revolution, but it was not and was never intended to be, despite the lofty rhetoric. (p. 228)

They ultimately conclude that school choice (presumably in the form of vouchers) is the only viable way to implement the findings from the research.

Chubb and Moe offer compelling evidence. In brief, they demonstrate that the more district-level control or constraints put

on a school, the lower the chances of the school being organized in an effective manner. According to Chubb and Moe, centralized control over personnel can be particularly debilitating to a school's effectiveness:

> Among the reasons why direct external control may interfere with the development of an effective school, perhaps the most important is the potentially debilitating influence of external control over personnel. If principals have little or no control over who teaches in their schools, they are likely to be saddled with a number of teachers, perhaps even many teachers, whom they regard as bad fits. In an organization that works best through shared decisionmaking [sic] and delegated authority, a staff that is in conflict with the leader and with itself is a serious problem. . . . Personnel policies

that promote such conflict may be a school's greatest external burden. (p. 152)

It is a small step from here to the necessity of vouchers and charter schools. Much of Chubb and Moe's argument has been criticized as "ideologically driven" (Berliner & Biddle, 1995, p. 75) as opposed to objectively driven by research results, but I believe their point is well taken. In effect, we stand at a crossroads—will we implement the research-based guidelines to produce schools that don't just work but that work remarkably well? To do so requires a powerful commitment to change the status quo.

How This Book Is Organized

Following the categorization scheme used by many researchers (Carroll, 1963; Cotton, 1995; Creemers, 1994; Elberts & Stone, 1988; Goldstein, 1997; Raudenbush & Byrk, 1988; Raudenbush & Willms, 1995; Rowe, Hill & Holmes-Smith, 1995; Scheerens, 1992; Scheerens & Bosker, 1997; van der Werf, 1997; Walberg, 1984; Wright, Horn, & Sanders, 1997), I've organized the results of 35 years of research into three general factors that influence student academic achievement: (1) school-level factors, (2) teacher-level factors, and (3) student-level factors.

School-level factors are primarily a function of school policy and schoolwide decisions and initiatives (a guaranteed and viable curriculum, challenging goals and effective feedback, parent and community involvement, a safe and orderly environment, and collegiality and professionalism).

Teacher-level factors are primarily under the control of individual teachers (specific instructional strategies, classroom management techniques, and classroom curriculum design). **Student-level factors** are generally associated with student background (home environment, learned intelligence and background knowledge, and motivation). Figure 1.4 depicts this model.

FIGURE 1.4
Factors Affecting Student Achievement

Factor	Example
School	• Guaranteed and viable curriculum • Challenging goals and effective feedback • Parent and community involvement • Safe and orderly environment • Collegiality and professionalism
Teacher	• Instructional strategies • Classroom management • Classroom curriculum design
Student	• Home atmosphere • Learned intelligence and background knowledge • Motivation

Implicit in Figure 1.4 is the notion that the school (as opposed to the district) is the proper focus for reform. Indeed, this is a consistent conclusion in the research literature (Scheerens & Bosker, 1997; Reynolds & Teddlie, 2000; Wang, Haertel & Walberg, 1993). While I share Chubb and Moe's concern that district-level central administration can sometimes impede school reform, I believe that the current structure of public education is malleable enough to benefit from the changes recommended in this book.

In keeping with the organization depicted in Figure 1.4, this book is divided into the following major sections. Section I deals with the five school-level factors, Section II deals with the three teacher-level factors, and Section III deals with the three student-level factors. Finally, Section IV addresses how a school might use the information in the three previous sections to engage in substantive change.

Summary

Thirty-five years of research provides remarkably clear guidance as to the steps schools can take to be highly effective in enhancing student achievement. Although the guidance from the research is clear, researchers and the public continue to debate whether public education is up to the task of following it. Following the lead of other studies, I have organized the research into three broad categories: school-level factors, teacher-level factors, and student-level factors.

Section I

SCHOOL-LEVEL FACTORS

List of Figures in Section I

THE SCHOOL-LEVEL FACTORS

We begin our discussion with an exploration of the five school-level factors introduced in Figure 1.4 (p. 10). I refer to them as school-level factors because, for the most part, they are under the jurisdiction of the school as a whole. That is, changes in these factors are usually a result of formal or informal policy decisions.

Anyone familiar with the last 35 years of research on school effectiveness is aware that there have been many proposed lists of school-level factors. In this chapter, I collapse those previous lists into these five factors:

1. Guaranteed and viable curriculum
2. Challenging goals and effective feedback
3. Parent and community involvement
4. Safe and orderly environment
5. Collegiality and professionalism

These categories represent the most current thinking on school-level factors, and the order in which I list them represents their order of impact on student achievement. That is, a guaranteed and viable curriculum is the school-level factor with the most impact on student achievement, followed by challenging goals and effective feedback, and so on down the list. In making my case for this order, I use the results of five previous attempts to synthesize the research on school-level factors (although more proposed lists could have been included with the same results). For more extensive discussions on these syntheses, see Good & Brophy, 1986; Marzano, 2000a; Scheerens & Bosker, 1997; Reynolds & Teddlie, 2000. In constructing my five school-level factors, I have considered only those that can be addressed without a drastic addition of resources. By definition, then, interventions that would require a drastic increase in the time spent in school (e.g., lengthening the school year or implementing after-school programs) or additional personnel (e.g., lower teacher-to-student ratios or tutoring for every student) or equipment not readily available at the present time (e.g., personal computers for every student) are not addressed in this book. Although these would probably have a significant impact on student achievement, my emphasis is on school reform efforts that can be implemented within the general boundaries of the resources available.

School-Level Factors: A Comparison Across Researchers

The most famous list of school-level factors came out of the school effectiveness research from the 1970s. (For a review see Good & Brophy, 1986; Marzano, 2000a.) Some of the well-known researchers of that era were Ron Edmonds (Edmonds, 1979a, 1979b, 1979c, 1981a, 1981b), Michael Rutter (Rutter, Maughan, Mortimore, Ouston & Smith, 1979), and Wilbur Brookover (Brookover, Schweitzer, Schneider, Beady, Flood, & Wisenbaker, 1978; Brookover, Beady, Flood, Schweitzer, & Wisenbaker, 1979). Of this list, Edmonds is the figurehead of the school effectiveness movement. As Good and Brophy (1986) note

> Until his untimely death in 1983 [Edmonds] had been one of the key figures in the school effectiveness movement ... Edmonds, more than anyone, had been responsible for communication of the belief that *schools* can and do make a difference. (p. 582)

These school-level factors were associated with the school effectiveness movement of the 1970s:

- strong administrative leadership,
- an emphasis on basic skill acquisition,

- high expectations for student achievement,
- a safe and orderly atmosphere conducive to learning, and
- frequent monitoring of student progress.

Although there is some variation from researcher to researcher (see Purkey & Smith, 1982, for a discussion), these five "correlates" of effective schools (so named because of their strong correlation with student achievement) became the focal point of reform in the 1970s and early 1980s. Although it is probably more accurate to credit these correlates to the entire school effectiveness movement, for ease of discussion, I attribute them to Edmonds in this and subsequent chapters.

Another list of school-level factors that has been widely used is one developed by Daniel Levine and Lawrence Lezotte (1990). In their review of the research literature, they relied heavily on case studies using what might be thought of as an "outlier design," for example, focusing on the characteristics of the top 25 percent of schools as opposed to the bottom 25 percent. Their analysis produced the following factors:

- productive climate and culture,
- focus on central learning skills,
- appropriate monitoring,
- practice-oriented staff development,
- strong leadership,
- salient parent involvement, and
- high expectations and requirements.

I should note that the list by Levine and Lezotte included effective instructional arrangement and implementation. In this discussion, it is classified as a teacher-level factor.

Pam Sammons and her colleagues (Sammons, 1999; Sammons, Hillman, & Mortimore, 1995) performed an analysis similar to that by Levine and Lezotte (1990). However, they relied less on case study evidence and included more quantitative studies such as the British Junior School Project (Mortimore et al., 1988). Their review produced the following school-level factors:

- professional leadership,
- concentration on teaching and learning,
- shared vision and goals,
- a learning environment,
- high expectations,
- positive reinforcement,
- monitoring progress,
- pupil rights and expectations,
- home-school partnership, and
- a learning organization.

Again, the complete list contains purposeful teaching as a factor, but I've classified that among the teacher-level factors.

From a quantitative perspective, one of the most rigorous reviews of the research on school-level factors was conducted by Jaap Scheerens and Roel Bosker (Scheerens & Bosker, 1997; Scheerens, 1992; Bosker, 1992; Bosker & Witziers, 1995, 1996). They identified eight school-level factors. Perhaps their major contribution to the previous work was that they were able to rank order these factors in terms of their impact on student achievement. (See Figure 2.1.)

The Scheerens and Bosker ranking was the first of its kind and significantly increased our understanding of the school-level factors associated with enhanced academic achievement.

FIGURE 2.1

Ranking of School-Level Factors Based on Scheerens and Bosker

Rank	Factor
1	Time
2	Monitoring
3	Pressure to Achieve
4	Parental Involvement
5	School Climate
6	Content Coverage
7	School Leadership
8	Cooperation

Note: Scheerens and Bosker included a ninth factor in their list—homework. In the context of the present discussion, however, it is more of a teacher-level factor than a school-level factor. For a discussion, see Marzano, 2000a.

Source: Scheerens, J., & Bosker, R. (1997). The foundations of educational effectiveness. New York: Elsevier.

The final review of the research that forms the basis of the five school-level factors presented in this book is one I conducted (Marzano, 2000a). My review was basically a reanalysis and updating of the review by Scheerens and Bosker. The findings from this review are reported in Figure 2.2 (p. 18).

FIGURE 2.2

Ranking of School-Level Factors Based on Marzano, 2000a

Rank	Factor
1	Opportunity to learn
2	Time
3	Monitoring
4	Pressure to Achieve
5	Parental Involvement
6	School Climate
7	Leadership
8	Cooperation

Source: Marzano, R. J. (2000a). *A new era of school reform: Going where the research takes us.* Aurora, CO: Mid-continent Research for Education and Learning. (ERIC Document Reproduction Service No. ED454255)

The basic difference between the lists in Figures 2.1 and 2.2 is that content coverage from the Scheerens and Bosker study has been renamed "opportunity to learn" and its rank elevated from sixth to first. This is not a trivial change. As I explain in Chapter 3, the research on opportunity to learn demonstrates its primacy in terms of impact on student achievement.

Although the five lists of school-level factors might seem somewhat disparate at first glance, careful examination reveals that,

except for wording differences, they address the same basic factors. Figure 2.3 depicts the commonality in these different lists and demonstrates how I have collapsed them into the five school-level factors that are the subject of the next five chapters.

An examination of Figure 2.3 illustrates how different researchers use slightly different terms to describe the same factors. For example, consider the following for "challenging goals and effective feedback":

- "High expectation for student achievement" and "frequent monitoring of student progress" from Edmonds
- "Appropriate monitoring" and "high expectations and requirements" from Levine and Lezotte
- "High expectations" and "monitoring progress" from Sammons
- "Monitoring" and "pressure to achieve" from Scheerens and Bosker
- "Monitoring" and "pressure to achieve" from Marzano

All these examples address setting academic goals for all students that do not underestimate their potential and that provide feedback as to progress. Therefore, I have organized them into the single category "challenging goals and effective feedback." As a result, Figure 2.3 does not convey the depth or complexity of the factors identified by other researchers. For example, in Figure 2.3, I have classified Sammons's "positive reinforcement" as an aspect of a safe and orderly environment, which of course is one of my five school-level factors. In fact, Sammons defines this factor as involving clear and fair discipline as well as feedback. Part of Sammons's factor

FIGURE 2.3						
Comparing School-Level Factors Across Researchers						
The School-Level Factors	Rank*	Marzano	Scheerens and Bosker	Sammons	Levine and Lezotte	Edmonds
Guaranteed and Viable Curriculum	1	Opportunity to Learn	Content Coverage	Concentration on Teaching and Learning	Focus on Central Learning Skills	Emphasis on Basic Skill Acquisition
		Time	Time			
Challenging Goals and Effective Feedback	2	Monitoring	Monitoring	High Expectations	High Expectations and Requirements	High Expectations for Student Success
		Pressure to Achieve	Pressure to Achieve	Monitoring Progress	Appropriate Monitoring	Frequent Monitoring of Student Progress
Parental and Community Involvement	3	Parental Involvement	Parental Involvement	Home-School Partnership	Salient Parental Involvement	
Safe and Orderly Environment	4	School Climate	School Climate	A Learning Environment	Productive Climate and Culture	Safe and Orderly Atmosphere Conducive to Learning
				Positive Reinforcement		
				Pupil Rights and Expectations		
Collegiality and Professionalism	5	Leadership	Leadership	Professional Leadership	Strong Leadership	Strong Administrative Leadership
				Shared Vision and Goals		
		Cooperation	Cooperation	A Learning Organization	Practice-Oriented Staff Development	

*Author has ranked these factors by order of impact on student achievement

of positive reinforcement, then, would fall under my school-level factor of challenging goals and effective feedback. In short, Figure 2.3 is not a perfectly accurate correlation of the work of others with my five school-level factors. It does, however, convey the basic message—that school-level factors identified by several researchers generally fall into five basic categories.

My five school-level factors are listed in rank order in terms of their impact on student achievement, which is derived from the ranking in *A New Era of School Reform: Going Where the Research Takes Us* (Marzano, 2000a). Specifically, the first school-level factor—a guaranteed and viable curriculum—is a composite of "opportunity to learn" and "time," which hold the ranks of first and second respectively. The second factor—challenging goals and effective feedback—is a composite of "monitoring" and "pressure to achieve," which hold the ranks of third and fourth respectively.

Although I stand firmly behind this rank ordering, I do not mean to imply that those factors with lower rank are not critical to the effective running of a school. Those factors with weaker statistical relationships with student achievement positively impact achievement up to a certain point only. Such relationships are typically referred to as nonlinear. As Good and Brophy (1986) explain: "Many of the school effects variables probably have a nonlinear relationship with outcomes" (p. 588). For example, consider collegiality and professionalism, which is ranked last of the five school-level factors. Taken at face value, you might conclude that establishing an atmosphere of collegiality and professionalism is not critically important to student achievement. However, if it has a nonlinear relationship with achievement, it could mean that it is highly important to student achievement up to a point where the relationship tapers off. This hypothesis not only makes good statistical sense, but it also makes good common sense. An atmosphere of collegiality and professionalism among teachers and administrators in a school might be a necessary condition for student achievement. But after a certain level of collegiality

and professionalism has been attained, an increase in this factor has no further effect on achievement.

The absence of the factor "leadership" from my list of school-level factors is not an oversight, although it was mentioned explicitly in the other five lists. Virtually all descriptions of leadership were either very narrow or so broad as to encompass virtually all other categories. For example, in the Scheerens and Bosker (1997) review, leadership was rather narrowly focused on what might be referred to as quality control. This narrow definition probably accounts for the fact that it is rated next to last in their analysis. In contrast, Levine and Lezotte (1990) define leadership as encompassing the following elements: high expenditure of time and energy for school improvement; superior instructional leadership; frequent, personal monitoring of school activities and "sense-making"; and acquisition of resources. Such broad descriptions of leadership were also characteristic of the interpretations by Sammons and Edmonds. I have chosen to exclude leadership from the list of school-level factors. Its proper place is as an overarching variable that impacts the effective implementation of the school-level factors, the teacher-level factors, and the student-level factors. See Chapter 18 for information on the critical role of leadership in school reform.

Each of the next five chapters in this section addresses one school-level factor. In each chapter, the research pertaining to the factor is first reviewed and discussed. Then, a set of recommended "action steps" is described and exemplified.

Summary

This chapter has introduced the five school-level factors. In addition to showing how they encompass the findings from five previous research synthesis efforts, I have provided a rationale for my rank ordering of their impact on student achievement.

A Guaranteed and Viable Curriculum

The first school-level factor is a "guaranteed and viable curriculum." I rank this as the first factor, having the most impact on student achievement. As indicated in Figure 2.3 (p. 19), a guaranteed and viable curriculum is primarily a combination of my factors "opportunity to learn" and "time" (Marzano, 2000a). Both have strong correlations with academic achievement, yet they are so interdependent that they constitute one factor.

Opportunity to Learn

Opportunity to learn (OTL) has the strongest relationship with student achievement of all school-level factors identified in Marzano (2000a). It was first introduced to the research literature more than 30 years ago by the International Association for the Evaluation of Educational Achievement (Wilkins, 1997) when it became a component of the First, and then later, the Second International Mathematics Study (FIMS and SIMS, respectively) (Burstein, 1992; Husen, 1967a, 1967b). Apparently, OTL began as an afterthought in FIMS when researchers became concerned that all students might not have had an equal opportunity to learn the items being used to assess their mathematics achievement (Wilkins, 1997). Consequently, various measures of OTL were devised and its relationship to mathematics achievement examined. The findings, which seem self-evident now, were somewhat of a surprise to the FIMS researchers as indicated by the following quote from a FIMS technical report (Husen, 1967b):

> One of the factors which may influence scores on an achievement examination is whether or not students have had an opportunity to study a particular topic or learn how to solve a particular type of problem presented by the test. (pp. 162–163)

Within a relatively short period of time, OTL had a profound impact on the thinking of researchers and practitioners alike. According to Jesse Wilkins (1997), "This new idea of OTL changed the course of educational research" (p. 13).

Although OTL was first introduced during FIMS, three types of curricula were identified in SIMS: the *intended curriculum*, the *implemented curriculum*, and the *attained curriculum*. The intended curriculum is content specified by the state, district, or school to be addressed in a particular course or at a particular grade level. The implemented curriculum is content actually delivered by the teacher, and the attained curriculum is content actually learned by students. The discrepancy between the intended curriculum and the implemented curriculum makes OTL a prominent factor in student achievement—a factor that since SIMS has continued to show a very strong relationship with student achievement (Brewer & Stacz, 1996; Herman, Klein, & Abedi, 2000; Robitaille, 1993).

The possible discrepancy between the intended curriculum and the implemented curriculum comes as a surprise to noneducators and educators alike. The surprise is probably because public education provides so much guidance on content standards for specific courses and specific grade levels. The existence of state-level standards documents and district-level or school-level curriculum guides does not necessarily imply that the implemented curriculum and the intended curriculum are identical. E. D. Hirsch, in *The Schools We Need and Why We Don't Have Them* (1996), noted this situation:

> We know, of course, that there exists no national curriculum, but we assume, quite reasonably, that agreement has been reached locally regarding what should be taught to children at each grade level—if not within the whole district, then certainly within an individual school. . . . The idea that there exists a coherent plan for teaching content within the local district, or even within the individual school, is a gravely misleading myth. (p. 26)

Hirsch explains that the notion of a coherent implemented curriculum is simply accepted by most educators as a matter of faith. Upon examination, however, most who hold this notion find that it is a myth. To illustrate, Hirsch relates the following anecdote:

> Recently, a district superintendent told me that for twenty years he had mistakenly assumed each of his schools was determining what would be taught to children at each grade level, but was shocked to find that assumption entirely false; he discovered that no principal in his district could tell him what minimal content each child in a grade was expected to learn. (pp. 26-27)

Although I find Hirsch's solution to this problem flawed (see Marzano, Kendall, & Gaddy, 1999), I strongly agree with his framing of the issue primarily because research supports his assertions. For example, studies (Doyle, 1992; Stodolsky, 1989; Yoon, Burstein, & Gold, n.d.) indicate that even when highly structured textbooks are used as the basis for a curriculum, teachers commonly make independent and idiosyncratic decisions regarding what should be covered and to what extent. This practice frequently creates huge holes in the continuum of content. In their book *The Learning Gap*, Stevenson and Stigler (1992) illustrate the point:

Daunted by the length of most textbooks and knowing that the children's future teachers will be likely to return to the material, American teachers often omit some topics. Different topics are omitted by different teachers thereby making it impossible for the children's later teachers to know what has been covered at earlier grades—they cannot be sure what their students know and do not know. (p. 140)

The concept of OTL, then, is a simple but powerful one—if students do not have the opportunity to learn the content expected of them, there is little chance that they will. OTL addresses the extent to which the curriculum in a school is "guaranteed." This means that states and districts give clear guidance to teachers regarding the content to be addressed in specific courses and at specific grade levels. It also means that individual teachers do not have the option to disregard or replace assigned content.

Time and Viability

A viable curriculum is unattainable without the benefit of time. The content that teachers are expected to address must be adequately covered in the instructional time teachers have available. This might sound obvious, and you might assume that the content identified in state standards documents and district- and school-level curriculum guides fits nicely into the school day. However, this is not the case. To illustrate, researchers at Mid-continent Research for Education and Learning (McREL) identified some 200 standards and 3,093 benchmarks in national- and state-level documents for 14 different subject areas (Kendall & Marzano, 2000). Classroom teach-

ers then estimated that the amount of time it would take to *adequately* address the content articulated in these documents was 15,465 hours (Marzano, Kendall, & Gaddy, 1999).

Just how much time is actually available for instruction?

In general, K–12 schools employ a 180-day school year. However, some noteworthy variations exist. For example, Karweit (1983) found that the number of scheduled school days in the U.S. ranged from 175 to 184 days, with an average of 179. The *Prisoners of Time* study (National Education Commission on Time and Learning, 1994), found that, as of 1994, 11 states permitted school terms of 175 days or less, and only one state required more than 180 days.

The length of the school day is far less standard. Reuter (1963) found that length varied from four to six hours. In the late 1970s, a large-scale study known as the Beginning Teachers Evaluation Study (BTES) found that 2nd graders were in school 5.5 hours, whereas 5th graders were in school for 6.0 hours (Fisher et al., 1978). One study even found that the length of the school day within the same district could vary as much as 45 minutes (Harnischfeger & Wiley, 1978). The 1994 *Prisoners of Time* study reported that, on average, schools offer a six-period day with about 5.6 hours of class time per day.

If we assume that 5.6 hours each day are devoted to classroom time and 180 days are spent in school per year, then K–12 students spend about 13,104 total hours in class (13 years of instruction x 1,008 hours per year). Thus, teachers have a maximum of 13,104 hours to address the 200 standards and 3,093 benchmarks identified by the McREL researchers.

And not all of the available classroom time is actually *used* for instruction. Classroom disruptions, socializing, informal breaks, and other noninstructional activities use up some of the classroom time. Estimates of how much class time is actually devoted to instruction vary widely from a low of 21 percent to a high of 69 percent (Conant, 1973; Marzano & Riley, 1984; National Education Commission on Time and Learning, 1994; Park, 1976). If we take the highest estimate of 69 percent as the upper boundary, we can conclude that of the 13,104 classroom hours theoretically available, only 9,042 hours are actually used for instruction. This comes to about 695.5 hours per year (9,042 hours ÷ 13 years of instruction) or about 3.9 hours per day (695.5 hours ÷ 180 days).

We now have a quantitative basis with which to answer the question: Can the 200 standards and 3,093 benchmarks be taught in the actual time available for instruction? The answer is a resounding *no*! Quite obviously, 15,465 hours of standards do not fit into 9,042 hours of instructional time.

These calculations put a new face on the concept of viability. In the current era of standards-driven curriculum, viability means ensuring that the articulated curriculum content for a given course or given grade level can be adequately addressed in the time available. However, the standards movement as currently implemented has created a situation that violates the viability criterion.

In summary, the first school-level factor is a straightforward one: implement a curriculum that is both guaranteed and viable. Yet, enacting this research-based principle of school reform is one of the most significant challenges currently facing U.S. schools.

Action Steps

I recommend five action steps to implement a guaranteed and viable curriculum.

Action Step 1. Identify and communicate the content considered essential for all students versus that considered supplemental or necessary only for those seeking postsecondary education.

[handwritten marginal note: decide what needs to be taught when]

The preceding discussion dramatically demonstrates that there is simply not enough time in the current system to address all the content in state-mandated standards and benchmarks. One obvious solution is to increase the amount of available instructional time. In fact, from the beginning of the standards movement, professionals from the various subject areas assumed that more time for instruction would be needed. To illustrate, during hearings by the National Education Commission on Time and Learning (1994) regarding what would be required to implement various national-level standards, subject matter representatives made the following comments:

> Arts: "I am here to pound the table for 15 percent of school time devoted to arts instruction," declared Paul Lehman of the Consortium of National Arts Education Association.

> English: "These standards will require a huge amount of time, for both students and teachers," Miles Myers of the National Council of Teachers of English told the Commission.

> Geography: "Implementing our standards will require more time. Geography is hardly taught at all in American schools today," was

the conclusion of Anthony DeSouza of the National Geographic Society.

Science: "There is a consensus view that new standards will require more time," said David Florio of the National Academy of Sciences. (p. 21)

Indeed, this option seems imminently logical especially when one compares the amount of time U.S. students spend in school versus students in countries such as Japan, Germany, and France. Commenting on this disparity, the *Prisoners of Time* study (National Education Commission on Time and Learning, 1994) notes:

No matter how the assumptions underlying the figure are modified, the result is always the same—students abroad are required to work on demanding subject matter at least twice as long [as U.S. students]. (p. 25)

The research generally supports the positive impact of increasing the amount of student instructional time. For example, Herbert Walberg (1997) found a positive relationship between increased instructional time and learning in 97 percent of 130 studies.

Although increasing the amount of instructional time appears to be a straightforward solution, it is an impractical one for U.S. schools, at least at the present time. To illustrate, I have shown that the standards identified across 14 subject areas would require 15,465 hours to address adequately, but there are only 9,042 hours of instruction currently available. This means that schools would have to increase the amount of instructional time by about 71 percent. As the current school year is structured, schooling would have to be extended from kindergarten to grade 21 or

22 to accommodate all the standards and benchmarks in the national documents. In other words, the change required is impractical if not impossible to implement, especially given the extreme cost involved in adding even a few days to the length of a school year (Walberg, 1997).

Even if it were possible to lengthen the school year, it may not be wise to teach all the content identified in the national and state standards documents. This point was dramatically illustrated in the *Third International Mathematics and Science Survey* (TIMSS). Specifically, one conclusion of TIMSS was that U.S. teachers are expected to cover far more content than teachers in other countries. For example, U.S. 4th and 8th grade mathematics textbooks cover between 30 and 35 topics, whereas textbooks in Germany and Japan cover 20 and 10 topics, respectively. Although U.S. 4th, 8th, and 12th grade science textbooks address between 50 and 65 topics, Japanese textbooks cover between 5 and 15 topics, and German textbooks cover 7 topics (at least at the 8th grade level). In short, the TIMSS study indicates that U.S. mathematics textbooks address 175 percent as many topics as do German textbooks and 350 percent as many topics as do Japanese textbooks. The science textbooks used in the United States cover more than nine times as many topics as do German textbooks and more than four times as many topics as do Japanese textbooks. Yet German and Japanese students significantly outperform U.S. students in mathematics and science (Schmidt, McKnight, & Raizen, 1996).

What, then, is a school to do if it cannot lengthen the school year and should not attempt to teach all the standard content?

The answer is straightforward: *Schools should drastically reduce the amount of content teachers are required to address in class.* To illustrate how this might be done, consider the following study I conducted on mathematics content (Marzano, 2002).

My first step was to "unpack" the benchmark statements in the standards document. This is necessary because most benchmark statements contain multiple types of knowledge and skill. The following benchmark from the mathematics standards published by the National Council of Teachers of Mathematics (NCTM) (2000) represents what students should know and be able to do by the end of the 5th grade:

- Develop fluency in adding, subtracting, multiplying, and dividing whole numbers. (p. 392)

This benchmark contains at least four elements that might be the focus of a unified set of lessons: adding whole numbers, subtracting whole numbers, multiplying whole numbers, and dividing whole numbers. When I performed this "unpacking" process on the mathematics standards and benchmarks, I identified 741 "instructional concepts."

This in itself is quite interesting. There are only 241 benchmark statements in the NCTM (2000, pp. 392–402) standards document—a number that appears quite manageable given the 9,042 hours of actual instruction time available. However, this number is misleading because there are more than three times as many instructional concepts that would logically form individual sets of lessons. This is a pattern I have observed in virtually every state and national standards document I have analyzed. Although the number of benchmarks might be small, the actual number of instructional concepts is quite large.

My next step was to present the 741 instructional concepts to 10 mathematics educators. (A school or district performing the same process would undoubtedly use a larger pool of educators. For a discussion of how one district surveyed all members of its community, see Marzano & Kendall, 1996). The question I posed to the educators was quite simple: Which of these 741 instructional concepts are essential for students to know, regardless of whether they intend to go to college? The results are depicted in Figure 3.1, p. 28.

To interpret Figure 3.1, consider the first row of the figure. The first row indicates that 299 concepts (column 2) were identified by 10 educators (column 1) as essential for all high school graduates to know. The percentage of concepts identified as essential (299 out of 741 potential concepts) is 40.4 percent.

Row 2 shows 17 additional math concepts were identified by 9 educators as essential for high school graduates to know. If we combine the results of row 1 and row 2, we find that 316 concepts were identified as essential by nine or more educators (299 + 17 + 316). Column 4 gives that result as a cumulative number of concepts identified as essential by the given number of educators (9 or more educators identified 316 concepts as essential).

The survey results are interesting in that they indicate that there was not a great deal of agreement as to which concepts are essential. Of course, the criterion as to the percentage of mathematics educators who must identify an instructional concept as essential is arbitrary. However, if one accepts

FIGURE 3.1

Mathematics Concepts Deemed Essential for All High School Graduates

Number of educators who agreed that a given concept is essential	Number of concepts on which they agreed	Percentage	Cumulative agreement
10	299	40.4	
9	17	2.3	9 or more 316
8	39	5.3	8 or more 355
7	26	3.5	7 or more 381
6	23	3.1	6 or more 404
5	69	9.3	5 or more 473
4	53	7.2	4 or more 526
3	8	1.4	3 or more 534
2	23	3.1	2 or more 598
1	41	5.5	
0	143	19.3	

the intuitively appealing criterion of "a majority of mathematics educators" (i.e., six or more in the context of my study), then 404 of the 741 instructional concepts are necessary for all students to know prior to high school graduation (see Figure 3.1, column 4).

Whatever the appropriate criterion might be, these findings indicate that not all of the content in the mathematics standards is considered essential. Indeed, 143 or 19.3 percent of the instructional concepts were not identi-fied by any of the mathematics educators as essential (see the last row of Figure 3.1). Again, this finding underscores the problem inherent in the current standards movement in the U.S.—there is simply too much content to address in an adequate manner.

Thus, schools should provide clear delineation of content that is essential versus that which is supplemental or intended for those seeking postsecondary education only.

Action Step 2. Ensure that the essential content can be addressed in the amount of time available for instruction.

The most straightforward way to address this issue is simply to ask teachers how much time it would take to adequately address essential content. In a study conducted at McREL (Marzano, 1998b), 350 teachers were asked how many hours it would take them to adequately address each benchmark articulated for a variety of standards and subject areas. (If benchmarks are unpacked as I recommend, it is better to ask teachers to comment on each instructional concept.) The average number of hours for each benchmark was then considered the most stable estimate of the amount of time it would take to address the content. Other researchers have used this process to obtain viable estimates of time needed for coverage (Florian, 1999).

Fenwick English (2000) recommends another useful approach. His method requires teachers to estimate how many "class periods" are required for students to reach mastery for each instructional concept. He casts these estimates in terms of "least amount of time" and "most amount of time." According to English, the *least amount of time* estimate represents an ideal, that is "when everything goes right" (p. 55). The *most amount of time* estimate "essentially should be seen in terms of Murphy's Law; that is, given the likelihood that everything could go wrong, it does!" (p. 55).

Obviously, the time necessary to address content standards should not exceed the time available for instruction. Referring to his technique, English notes

When the "least amount of time" column is summed, the total number of class periods should not exceed the total possible in a quarter, semester, or year (whatever the official length of time is for the class) or *there is too much curriculum for the real time available.* [original emphasis] (p. 55)

To determine how much time is available for instruction, a school might undertake a formal "time audit," the process for which has been described elsewhere (Marzano, Kendall, & Gaddy, 1999). At a less formal level, a school can simply determine how much time in the day is devoted to actual instruction within scheduled classes. The school then estimates how much time in class is generally taken up by noninstructional class time such as taking roll, transitioning between activities, collecting or passing out material, socializing, and disciplining.

Armed with these time estimates, a school might be tempted to assume that all is well if the necessary instructional time is less than the available instructional classroom time. To illustrate, one middle school determined that over a three-year period about 2,200 hours of classroom instructional time were available, and the essential content would take about 2,000 hours to adequately address. At first blush, the issue was solved. However, the teachers involved in the study quickly realized that the essential content took up about 91 percent of the available instructional time. This meant that there was very little time left to address topics that arose serendipitously but were important to address (e.g., the War on Terrorism), even if it meant straying from the intended curriculum. These teachers decided that they wanted to keep at least 30 percent of the instructional class time available for such eventualities. They then went back to the task of deleting more "essential content" to make room for serendipitous instructional opportunities. The point is that schools should consider carefully how much of their available classroom instructional time they wish to fill with essential content.

Action Step 3. Sequence and organize the essential content in such a way that students have ample opportunity to learn it.

Once a viable amount of essential content has been established, it should be organized and sequenced to optimize the learning experience. It is useful to follow a basic curriculum principle articulated by NCTM (2000): "Big ideas encountered in a variety of contexts should be established carefully, with important elements such as terminology, definitions, notations, concepts, and skills emerging in the process" (p.15). The message here is to organize the essential instructional concepts into categories that form a realistic and logical sequence—fortunately, much of this work has already been done by John Kendall (Kendall, 2000). He and other researchers at McREL have organized the content from 14 different subject areas into categories that he refers to as "topics."

To understand a topic's nature (i.e., NCTM's "big idea"), consider the following instructional concepts I identified for mathematics study (Marzano, 2002):

- unit differences,
- standard versus nonstandard units,
- cubic units,
- linear units,
- square units,
- unit size, and
- unit analysis.

These instructional concepts quite logically can be organized into a single topic or category with the title *units*. In my study, I organized the 741 instructional concepts into 52 topics. I then sequenced them across four grade-level intervals: K–2, 3–5, 6–8, 9–12. This is depicted in Figure 3.2 (pp. 32–33).

As indicated in Figure 3.2, some topics (like *probability*) are addressed across all grade level intervals; some topics (like *direction, position, location*) are at the K–2 level only; some topics (like the *Pythagorean theorem*) are at the 9–12 level only.

Of course a school or district might articulate a very different scope and sequence from that depicted in Figure 3.2. The important point is that a school or district has taken the time to (1) identify the essential instructional concepts, (2) organize these into "big ideas" or "topics," and (3) establish a sequence for the topics or big ideas.

Action Step 4. Ensure that teachers address the essential content.

Ensuring that teachers address the essential content is necessary to implement a guaranteed and viable curriculum. As discussed, it is not uncommon for teachers to make idiosyncratic decisions regarding what to cover and what to leave out even within the context of highly structured curricula.

To implement this criterion, administrators must monitor the coverage of the essential content. This does not necessarily mean that administrators have to "observe" the actual teaching of the content. This would be so labor intensive as to be impossible.

However, an administrator could ask teachers for evidence of adequate coverage in the form of lesson plans, unit plans, or both. Administrators might also have a conference with teachers on a quarterly or semester basis. These conferences could be used as a platform for fruitful discussions not only about essential content coverage but also about effective instructional practices and engaging learning experiences for students. Monitoring should not be a police action, but it can be a powerful professional development tool executed in the spirit of what Jo Blase and Joseph Blase (1998) refer to as "reflective supervision," in which the administrator poses questions that help teachers think through their instructional decisions.

Action Step 5. Protect the instructional time that is available.

Lengthening the school year or the school day is probably impractical given the current resource constraints in public education. Consequently, I have (partially) addressed the issue of time by recommending a reduction in content considered essential. Schools can also protect the instructional time by decreasing the amount of scheduled time not devoted to actual instruction. This means being as efficient as possible about lunch, recess, breaks between classes, and announcements. Schools should make every effort to convey the message that class time is sacred time and should be interrupted for important events only, a message that is commonly conveyed in other countries. For example, in their book *The Teaching Gap*, James Stigler and James Hiebert (1999) relate the following incident that occurred when a group of Japanese teachers were observing a video-taped lesson from a U.S. 8th grade mathematics class:

> The teacher in the video was standing at the chalkboard, in the midst of demonstrating a procedure, when a voice came over the public address system: "May I have your attention, please. All students riding in bus thirty-one, you will meet your bus in the rear of the school today, not in the front of the school. Teachers please take note of this and remind your students."
>
> A Japanese member of our team reached over and pushed STOP on the VCR. "What was that?" he asked. "Oh nothing," we replied as we pushed the PLAY button. "Wait," protested our Japanese colleague. "What do you mean, nothing?" As we patiently tried to explain that it was just a P.A. announcement, he became more and more incredulous. Were we implying that it was normal to interrupt a lesson? How could that ever happen? Such interruptions would never happen in Japan, he said, because it would ruin the flow of the lesson. (p. 55)

Although Stigler and Hiebert warn that it is dangerous to draw inferences from single examples like this one, they did find that lessons in the United States are more frequently interrupted than lessons in Japan: "As claimed by our Japanese colleague, this never occurred during the Japanese lessons. But they did occur in . . . 33 percent of the American lessons" (p. 62).

The sanctity of instructional time might be communicated in a variety of ways. Here are some of the more creative methods of preserving instructional time: (1) providing teachers with a sign they can place outside their door when they wish no interruptions, (2) decreasing or eliminating announcements,

FIGURE 3.2

Mathematics Topics by Grade-Level Intervals

Topic	Grade-Level Interval			
	K–2	3–5	6–8	9–12
Addition	•	•		
Area		•	•	•
Central tendency & variability		•	•	•
Charts & graphs	•	•	•	
Computation (general)	•	•	•	
Coordinate systems		•	•	•
Data collection & samples	•	•	•	•
Data distributions		•	•	•
Decimals		•	•	
Direction, position, location	•			
Division		•	•	
Equations & inequalities		•	•	•
Estimation	•	•	•	
Experiments		•	•	•
Exponents, logs, roots			•	•
Expressions			•	•
Factors, multiples, primes		•		
Figures & shapes	•	•	•	•
Fractions		•	•	
Functions		•	•	•
Length, width, height	•	•	•	
Lines & angles		•	•	•
Math reasoning	•	•	•	•
Matrices & vectors				•
Measurement	•	•	•	•
Metric system		•	•	
Money	•			

FIGURE 3.2 (*continued*)

Mathematics Topics by Grade-Level Intervals

Topic	Grade-Level Interval			
	K–2	3–5	6–8	9–12
Motion geometry	•	•	•	•
Multiplication	•	•	•	•
Numbers & number systems	•	•	•	•
Patterns	•	•	•	
Perimeter & circumference		•	•	
Polynomials				•
Precision & accuracy				•
Probability	•	•	•	•
Problem-solving strategies	•	•	•	•
Proof			•	•
Pythagorean theorem				•
Rate & velocity			•	•
Ratio, proportion, percent		•	•	
Regression & correlation				•
Scale		•	•	
Sequences & series			•	•
Similarity & congruence		•	•	•
Statistics				•
Subtraction	•	•		
Temperature	•			
Time	•	•		•
Trigonometry				
Units	•	•	•	
Volume, mass, capacity	•	•	•	
Weight	•	•		

Source: R. J. Marzano. (2002). *Identifying the primary instructional concepts in mathematics: A linguistic approach.* Englewood, CO: Marzano & Associates. Copyright © 2002, Marzano & Associates, reprinted by permission.

and (3) referring to specific parts of class time as "academic learning time" so students understand that these times require more attention than others.

Summary

A guaranteed and viable curriculum is, for the most part, a composite of OTL and time. Although this school-level factor has the most impact on student achievement, it probably is the hardest to implement, especially within the context of the current standards movement. Schools must identify essential versus supplemental content and ensure that the essential content is sequenced appropriately and can be adequately addressed in the instructional time available. Schools must also ensure that teachers cover the essential content and protect the instructional time available.

4

CHALLENGING GOALS AND EFFECTIVE FEEDBACK

The second school-level factor is "challenging goals and effective feedback." The factor is primarily a combination of what other researchers have referred to as "high expectations" (or "effective monitoring" as referred to in Marzano, 2000a) and "pressure to achieve" (see Figure 2.3, p. 19). In my terminology, high expectations and pressure to achieve refer to establishing *challenging goals* for students. Monitoring refers to *feedback*—tracking the extent to which goals are met. Given that these elements hold the ranks of third and fourth respectively in my previous study (Marzano, 2000a), I've combined them and ranked them second in the list of the five school-level factors.

Pressure to Achieve: Establishing Academic Goals

In reviewing the research underlying this factor, let's first consider the academic impact of goal setting. Figure 4.1 (p. 36) provides a brief review of some of that research.

Specifically, Figure 4.1 reports the research using the metric of effect sizes (ES) translated into percentile gains. (For a detailed explanation of effect sizes, see Technical Note 4, pp. 190–191.) For example, Mark Lipsey and David Wilson (1993) examined 204 different studies and found that, on average, the act of setting academic goals had an effect size of 0.55. This means that the achievement scores in classes where clear learning goals were exhibited were 0.55 standard deviations higher than the achievement scores for classes where clear learning goals were not established. This differential translates into a 21-percentage point difference in achievement. Considered together, the findings reported in Figure 4.1 are compelling. Specifically, the reported impact of setting goals on student achievement ranges from a low of 18 percentile points to a high of 41 percentile points.

In addition to its impact on achievement, Mike Schmoker (1999) notes that setting academic goals for the school as a whole has

---

FIGURE 4.1

Research on the Importance of Goal Setting

Synthesis Study	Number of Effect Sizes	Average Effect Size	Percentile Gain
Wise & Okey, 1983*	3	1.37	41
	25	0.48	18
Walberg, 1999	21	0.46	18
Lipsey & Wilson, 1993	204	0.55	21

*Two effect sizes are listed because of the manner in which effect sizes were reported. Readers should consult the study for more details.

---

a powerful, coalescing effect on teachers and administrators: "Goals themselves lead not only to success but also to the effectiveness and cohesion of a team" (p. 24). Judith Little (1990) corroborates Schmoker's opinion. She found that shared responsibility for common goals was more important in establishing collegiality than interpersonal friendships. Unfortunately, shared goals do not seem to be the norm in schools across the country (Little, 1990; Lortie, 1975). For example, commenting on the research of Susan Rosenholtz (1991), Schmoker (1999) notes

> The existence of common goals in schools was . . . rare, and the lack of agreed-upon goals makes schools unique among organizations. She found that there was very little goal consensus—a collective agreement about what to work toward—even though her studies revealed that this element was the heart of what accounted for progress and success. (p. 25)

The act of establishing academic goals, then, has strong support as an important factor in effective schooling. In addition, another critical aspect of academic goal setting is important though less obvious—academic goals should be challenging for *all* students. This proviso comes directly from the research on expectations.

Ron Edmonds, an icon for the school effectiveness movement of the 1970s, believed that a school must challenge all students to be truly effective. More precisely, he noted that schools must close the achievement gap between those students from low socioeconomic status (SES) backgrounds and those from high SES backgrounds. In fact, high expectations for students, particularly those from low SES backgrounds, are a cornerstone of the school effectiveness research. David Reynolds and Charles Teddlie (2000) comment on the ubiquitous nature of this finding:

> High expectations of students has been one of the most consistent findings in the literature. . . . Virtually every review of the topic mentions the importance of this factor, whether British . . . Dutch . . . or American. (p. 148)

Reynolds and Teddlie further explain that teachers should communicate high expectations directly to students, which implies that clear goals for all students should be established.

Monitoring: The Need for Feedback

How do we know if goals are met if effective feedback is not in place? As is the case with goal setting, a strong and broad research base supports the effect of feedback. To illustrate, Figure 4.2 reports findings from several synthesis studies.

Again, these are impressive results. The reported impact of feedback in achievement ranges from a low of 21 percentile points to a high of 41. Both of these indicate that academic achievement in classes where effective feedback is provided to students is considerably higher than the achievement in classes where it is not. In fact, a review of almost

8,000 studies led John Hattie (1992) to comment, "The most powerful single modification that enhances achievement is feedback. The simplest prescription for improving education must be 'dollops of feedback.'" (p. 9)

Some research findings regarding feedback, however, might temper Hattie's enthusiastic endorsement. To impact student achievement, feedback must have two specific characteristics.

First, it must be timely. Students must receive feedback throughout the learning process—ideally multiple times throughout the school year (Bangert-Drowns, Kulik, Kulik, & Morgan, 1991). Timely feedback provided throughout a learning experience is referred to as "formative" assessment (as opposed to "summative" assessment that occurs at the end of a learning experience only) (Airasian, 1994; McMillan, 2000). In fact, some researchers assert that appropriate and systematic use of formative assessment could drastically improve the achievement of

FIGURE 4.2

Research on the Importance of Feedback

Synthesis Study	Number of Effect Sizes	Average Effect Size	Percentile Gain
Walberg, 1999	20	0.94	33
Bloom, 1976	7	0.54	21
Scheerens & Bosker, 1997	—	1.09	36
Kumar, 1991	5	1.35	41
Haller, Child, & Walberg, 1988	20	0.71	26

U.S. students. For example, in a major review of the research on assessment, Paul Black and Dylan Wiliam (1998) noted

> The research reported here shows conclusively that formative assessment does improve learning. The gains in achievement appear to be quite considerable, and as noted earlier, amongst the largest ever reported for educational interventions. As an illustration of just how big these gains are, an effect size of 0.7, if it could be achieved on a nationwide scale, would be equivalent to raising the mathematics achievement score of an 'average' country like England, New Zealand or the United States into the 'top five' after the Pacific rim countries of Singapore, Korea, Japan and Hong Kong. (p. 61)

These findings and conclusions create a dilemma for schools that rely primarily on state tests or external standardized tests as their vehicle for feedback. By definition, such feedback is summative.

Second, effective feedback must be specific to the content being learned (Bangert-Drowns, et al., 1991). George Madaus and colleagues found that tests that are not specifically designed to assess a particular school's curriculum frequently underestimate the true learning of students (Madaus, Kellaghan, Rakow, & King, 1979; Madaus, Airasian, & Kellaghan, 1980). Madaus and colleagues (1979) noted

> Several of our results clearly indicate that what we call curriculum-sensitive measures are precisely that. Compared to conventional standardized tests, they are clearly more dependent on the characteristics of schools and what goes on in them. (pp. 223–224)

The message is clear. Unless a school employs assessments that are specific to the curriculum actually taught, it cannot accurately determine how well its students are learning.

Today, many schools rely on the results from standardized state tests to assess student learning. Although it is true that state tests more accurately reflect the content deemed important by individual states, they are still problematic because the items on such tests sample the content in state standards documents. Indeed, sampling the content within a subject area is the basis for all large-scale assessments. To illustrate, in a report on the nature and function of state-level tests and standardized tests, the National Research Council (1999) noted

> No test can possibly tap all the concepts and processes embodied in a subject area. . . . Instead, test makers construct a sample from the entire subject matter, called a domain. The samples that different test makers choose differ substantially. Thus, one can conclude that not only are the domains of [various subject areas] complex, but there are many subdomains and subsets of test elements . . . that can be used to measure them. (p. 67)

State tests are also problematic in their use of very general performance categories. These categories often provide little feedback on specific knowledge and skills (Cizek, 2001; Hambleton, 2001). For example, the state standard examples in Figure 4.3, p. 39, are modeled after descriptions of novice, apprentice, and proficient mathematics performance for 8th graders.

Clearly the descriptions of the three performance levels in Figure 4.3 are too broad to provide effective feedback on specific skills and abilities. For example, what is the difference between exhibiting *minimal* understanding of *rudimentary* concepts and skills (novice) and exhibiting *partial* understanding of *basic* concepts and skills (apprentice)? Figure 4.3 is a composite for illustration only, yet all too often schools rely solely on state tests with performance levels like these as their primary feedback mechanism.

Action Steps

I recommend three action steps to implement challenging goals and effective feedback.

Action Step 1. Implement an assessment system that provides timely feedback on specific knowledge and skills for specific students.

Effective feedback is specific and formative in nature. Certainly feedback once a year from a state test or standardized test falls well below the minimum frequency level. At a minimum, students should receive quarterly feedback on their academic performance. Consequently, schools must establish an assessment system that provides feedback on specific knowledge and skills at least every nine weeks. This automatically rules out state-developed tests on standards, off-the-shelf standardized tests, or even both working in tandem. For all practical purposes, a school has two primary options.

The first is to construct a series of quarterly tests that are specifically designed to assess student competence in essential school-identified content (see action steps 1 and 2 from Chapter 3). Although this is a viable option (see McMillan, 1997, for a discussion), it is usually an expensive one because most schools and districts do not have the time or

FIGURE 4.3

Model of Performance Categories for State Standards

Novice	• Demonstrate minimal understanding of rudimentary concepts and skills. • Occasionally make obvious connections among ideas, providing minimal evidence or support for inferences and solutions. • Have difficulty applying basic knowledge and skills. • Communicate in an ineffective manner.
Apprentice	• Demonstrate partial understanding of basic concepts and skills. • Make simple or basic connections among ideas, providing limited supporting evidence for inferences and solutions. • Apply concepts and skills to routine problem-solving situations. • Communicate in a limited manner.
Proficient	• Demonstrate general understanding of concepts and skills. • Make meaningful, multiple connections among important ideas or concepts and provide supporting evidence for inferences and justification of solutions. • Apply concepts and skills to solve problems using appropriate strategies. • Communicate effectively.

resident expertise to construct such tests and must rely on companies that specialize in their design.

A second and much better option is to redesign report cards and grading practices to reflect student competence in specific or "essential" knowledge and skills. I have detailed what this would entail in *Transforming Classroom Grading* (Marzano, 2000b) and will only briefly address it here. Figure 4.4 presents a reporting system that would provide this type of feedback.

The top section of the report card in Figure 4.4 looks quite traditional in that it presents overall subject matter grades. Of course, overall grades do not provide specific feedback. (For a discussion of report card options that do not include overall grades, see Marzano, 2000b.) The bottom section contains information about student performance on specific topics and skills. This particular example employs a 100-point scale for each subject matter topic as well as for nonacademic factors such as participation, assignments, working in groups, and following rules.

Many other schemes can be used. A four-point scale might be used for the nonacademic factors or for the nonacademic factors as well as the subject matter topics (for examples of such report cards, see Marzano, 2000b). Figure 4.4 indicates that the student, Cecelia Haystead, is doing relatively well in the mathematics topics of charts and graphs and problem-solving strategies, but she is not faring well in functions. These scores are the aggregate results of formative assessments collected over a period of nine weeks. Thus, the report card depicts the conclusions from a classroom-based assessment system that is both specific and formative.

The information in a nine-week report card like that in Figure 4.4 could be aggregated into a transcript-like report as shown in Figure 4.5, pp. 43–45.

Figure 4.5 represents topic scores from formative assessments collected over a three-year period for grades 6, 7, and 8. The report provides feedback on a wide variety of mathematics and science topics. What is most important about this report is that it would require teachers to keep track of student achievement on only about six topics per quarter. To illustrate, 38 mathematics topics are addressed in Figure 4.5. Some of these topics have two ratings or scores. Some have only one. A teacher provided each rating at the end of a nine-week grading period. In all, there are 69 ratings of the 38 mathematics topics. Given that the transcript covers a three-year period (grades 6, 7, and 8), ratings in mathematics topics were made four times a year or 12 times in three years. If teachers rated six mathematics topics each quarter, 72 (i.e., 6 x 12) ratings would be made in three years. Of course, computer grade books make this much less labor- and time-intensive. In fact, I commonly tell schools to become acquainted with the various computer grade books and report cards before they start developing their record-keeping and reporting system. (For a thorough discussion of computer grade books, see Marzano, 2000b.)

Action Step 2. Establish specific, challenging achievement goals for the school as a whole.

If an effective assessment system is in place, achievement goals can be set for the school as a whole. Mike Schmoker (1999, 2001) provides clear guidance on setting and using

FIGURE 4.4

Sample Report Card

Student: Cecelia Haystead
Grade: 8
Homeroom: Ms. Becker

Mathematics:	79.7	C		*Participation:*	90.8	B
Science:	79.4	C		*Assignments:*	87.6	B
Language Arts:	93.8	A		*Working in Groups:*	78.2	C
History/Geography:	82.9	C		*Following Rules:*	87.1	B
Art:	97.7	A				
Civics:	85.4	B				

Mathematics		
Central tendency & variability	76.5	
Charts & graphs	87.2	
Data collection & samples	78.2	
Functions	68.3	
Problem-solving strategies	88.2	
Participation	94.2	
Assignments	82.1	
Working in groups	70.5	
Following rules	78.4	

Science		
Motion of Earth/moon	71.0	
Energy in Earth's system	82.3	
The solar system	79.1	
The universe	83.9	
Seasons/weather/climate	80.7	
Participation	90.2	
Assignments	84.7	
Working in groups	71.5	
Following rules	82.4	

FIGURE 4.4 (*continued*)

Sample Report Card

Language Arts		
Writing:		
The writing process	94.7	
Organization & development	95.0	
Diction	89.9	
Style	95.2	
Reading:		
Reading comprehension	92.6	
Critical reading	95.8	
Understanding genre	93.8	
Participation	97.1	
Assignments	94.7	
Working in groups	87.2	
Following rules	92.9	
History/Geography		
Colonies & colonialism	88.3	
Empires & imperialism	77.9	
Causes & consequences of slavery	79.5	
Adaptation to the environment	83.4	
Types of regions	84.9	
Participation	77.4	
Assignments	75.1	
Working in groups	69.8	
Following rules	88.1	
Art		
Purposes of art	98.5	
Art skills	97.7	
Art & culture	96.9	
Participation	92.4	
Assignments	99.3	
Working in groups	89.2	
Following rules	96.0	
Civics		
Human & civil rights	85.3	
Government representation	81.6	
Personal responsibility	89.4	
Participation	90.5	
Assignments	89.7	
Working in groups	81.2	
Following rules	84.8	

FIGURE 4.5

Sample Mathematics Transcript

Mathematics	Average Rating	Number of Ratings	Most Recent Rating	Highest Rating	Lowest Rating
Area	81.9	2	82.7	82.7	81.0
Central tendency & variability	78.0	2	76.5	79.5	76.5
Charts & graphs	86.1	2	87.2	87.2	84.9
Computation (general)	88.8	2	94.1	94.1	82.7
Coordinate systems	91.2	1	91.2	91.2	91.2
Data collection & samples	77.7	2	78.2	78.2	77.2
Data distributions	82.1	2	81.6	82.9	81.6
Decimals	86.7	2	85.9	87.4	85.9
Division	88.1	2	91.4	91.4	85.6
Equations & inequalities	79.9	1	79.9	79.9	79.9
Estimation	86.9	2	82.3	91.5	82.3
Experiments	84.1	1	84.1	84.1	84.1
Exponents, roots, logs	80.7	2	79.1	82.2	79.1
Expressions	85.5	1	85.5	85.5	85.5
Figures & shapes	85.4	2	87.1	87.1	83.7
Fractions	81.1	2	78.2	84.0	78.2
Functions	69.7	2	68.3	71.0	68.3
Length, width, height	75.2	1	75.2	75.2	75.2
Lines & angles	83.0	2	82.2	83.8	82.2
Mathematical reasoning	85.7	2	84.7	86.6	84.7
Measurement	81.0	2	79.2	84.7	79.1
Metric system	85.2	2	85.5	85.5	84.9
Motion geometry	82.2	1	82.2	82.2	82.2
Multiplication	75.6	2	74.1	77.0	74.1
Numbers & number systems	76.2	2	77.1	77.1	75.2
Patterns	77.1	2	81.0	81.0	75.2
Perimeter, circumference	74.0	2	72.1	75.8	72.1
Probability	69.4	2	70.0	70.0	68.8
Problem-solving strategies	84.4	2	88.2	88.2	79.8

FIGURE 4.5 (*continued*)

Sample Mathematics Transcript

Mathematics	Average Rating	Number of Ratings	Most Recent Rating	Highest Rating	Lowest Rating
Proof	87.1	1	87.1	87.1	87.1
Rate & velocity	81.9	2	79.2	84.7	79.0
Ratio, proportion, percent	81.0	2	77.1	84.9	77.1
Scale	83.3	2	81.7	84.9	81.7
Sequences & series	86.7	2	89.1	89.1	84.2
Similarity & congruence	80.9	2	80.7	81.1	80.7
Statistics	47.0	2	44.9	51.2	44.9
Units	84.9	1	84.9	84.9	84.9
Volume, mass, capacity	68.5	2	71.9	71.9	65.1
Overall mathematics	80.7		80.6	82.3	77.1

Sample Science Transcript

Science	Average Rating	Number of Ratings	Most Recent Rating	Highest Rating	Lowest Rating
Atoms & molecules	75.4	2	71.9	78.8	71.9
Characteristics of organisms	74.1	1	74.1	74.1	74.1
Chemical reactions	69.2	1	69.2	69.2	69.2
Classes of organisms	69.0	3	70.9	70.9	68.7
Conservation of matter, energy	77.9	3	77.8	81.7	74.3
Earth systems	75.9	3	77.7	77.9	72.1
Earth's atmosphere	70.2	3	68.5	73.9	68.3
Earth's history	71.5	2	71.1	71.8	71.1
Earth's surface features	79.0	3	78.7	82.1	76.2
Energy in Earth's system	81.0	3	82.3	82.3	77.0
Forces & motion	64.6	1	64.6	64.6	64.6
Forms of energy	71.8	1	71.8	71.8	71.8
Gravity	73.6	2	74.9	74.9	72.2
Life cycles	80.8	3	81.4	81.8	79.2
Motion of Earth, moon	75.2	3	71.0	79.2	75.7

FIGURE 4.5 (*continued*)
Sample Science Transcript

Science	Average Rating	Number of Ratings	Most Recent Rating	Highest Rating	Lowest Rating
Organism & environment	66.8	1	66.8	66.8	66.8
Position & motion	41.2	1	41.2	41.2	41.2
Reproduction	74.5	2	71.8	77.2	71.8
Rock cycle	85.5	3	91.7	91.7	81.6
Rocks, minerals, soil	74.9	3	71.9	79.9	71.9
Seasons, weather, climate	80.5	3	80.7	80.7	80.0
Scientific data	68.5	2	69.9	69.9	67.1
Scientific explanations	72.6	2	74.2	74.2	71.0
Scientific investigation	76.7	2	74.3	79.0	74.3
Solar system	80.3	3	79.1	84.1	77.7
The universe	83.4	3	83.9	87.2	79.1
Vibrations & waves	90.1	1	90.1	90.1	90.1
Water	87.8	3	89.1	89.1	84.2
Water in Earth's system	83.0	3	82.4	85.7	81.0
Overall science	75.0		74.9	72.9	72.2

schoolwide goals. One critical aspect is not to set too many. For example, commenting on the research of Michael Fullan and Andy Hargreaves, he notes: "Many of the schools tackle only one or two achievement goals annually to prevent the over-load that is so clearly the enemy of improvement" (2001, p. 37).

Schmoker identifies a second feature that he refers to as the principle of "rapid results" (Schmoker, 1999). Although he does not necessarily advocate a short-term view of school reform, he asserts that obtaining results in the first year is critical to providing a foundation of success on which to build. His advice is logical and practical—and it works. Among

others, Schmoker (1999, p. 57) lists the following examples of schools that produced observable results in a year or less:

- Between 1997 and 1998, Bessemer Elementary School in Pueblo, Colorado, increased the percentage of students who are at or above grade level in reading from 12 percent to 64 percent.
- George Washington Vocational and Technical School in downtown Brooklyn, New York, reduced the number of students failing every class from 151 to 11 in one semester.
- Amphitheater Middle School reduced

the number of referrals from 250 to 95 in a year's period of time.

As these examples indicate, schoolwide goals can be quite varied. However, setting a few goals that can be accomplished in a short period of time is so potentially powerful that Schmoker (1999) refers to it as a "breakthrough strategy" (p. 56).

Action Step 3. Establish specific goals for individual students.

Establishing goals for individual students is perhaps more powerful than setting a few schoolwide goals. Individual goals have been a staple of special education for decades and are usually presented in the form of Individualized Educational Plans (IEPs).

Martin Covington (1992) maintains that individual student goals are most effective when students are involved in setting them. Schoolwide goals certainly have their place, but they are usually expressed as a percentage of students exhibiting a certain level of achievement in some area. For example, a school might strive for 90 percent of students achieving at or above grade level in reading by year's end. What about the 10 percent of

students who do not meet this goal? Setting schoolwide goals only risks this sector of the student population being systematically excluded from the powerful effects of establishing goals and monitoring progress. Using a report card and transcript like those in Figure 4.4 and Figure 4.5, students, with the help of a counselor or a homeroom teacher, can set quarterly achievement goals for specific topics within specific subject areas.

Summary

Two key elements are required to implement challenging goals and effective feedback: first, challenging goals must be established for all students; second, effective feedback must be specific and formative. I recommended three action steps to establish an assessment system that provides feedback on specific topics to individual students at least once per quarter. To accomplish this, I suggest innovative report cards that use formative classroom assessments. With such a system in place, schoolwide achievement goals, as well as individual student goals, can be set and monitored.

PARENT AND COMMUNITY INVOLVEMENT

The third school-level factor is "parent and community involvement." It has to do with the extent to which parents (in particular) and the community at large (in general) are both supportive of and involved in a school. One or both of these two groups is identified in most attempts to synthesize the research on effective schooling. Parental and community involvement is mentioned explicitly in four of the five lists of school-level factors summarized in Figure 2.3, p. 19. (Edmonds excludes both.)

Not all types of parental or community involvement are beneficial to the effective running of a school. Speaking of parental involvement in particular, David Reynolds and Charles Teddlie (2000) explain

> It is clear that parental involvement in such areas as criticism of the school or visits to the school to complain are likely to generate negative effectiveness at [the] school level. . . . On the other hand, there is too much evidence of the positive effects of parental involvement . . . (p. 151)

Although community involvement is not addressed in the research as frequently as is parent involvement, it is commonly implicit in the broad descriptions applied to parent involvement. For example, Charles Teddlie, Sam Stringfield, and David Reynolds (2000) indicate that many of the studies examining the impact of parent involvement commonly include elements of community involvement. Sandra Tangri and Oliver Moles (1987) reach the same conclusion. In addition, the national standards for Parent/Family Involvement Programs established by the Parent Teacher Association (1997) explicitly note the need for involvement by both parents and community.

Three features define effective parental and community involvement: communication, participation, and governance.

Communication

One of the defining features of effective parent and community involvement appears to be good communication (Antunez, 2000)—from schools to parents and community and vice versa. This does not imply that schools should provide parents and the community with an open invitation to criticize school policy. In fact, this dynamic has been shown to have a negative effect (Brookover & Lezotte, 1979; Hallinger & Murphy, 1986; Teddlie & Stringfield, 1993).

Home-to-school communications in particular may be constrained by conditions such as legal regulations, district policies, and history. The National Education Association (1982) points out that parents have no obligation to communicate with the school. Therefore, it is the responsibility of the school to initiate communication and provide an atmosphere in which parents desire such communication. Yet, one study of four federal education programs found that the most frequently used school-to-home communication mechanisms were newsletters, bulletins, and flyers, all of which provide little opportunity for parents to respond (Melaragno, Keesling, Lyons, Robbins, & Smith, 1981).

Participation

A second feature of effective parent and community involvement is participation in the day-to-day running of the school such as working as teacher aides or guest lecturers (Comer, 1984, 1988; Epstein, 1991; Epstein & Becker, 1982; Paulsen, 1994a, 1994b). Involved parents sense that the school values and welcomes not only their ideas but also their physical participation. As an added benefit, parent and community involvement can significantly add to a school's resource base.

According to Tangri and Moles (1987), benefits include

- expanded expertise on specific topics and subject areas,
- expanded contacts for teachers and administrators with resources in the community,
- direct financial contributions resulting from business support, and
- donation of equipment from businesses.

Finally, schools that involve parents and community in their day-to-day operations have reported lower absenteeism, truancy, and dropout rates (Bucknam, 1976) attesting to a possible "spill over" effect into the home environment.

Governance

Governance requires the establishment of specific structures that allow parents and community some voice in key school decisions. Sandra Tangri and Oliver Moles (1987) explain the rationale for parent (and by extension, community) involvement in school governance:

> The concept of parent participation in educational decision making is closely linked to democratic ideals of citizen participation in the affairs of government. It has been defended on both ideological and practical grounds. The ideological rationale is that people affected by decisions of public instruction should be involved in making those decisions. The practical one is that enduring and positive change is most likely when those affected are involved in the planning and decision making. (p. 520)

Public participation in school governance was given a major boost in the 1960s and early 1970s with federal requirements for the establishment of parent advisory councils (PACs) under Title I of the Elementary and Secondary Education Act, Head Start, Follow Through, and the Education for All Handicapped Children Act. Although the requirement for PACs has been lifted, the effects of these legislative mandates are still felt in public education.

How interested are parents and the community in making these types of decisions? One large survey study of parents in six southwestern states (Stallworth & Williams, 1982) found little interest in decisions regarding the hiring and firing of teachers or principals. However, parents were very interested in decisions regarding programs and practices that bore directly on the achievement of their children.

Action Steps

I recommend three action steps to promote effective involvement of parents and community.

Action Step 1. Establish vehicles for communication between schools and parents and the community.

Communication does not occur automatically. Rather, specific vehicles must be established to facilitate the flow of information to and from the school. Beth Antunez (2000) offers the stated policies of the San Francisco Unified School District (SFUSD) as a noteworthy example. As described by Antunez, SFUSD established the policy that each preschool through high school must develop a long-range plan to enhance communication between the school site and parents. Suggestions include

- All school communications should be issued in the major languages of the school's linguistically diverse students.
- All public meetings should be translated from English into the major languages of the linguistically diverse students. Public meetings should be conducted on a regular basis in the languages of the parents and translated into English.

One of the more important aspects of the SFUSD initiative is that it doesn't stop at simply listing ways that a school might enhance the flow of information. It also addresses perhaps the most important feature of this communication—making information easily and readily available.

Specific ways for schools to establish effective lines of communication, particularly with parents, have been in place for some time and include phone calls, the Internet, home visits, and parent-teacher conferences.

Studies indicate that **phone calls** to parents by the principal are particularly effective in decreasing truancy and absenteeism (Parker & McCoy, 1977; Sheats & Dunkleberger, 1979). The major problem with phone calls is that they are time consuming and labor intensive (National Education Association, 1982). Recorded telephone messages have been used effectively to inform parents about school activities (Bittle, 1975).

In the last decade, the **Internet** has greatly expanded the options for parent and school interaction. Some schools provide weekly or even daily access to information.

Indeed, schools now commonly establish their own Web sites to provide information to parents and the community in general.

Home visits are common but they are labor intensive and have shown inconsistent results in changing student behavior or enhancing academic achievement (Tangri & Moles, 1987). Evidence exists that home visitations bring long-term benefits (Olmsted, 1983).

Finally, the time-honored **parent-teacher conference** is used widely. Protocols for effective parent-teacher conferences commonly include suggestions regarding general teacher dispositions such as warmth, attentiveness, and responsiveness (Rotter & Robinson, 1982) and suggestions on handling parents' resistance to negative information (Losen & Diament, 1978).

Action Step 2. Establish multiple ways for parents and community to be involved in the day-to-day running of the school.

Researchers indicate that nothing creates more of a sense of ownership than being involved in day-to-day school activities (Antunez, 2000; Center for Community Education, 1989; Onikama, Hammond, & Koki, 1998; Parent Teacher Association, 1997). Using volunteers is the most common vehicle for this type of involvement (Tangri & Moles, 1987) One study estimates that volunteers are used in some capacity in 79 percent of the public school districts in the country (Thomas, n.d.).

Volunteers are used in a wide variety of ways, such as

- classroom aides,
- hallway, lunchroom, and playground monitors,
- office clerical assistants, and
- guest lecturers and presenters.

According to Tangri and Moles (1987), factors that appear critical to the success of volunteer programs include

- appropriate recruiting and training techniques,
- orientation workshops,
- staff training on appropriate volunteer use, and
- consideration of legal and financial aspects of volunteer programs.

Some volunteer programs are specifically designed to involve businesses. Sometimes referred to as "adopt-a-school" models, they allow the sponsoring business to "take students on tours of the business, let them try out equipment, give demonstrations of new technology, and develop minicourses" (Tangri & Moles, 1987, p. 541). Specific programs designed to involve the business community in school operations include The Community as a Classroom, The Community as Textbook, and Learning from Volunteering and Other Roles (Gonder, 1981).

Action Step 3. Establish governance vehicles that allow for the involvement of parents and community members.

Governance structures are the most formal vehicles for parent and community involvement. James Comer's work (1984, 1988) is the most recognized and well researched on this issue. Comer's School Development

Program (SDP) was first implemented in two elementary schools in New Haven, Connecticut and now operates in more than 700 schools (American Institute for Research, 1999).

Central to Comer's model are three "mechanisms"—the School Planning and Management Team, the Student and Staff Support Team, and the Parent Team. All deal with school governance; two involve parents or community members.

Led by the principal, the **School Planning and Management Team** is composed of approximately a dozen teachers, parents, professional support staff (e.g., school psychologists, social workers), and paraprofessional staff (e.g., secretaries, janitors, classroom aides). The purposes of this team include

- establishing policies that affect the curriculum, the overall school environment, and staff development;
- carrying out school planning activities, implementing programs, and evaluating the effectiveness of schoolwide initiatives;
- coordinating the activities of the various groups functioning in the school; and
- working with parents and the community to establish a calendar for social and informational activities.

The **Student and Staff Support Team** does not explicitly involve parents and community members but is composed of teachers, school psychologists, social workers, special education teachers, counselors, and other support staff. The team provides input to the School Planning and Management Team on learning and development needs and teacher efforts to work with students who are having behavior or learning problems.

By definition, the **Parent Team** most directly addresses the involvement of parents. As the American Institute for Research (1999) describes it:

> There are different levels of participation, so parents can choose how involved they wish to be. All parents are encouraged to participate in several school-sponsored activities each year, such as a field trip to a museum. These activities allow parents to get to know members of the school staff, so they feel more comfortable with the school. Parents who wish to be involved more directly are encouraged to participate as classroom assistants, tutors, or aides. Finally, parents who are committed to being highly involved can participate as members of the School Planning and Management Team. (pp. 111–112)

Of course, many types of governance structures exist that involve parents and community members other than those within Comer's model. For example, the School/Community-Based Management (SCBM) program (Onikama et al., 1998) uses a more site-based management approach. Like Comer's SDP, SCBM utilizes specific governance structures that involve parents and community. According to Onikama and colleagues:

> An evaluation of SCBM by the Far West laboratory (now WestEd) revealed that SCBM has a significant impact on school decision-making practices. It was also found that decision-making and school-community connections are strongly linked. (p. 16)

Summary

Where the importance of parental involvement is explicit in the research, the importance of community involvement is more implicit. Three aspects of this third school-level factor are important to student achievement: mechanisms for communication, involvement in the day-to-day running of the school, and the use of governance structures. I recommended three action steps to address these three aspects and to promote effective parent and community involvement in schools.

SAFE AND ORDERLY ENVIRONMENT

The fourth school-level factor is "a safe and orderly environment." Its importance is evident. If teachers and students do not feel safe, they will not have the necessary psychological energy for teaching and learning. This factor's fourth place rating among the five school-level factors does not imply that it is unimportant. Without a minimum level of safety and order, a school has little chance of positively affecting student achievement.

Safety and order (by other names) are addressed in all five of the studies reviewed in Chapter 2. Edmonds calls them "a safe and orderly atmosphere conducive to learning"; Levine and Lezotte use "productive climate and culture." Sammons calls them "learning environment," "positive reinforcement," and "pupil rights and expectations"; Bosker and Scheerens use the term "school climate."

Many other studies have singled out a safe and orderly environment as critical to academic achievement (Chubb & Moe, 1990; Mayer, Mullens, Moore, & Ralph, 2000). This

has even been noted at the federal level. For example, *Goals 2000: Educate America Act* (National Education Goals Panel, 1994) stated that by the year 2000, every school "will offer a disciplined environment conducive to learning" (p. 13).

A great deal of evidence suggests that safety in schools is also a major concern of parents (Coldron & Bolton, 1996). Indeed, local and national polls consistently demonstrate that the general public perceives safety as a primary issue (Sewall & Chamberlin, 1997). As Pedro Noguera (1995) notes

> In many school districts[,] concerns about violence have even surpassed academic achievement—traditionally the most persistent theme on the nation's agenda—as the highest priority for reform and intervention. (p. 189)

The perceptions regarding the lack of safety in U.S. schools might exceed the reality. For example, Leal (1994) comments on safety in the San Antonio, Texas, public schools.

Reading the city's major newspaper, one might get the impression that many school children are involved in crime and drugs. However, the reality is much different. (p. 39)

Phi Delta Kappa and the Gallup organization caution that the perceptions of violence might be due to extensive media coverage rather than actual incidents of school violence (Miller, 1994). Noguera (1995) explains: "Relatively speaking, young people may in fact be far safer in school than they are in their neighborhoods or, for that matter, at the park, the roller rink, or even in their homes" (p. 191).

Some evidence suggests that public concern about school violence has been used as a political tool. For example, Sewall and Chamberlin (1997) explain

There has also been the suggestion that the perception of school violence has been politicized. As the attitude of the public has become more harsh toward the incidence of crime and general lawlessness, there has been a tendency on the part of elected officials and school boards and administrators to adopt a "get tough" policy to convince the public that appropriate action is being taken. (p. 4)

Still, the data regarding school violence are sobering. For example, in the late 1990s, a spokesperson for the American Federation of Teachers reported that one out of 11 teachers is assaulted in schools and one out of four students experiences violence in U.S. schools. The executive director of the National School Safety Center noted that an estimated 5,000 teachers are assaulted each month. Of these, about 1,000 are injured seriously enough to require medical attention (Ward, 1998).

Data obtained from and about students are equally sobering. In a survey of 2,066 9th grade students in Lexington, Kentucky, 43 percent of the students reported that they had hit another student during a six-month period. Eight percent reported that they had hit a teacher, and 16 percent reported they had carried a weapon to school (Kingery, McCoy-Simandle, & Clayton, 1997). In a survey of a representative sample of high school students in Seattle, 6.6 percent reported that they had carried a handgun into school at some time (Callahan & Rivera, 1992).

Even if the incidents of violence are not higher than in previous years, the negative impact of violence and disorder in schools is well documented. In a study that controlled for background characteristics such as race, ethnicity, and socioeconomic status, students in schools with high levels of violence had lower math scores by 0.20 of a standard deviation and were 5.7 percentage points less likely to graduate (Grogger, 1997).

Although not commonly thought of as directly related to violence, truancy appears to be an important contributing factor. A strong relationship exists between truancy and criminal activity—a relationship that David Gullatt and Dwayne Lemoine (1997) refer to as the "truant-to-criminal evolution" (p. 7). In a related finding, Judith Levine (1992) found a negative correlation of –0.33 between absenteeism and student achievement.

Thus, a safe and orderly environment is a critical aspect of effective schooling. A school that does not attend to this factor risks undermining all other efforts at school improvement.

Action Steps

I recommend five action steps to achieve a safe and orderly environment.

Action Step 1. Establish rules and procedures for behavioral problems that might be caused by the school's physical characteristics or the school's routines.

The old saying that "an ounce of prevention is worth a pound of cure" applies nicely to the establishment of a safe and orderly environment. Rules and procedures simply lessen the chance for disruption and violence. J. Ron Nelson, Ron Martella, and Benita Galand (1998) refer to such rules and procedures as "ecological interventions." In a four-year study involving 600 students in grades 1 through 6, they found:

> . . . having students of similar grade levels participate in a recess period created congestion problems because same-age students tended to participate in the same activities. This led to more physical and undesirable social interactions among students. Mixing up the grade levels during the recess periods reduced the congestion problems. (p. 155)

Ecological interventions, then, are rules and procedures that counteract possible negative consequences of a school's physical characteristics (e.g., narrow hallways, limited access to and from certain areas) or schedule (e.g., overlapping lunch periods, staggered schedules). To implement ecological interventions, a school must examine its physical structure and routines with an eye to heading off possible problems. Ecological interventions recommended by Nelson and colleagues include

- reducing crowd density by using all entrances and exits to a given area,
- keeping wait time to enter and exit common areas to a minimum,
- decreasing travel time and distances between activities and events,
- using signs marking transitions from less controlled to more controlled space,
- using signs indicating behavioral expectations for common areas, and
- sequencing events in common areas to decrease the potential of overcrowding.

Nelson recommends a three-phase approach to teach and reinforce the rules and procedures for ecological interventions. During the first phase, lasting two to three weeks, students are taught the rules and procedures for the common areas. In the second phase, lasting two to three months, students receive periodic reviews of those rules and procedures. In the third phase, students receive review or "booster" sessions as needed.

Action Step 2. Establish clear schoolwide rules and procedures for general behavior.

Commonly, individual teachers establish rules and procedures governing classroom behavior. Schools should establish rules and procedures for expected behavior outside the classroom. A comprehensive list of behaviors (Bear, 1998; Billings & Enger, 1995; Green & Barnes, 1993) for which rules and procedures are commonly established includes

- bullying,
- verbal harassment,
- drug use,
- obscene language and gestures,
- gang behavior,

- sexual harassment,
- repeated class disruptions,
- disregarding others' safety,
- fighting,
- theft, and
- truancy.

Rules and procedures for expected behavior should be clearly communicated to students and made highly visible. Common approaches are to review schoolwide rules and procedures at the beginning of the school year, perhaps in an assembly format, and provide students and parents with a written copy. A school might also schedule an open house night to answer parents' questions.

Action Step 3. Establish and enforce appropriate consequences for violations of rules and procedures.

Consequences for violation must be fair and consistently administered. Research indicates that the types of consequences that administrators use seem to be remarkably consistent. James Green and Donald Barnes (1993) interviewed 100 middle school and 100 high school administrators representing four different sized schools and four different community types. They concluded that "Actions taken in response to offenses are consistent among the four school sizes and four community types" (p. 7).

The most common actions employed by administrators in their study included

- verbal reprimand,
- disciplinary notices to parents,
- conferences,
- after-school detention,

- out-of-school suspension, and
- expulsion.

This list is quite similar to that produced by Ward Billings and John Enger (1995) as a result of their study:

- verbal reprimand,
- detention,
- in-school suspension,
- out-of-school suspension, and
- expulsion.

Although the consequences for violation of schoolwide rules and procedures are fairly well established, their effectiveness is not. For example, little research exists as to the relative effectiveness of verbal reprimands versus detention.

However, John Winborn (1992) reports significant decreases in suspensions and expulsions as a result of "Saturday School" where high school students engaged in activities such as writing about discipline and engaging in behavior-improvement training activities. Kube and Ratigan (1992) describe a program for unexcused absences that includes a Saturday morning class from 8:00 to 11:30 during which students are required to complete missed assignments. Another Saturday class is assigned if students fail to complete those assignments.

David Gullatt and Dwayne Lemoine (1997) report the impact of a program for truancy that might be considered particularly harsh on parents and guardians:

> In the first three years of its implementation over 600 cases were prosecuted, resulting in 300 convictions in which a parent or

guardian was fined and received some form of counseling. Since its beginning in 1989, a 45% reduction in the dropout rate has occurred at practically no cost to the school district. By keeping 800 more students on the role, approximately $3,000 in both state and local reimbursement was received for each student based on the school district's average daily attendance. It was noted that for every 200 cases brought to court more than 400 students returned to school. (p. 7)

Although there appears to be some agreement regarding general consequences for violations, little research differentiates the impact of various types of consequences. Schools should consider examining the effectiveness of the consequences they employ.

Action Step 4. Establish a program that teaches self-discipline and responsibility to students.

Some theorists react quite negatively to suggestions like those in action steps 2 and 3. For example, in an article entitled "Discipline: The Great False Hope," Raymond Wlodkowski (1982) notes

> Because discipline is so often applied as control, it comes across to the student as a form of direct or implied threat. We essentially say to the student, "If you don't do what I think is best for you to do, I am going to make life in this classroom difficult for you." (p. 8)

Jim Larson (1998) echoes this sentiment noting: "School disciplinary procedures . . . tend to rely more on reactive administrative interventions such as suspensions and expulsions . . ." (p. 284). However, Larson offers a solution that involves students in the design and execution of schoolwide discipline policies:

> A code of discipline specifies what would be considered appropriate school conduct and alleviates controversies associated with arbitrary rule enforcement. . . . Unlike the older, legalistic code models with their heavy-handed authoritarian emphasis on rules and punishment, a modern code of discipline should be developed "bottom up" with collaborative input from students, teachers, support staff, and parents, and reviewed frequently for modification. (p. 285)

Larson goes on to explain that involving students develops self-discipline and responsibility. Ultimately, this is the most important benefit of such an approach. George Bear (1998) agrees:

> Self-discipline connotes internal motivation for one's behavior, the internalization of democratic ideals, and is most evident when external regulations of behavior are absent. (p. 16)

Much of the work of William Glasser (1969, 1986, 1990) is quite relevant to the discussion here. His approach includes showing students appropriate behavior (as opposed to telling them) and engaging their cooperation in the design of a schoolwide disciplinary program. Thomas Gordon's work also promotes self-discipline and responsibility (Gordon, 1970, 1974). Key features of his model include engaging students in "no-lose" agreements around problem issues such as what to do about fighting in the lunchroom. Solutions would be reached jointly by students and school staff.

Action Step 5. Establish a system that allows for the early detection of students who have high potential for violence and extreme behaviors.

Tary Tobin and George Sugai (1999) demonstrated the use and impact of early detection of such students in a longitudinal study involving 526 students. After examining student records in grade 6 to predict violence in grade 8, they reported the following:

> Results suggest that a discipline referral at Grade 6, for either violent or nonviolent behavior, should prompt educators and parents to intervene but with a positive behavior support plan likely to change the predicted trajectory of continual antisocial behaviors. Even a few discipline referrals in Grade 6 and, in some cases, even one referral should be recognized as a warning of more problems to come and thus a need to develop and implement preventative interventions. (p. 47)

Figure 6.1 reports the correlations computed in their study between violent behavior in grade 8 and certain types of referrals in grade 6. The figure lists four types of misbehavior and indicators of misbehavior: violent fighting, violent harassing, nonviolent misbehavior, and out-of-school suspension (as opposed to in-school suspension which is usually administered when misbehavior is not considered serious or habitual). Given that correlations in the social sciences are rarely greater than .50 (Cohen, 1988), those reported in Figure 6.1 are quite high, indicating that behaviors such as violent fighting, violent harassing, and even nonviolent misbehavior are good predictors of violent behavior. In short, data such as these should be used to help identify students with high potentials for extreme misbehavior. However, it is also important to note that these data should not be used to typecast students but to identify those who might need extra support or help to avoid potential negative consequences of behavioral tendencies.

Summary

This chapter has addressed the fourth school-level factor—a safe and orderly environment.

	FIGURE 6.1	
	Correlations Between Misbehavior Indicators in Grade 6 and Violent Behavior in Grade 8	
Type of Misbehavior Indicators in Grade 6	Violent Incidents in Grade 8	
	Girls	Boys
Violent fighting	0.61 (n = 142)	0.50 (n = 209)
Violent harassing	0.43 (n = 142)	0.33 (n = 209)
Nonviolent misbehavior	0.34 (n = 142)	0.35 (n = 209)
Out-of-school suspension	0.33 (n = 142)	0.32 (n = 209)

Source: Tobin, T. J., & Sugai, G. M. (1999). Using sixth-grade school records to predict school violence, chronic discipline problems, and high school outcomes. *Journal of Emotional and Behavioral Disorders, 7*(1), 40–53.

It was described as a necessary but not sufficient condition for academic achievement. I recommended five action steps to achieve a safe and orderly environment. These address establishing ecological interventions, establishing schoolwide rules and procedures and consequences for violating those rules and procedures, establishing programs for enhancing student self-discipline and responsibility, and implementing a system for the early detection of students at risk for violence or extreme behavior.

COLLEGIALITY AND PROFESSIONALISM

The fifth school-level factor is "collegiality and professionalism." This factor deals with the manner in which staff members in the school interact and the extent to which they approach their work as professionals. As shown in Figure 2.3 (p. 19), researchers use a variety of descriptive terms for this factor. Edmonds uses "administrative leadership"; Levine and Lezotte use "strong leadership" and "practice oriented staff development." Sammons calls it "professional leadership," "shared vision and goals," and "a learning organization"; Bosker and Scheerens and Marzano use "leadership" and "cooperation."

The early discussions of staff collegiality and professionalism were couched within the context of "school climate" in the 1970s. For some researchers, school climate was the umbrella defining effective schooling. This was certainly the case for Wilbur Brookover and his colleagues (Brookover & Lezotte, 1979; Brookover & Schneider, 1975; Brookover, et al., 1978; Brookover, et al.,

1979). In his analysis of the characteristics of effective schools versus ineffective schools (as defined by the academic achievement of those students from low socioeconomic backgrounds), Brookover and colleagues (1978) note

> . . . we believe that the differences in school climate explain much of the differences in academic achievement between schools that is normally attributed to composition. (p. 303)

Some researchers' descriptions of school climate are so broad as to encompass a wide variety of school-level factors such as leadership, classroom instruction, classroom management, the physical surroundings, and the nature and tone of relationships therein (Anderson, 1982; Gottsfredson, Hybl, Gottsfredson, & Castaneda, 1986).

What I refer to here as collegiality and professionalism is probably closest to Deal and Kennedy's (1983) conception of "organizational climate." They explain

COLLEGIALITY AND PROFESSIONALISM | 61

The organizational climate in a school has been defined as the collective personality of a school based upon an atmosphere distinguished by the social and professional interactions of the individuals in the school. (Deal and Kennedy, 1983, p. 14)

I use the phrase "collegiality and professionalism" instead of organizational climate for two reasons. First, it more accurately highlights aspects of previous treatments of climate that have strong statistical relationships with student achievement. That is, the studies that have found a statistically significant relationship between school climate and student achievement have focused on collegiality and professionalism. Second, it avoids confounding elements of the overall school climate with individual classroom climate. Some researchers believe that the overall school climate is little more than the aggregation of individual classroom climates (Johnson & Johnson, 1979). However, much research and theoretical evidence supports the convention of separating overall school climate from the classroom climate (Fraser, 1986).

To understand the impact of collegiality and professionalism on student achievement, let's consider each individually.

Collegiality

The specifics of this fifth school-level factor begin with collegiality—the manner in which teachers interact with one another. As Christine Villani (1996) notes

Collegial behavior is demonstrated by teachers who are supportive of one another. They openly enjoy professional interactions, are respectful and courteous of each other's needs. (p. 44)

Fullan and Hargreaves (1996) warn that collegiality cannot be "contrived" by requiring teachers to plan together or consult together, to engage in peer coaching, or the like. Rather, collegiality is characterized by authentic interactions that are professional in nature. According to Fullan and Hargreaves, these behaviors include

- openly sharing failures and mistakes,
- demonstrating respect for each other, and
- constructively analyzing and criticizing practices and procedures.

In effect, collegiality is characterized by tacit norms of professional behavior (Deal & Peterson, 1990; Lortie, 1975).

One important aspect of the definition of collegial behavior is what it does *not* include. Collegiality is commonly interpreted to involve social interactions and explicit friendships among teachers. Noah Friedkin and Michael Slater (1994) studied 17 elementary schools to examine the relationship between student achievement and the extent to which teachers discussed professional issues, sought advice regarding professional issues, and interacted as friends. The correlations between these types of interactions and student achievement are reported in Figure 7.1 (p. 62).

The most striking result is the negative correlation between student achievement and "friendship" interactions among teachers—the more friendship interactions, the lower students' academic achievement. Of course, findings based on correlations (with low numbers of cases involved at that) should be interpreted cautiously although they do cast doubt on the perception that teachers must

FIGURE 7.1

Relationship Between Types of Teacher Interactions and Student Achievement

Type of Interaction	Correlation
Discussion	0.326
Advice	0.222
Friendship	-0.252

Note that these are rank order correlations with n = 17
Rank order correlations depict the strength of relationship between the ranking by teachers of the importance of these factors with the ranking by principals of the importance of these factors.

Source: Friedkin, N. E., & Slater, M. R. (1994). School leadership and performance: A social network approach. *Sociology of Education*, 67, 139–157.

be friends or engage in social interactions for the school to be effective. Referring to friendship and social interactions among teachers as "network cohesion," and the leadership of the principal as "advice centrality" Friedkin and Slater note

> Our evidence does not support the conclusion that teacher network cohesion has a strong effect on school performance independent of [the] principal's advice centrality. (p. 151)

Professionalism

Certainly one aspect of professionalism is a sense of efficacy on the part of teachers. Kent Peterson (1994) explains that, among other things, efficacy is grounded in teachers' perception that they can effect change in their schools. To do this, they must be a valued and critical part of the school's policy-setting mechanisms.

Another widely researched aspect of professionalism deals with the level of teacher

experience. Ronald Ferguson (1991) performed one of the most frequently cited studies on the effects of teacher experience on student achievement. As Linda Darling-Hammond (1997a) describes the study:

> In an analysis of 900 Texas school districts Ronald Ferguson found that teachers' experience—as measured by scores on a licensing examination, master's degrees, and experience, accounted for about 40% of the measured variance in students' reading and mathematics achievement at grades 1 through 11, more than any other single factor. (p. 8)

The results of the Ferguson study (as reported by Darling-Hammond) are depicted in Figure 7.2.

The proportions reported in Figure 7.2 appear to contradict the basic model in Chapter 1 where I made the case that student background factors account for about 80 percent of the measured variance in student achievement while schooling accounts for about the other 20 percent. How can schools

---

FIGURE 7.2

Percentage of Variance in Student Achievement Accounted for by Various Factors

Factor	Percentage of Variance Accounted for in Student Achievement
Home and family	49%
Teacher qualifications	43%
Class size	8%

Source: Darling-Hammond, L. (1997a). *Doing what matters most: Investing in quality teaching.* NY: National Commission on Teaching and America's Future.

---

in general account for only 20 percent of the variance in student achievement when teacher qualifications alone account for 43 percent of the variance? This issue is discussed in some depth in Technical Note 5, p. 191, but I will briefly address it here.

The Ferguson study used *average* achievement for a school or a district as the primary dependent measure. Examining the relationship between average achievement for a district and the average score in a district for teacher qualification produces a correlation between these two factors that is much higher than if individual scores for students and teachers were used. Keep in mind that this form of data aggregation typically produces artificially high correlations. With the cautions above noted, it is useful to examine the research on the specific aspects of teacher experience that affect student achievement.

Teacher longevity and certification are often cited as experiential factors that have an impact on student achievement. For example, a study of high- versus low-achieving schools in New York City with demographically similar students found that

years of experience and levels of certification accounted for 90 percent of the variation in student achievement at the school level (Armour-Thomas, Clay, Domanico, Bruno, & Allen, 1989). Teacher licensing certainly seems justified. Indeed, in a landmark report entitled *What Matters Most: Teaching for America's Future* (National Commission on Teaching and America's Future, 1998), licensure was identified as one of three critical factors necessary to develop effective teachers. The report used the metaphor of a "three-legged stool" for quality assurance:

> The three-legged stool of quality assurance—teacher education program accreditation, initial teacher licensing, and advanced professional certification—is becoming more sturdy as a continuum of standards has been developed to guide teacher learning across the career. (p. 29)

Teacher subject-matter knowledge is also frequently cited as critical to student achievement (Andrews, Blackmon, & Mackey, 1980; Haney, Madaus, & Kreitzer, 1987; Schalock, 1979; Soar, Medley, & Coker, 1983). This was also one of the primary findings in *What Matters Most*. However, its relationship with student achievement is not as straightforward as you might think. Reviews of the research commonly reveal a spotty relationship between teacher subject-matter knowledge and achievement. For example, Byrne (1983) found that in 31 studies only 17 showed a positive relationship between the two. Ashton & Crocker (1987) found that only 5 of 14 studies exhibited a positive relationship. Monk (1994) found that teacher subject-matter knowledge was related to student achievement only up to a certain point. That is, a minimal level of subject-matter knowledge was a prerequisite for effective teaching. However, after a certain level was reached, an increase in subject-matter knowledge was not related to enhanced achievement. These findings imply that it would not be accurate to assume that the more a teacher knows about the subject matter, the better teacher he will be. Again, a critical minimum level is certainly needed, but beyond this point the relationship between teacher subject-matter knowledge and enhanced student achievement begins to taper off. Additionally, it is reasonable to assume that the critical level of knowledge is different from grade level to grade level. The knowledge requirements to teach 5th grade mathematics are certainly different from those for 12th grade trigonometry.

Pedagogical Knowledge

While subject-matter knowledge in itself might not be consistently associated with student achievement, pedagogical knowledge is. As Darling-Hammond (2000) notes

It may be that the positive effects of subject matter knowledge are augmented or offset by knowledge of how to teach the subject to various kinds of students. That is, the degree of pedagogical skill may interact with subject matter knowledge to bolster or reduce teacher performance. (p. 6)

The importance of the relationship between pedagogical knowledge and student achievement is also reported by others (Brown, Smith, & Stein, 1995; Byrne, 1983; Cohen & Hill, 1997; Wiley & Yoon, 1995). In a related study of 200 teachers, Ferguson and Womack (1993) found that the amount of courses teachers took in instructional techniques accounted for four times the variance in teacher performance than did subject-matter knowledge. Similarly, in a study involving some 7,500 8th grade students, Harold Weglinsky (2000) found that teacher participation in professional development activities accounted for significant amounts of variation in mathematics and science achievement. In fact, teacher experience and involvement in professional development activities accounted for about as much of the variance in student achievement as did student background. Professionalism, then, includes a certain level of knowledge about one's subject area, but perhaps more important, it also involves pedagogical knowledge of how best to teach that subject-matter content.

Action Steps

I recommend three action steps to foster staff collegiality and professionalism.

Action Step 1. Establish norms of conduct and behavior that engender collegiality and professionalism.

Many researchers and theorists directly or indirectly recommend the overt establishment of norms of behavior for teachers and administrators (Blase and Blase, 2001; Blase and Kirby, 2000; Fullan, 1993; Sergiovanni, 1992; Dickman & Stanford-Blair, 2002). Some of the commonly recommended areas around which to establish norms include

- how staff will resolve conflicts,
- how staff will address and solve professional problems,
- how staff will share information about students,
- how staff will communicate to third parties about other staff members, and
- how staff will behave during professional activities (e.g., staff meetings, workshops).

Ideally, norms in these areas are arrived at by teachers and administrators through consensus. Once established, these norms are made highly visible (e.g., as a reminder at staff and faculty meetings or prominently displayed in the staff handbook).

Action Step 2. Establish governance structures that allow for teacher involvement in decisions and policies for the school.

For teachers to develop a sense of efficacy, they must be represented in governance structures that establish direction and policy for the school. Again, Comer's School Development Program provides a noteworthy prototype. Recall that Comer's model employs three governance mechanisms: (1) the School Planning and Management Team, (2) the Student and Staff Support Team, and (3) the Parent Team. Two of these directly involve teachers. The School Planning Team is headed by the principal and includes teachers, parents, professional support staff, and paraprofessionals. This team is responsible for establishing major policies and directions. The Student and Staff Support Team involves teachers, school psychologists, social workers, special education teachers, counselors, and other support service staff. It provides direct input to the School Planning and Management Team and is charged with ensuring that the school environment supports learning and the concerns of individual classroom teachers.

Action Step 3. Engage teachers in meaningful staff development activities.

Perhaps the most obvious way to address the issue of professionalism is to engage teachers in meaningful staff development activities. Although many schools have regularly scheduled staff development sessions, much of what is done in these sessions is not necessarily meaningful or useful in terms of impacting student achievement. As Judith Little notes

> Much staff development or inservice communicates a relatively impoverished view of teachers, teaching, and teacher development. Compared with the complexity, subtlety, and uncertainty of the classroom, professional development is often a remarkably low-intensity enterprise. It requires little in the way of intellectual struggle or emotional engagement and takes only superficial account of teachers' histories or

circumstances. Compared with the complexity and ambiguity of the most ambitious reforms, professional development is too often substantively weak and politically marginal. . . . Professional development must be constructed in ways that deepen the discussion, open up the debates, and enrich the array of possibilities for action. (p. 14)

Michael Garet and his colleagues (Garet, Porter, Desmone, Birman, & Yoon, 2001) conducted one of the most extensive studies on the effects of staff development activities. Their survey of 1,000 teachers revealed that those features of staff development with the strongest relationship to reported change in teacher behavior are (1) focus on content knowledge, (2) opportunities for active learning, and (3) overall coherence of the staff development activities.

Focus on content refers to the extent to which staff development activities address specific strategies for specific subject areas. This is not to say that staff development activities must be subject-specific (e.g., staff development for mathematics, staff development for science), though this is certainly an effective option. At the very least, pedagogical knowledge must be presented to teachers in the context of their specific subject areas. Staff development activities that present generic strategies and do not provide opportunities for classroom application are probably not very effective in terms of actually changing teacher behavior.

Opportunities for active learning elaborates on the notion that teachers are able to apply the pedagogical knowledge they learn. The best application task they might engage in is to actually try out a particular instructional strategy. This means that they return to their classrooms and actually use the strategy in an action research environment—an environment in which they informally examine the impact of various strategies on student achievement.

Overall coherence means that the staff development program is perceived as a coherent, integrated whole with "staff development days" building on one another. Length and number of staff development activities are positively correlated with change in teacher behavior. Thus, the more staff development provided, the greater the change in teacher behavior.

It is easy to become disheartened with the staff development efforts in most schools. In my experience, most schools and districts violate virtually every principle in Garet's study by (1) presenting staff development sessions that are not tied to specific subject areas, (2) not providing opportunities for teachers to translate generic strategies into the context of specific subject areas, (3) not providing opportunities for teachers to field test the strategies presented during staff development days, and (4) providing only a few staff development days that are unrelated and disjointed.

The pattern of staff development as practiced in the United States stands in sharp contrast to that in Japan. Stevenson and Stigler (1992) note: "By Japanese law, beginning teachers must receive a minimum of twenty days of in-service training during their first year on the job" (p. 159). Additionally, Japanese staff development activities employ hands-on efforts to change specific lessons and units. Stigler and Hiebert (1999) note that this is done in the context of what the Japanese refer to as "lesson study" or *jugyou kenkyuu*, which is an aspect of *kounaikenshuu*, a comprehensive set of activities that form the crux of school improvement. While engaged in *kounaikenshuu*, teachers work together on various teams with various roles and functions:

> One of the most common components of *kounaikenshuu* is lesson study (*jugyou kenkyuu*). In lesson study, groups of teachers meet regularly over long periods of time (ranging from several months to a year) to work on the design, implementation, testing, and improvement of one or several "research lessons" (*kenkyuu jugyou*). By all indications, lesson study is extremely popular and highly valued by Japanese teachers, especially at the elementary level. It is the linchpin of the improvement process. (pp. 110–111)

Although it would probably be difficult to perform a wholesale transplant of lesson study as practiced by Japanese educators into the U.S. system, certain characteristics might be readily transported. To do this, Stigler and Hiebert recommend that teachers organize themselves into teams based on common interests or issues in teaching their subjects. They then systematically employ specific techniques in the context of specific lessons and observe each other doing so. They give each other feedback regarding what worked well and what could be changed in these trial lessons. Finally, they capture and archive collective knowledge gained from these efforts for others to build on.

Summary

Defining features of collegiality and professionalism includes the manner in which teachers interact with one another and the nature, scope, and sequence of professional development activities. Collegiality and professionalism involve interactions between teachers that are collaborative and congenial.

Section II

TEACHER-LEVEL FACTORS

List of Figures in Section II

THE TEACHER-LEVEL FACTORS

Now we turn our attention to those factors that affect individual students in the classroom—the independent impact that a teacher can have on student achievement. Naturally, an individual teacher is influenced by decisions the school makes (decisions that include a guaranteed and viable curriculum, challenging goals, and feedback). However, the teacher-level factors addressed here are primarily a function of decisions made by individual teachers, including instructional strategies, classroom management, and classroom curriculum design.

Before the mid-1980s, studies of effective schooling tended to look at school-level factors only, that is, the school as having a unitary and consistent impact on student achievement. Good and Brophy (1986) warned of the consequences of this perspective:

> Studies of large samples of schools yield important profiles of more and less successful schools, but these are *group averages* [original emphasis] that may or may not

describe how a single effective teacher actually behaves in a particular effective school. Persons who use research to guide practice sometimes expect all teachers' behavior to reflect the group average. Such simplistic thinking is apt to lead the literature to be too broadly and inappropriately applied. (p. 588)

A useful question, then, for anyone wishing to understand those factors that enhance student achievement is this: What influence does an individual teacher have apart from what the school does?

The Effect of Individual Teachers

Although most attempts to answer this question arrive at slightly different quantitative estimates, all researchers agree that the impact of decisions made by individual teachers is far greater than the impact of decisions made at the school level. Reporting on their analysis of achievement scores from five subject areas (mathematics, reading, language arts, social studies, and science) for some 60,000 students across grades 3 through 5, S. Paul Wright, Sandra Horn, and William Sanders (1997) note

> The results of this study will document that the most important factor affecting student learning is the teacher. In addition, the results show wide variation in effectiveness among teachers. The immediate and clear implication of this finding is that seemingly more can be done to improve education by improving the effectiveness of teachers than by any other single factor. *Effective teachers appear to be effective with students of all achievement levels regardless of the levels of heterogeneity in their classes* [emphasis in original]. If the teacher is ineffective, students under that teacher's tutelage will achieve inadequate progress academically, regardless of how similar or different they are regarding their academic achievement. (p. 63)

This study and others conducted by William Sanders and his colleagues (Sanders & Horn, 1994; Wright, Horn, & Sanders, 1997) rather dramatically illustrate the profound impact an individual teacher can have on student achievement. For example, Kati Haycock (1998) notes that Sanders' results are most revealing in determining the achievement differences between students who spend a year with a highly effective teacher as opposed to a less effective teacher. This difference is depicted in Figure 8.1. On the average, the most effective teachers produced gains of about 53 percentage points in student achievement over one year, whereas the least effective teachers produced achievement gains of about 14 percentage points over one year. To understand these results, consider the fact that researchers estimate that students typically gain about 34 percentile points in achievement during one academic year (see

---

FIGURE 8.1

Student Achievement Differences Affected by Teachers

Teacher	Student achievement gain in 1 year
Least effective	14 percentage points
Most effective	53 percentage points

Note: Sanders identified "most effective" versus "least effective" teachers by ranking them in terms of gains in student achievement and then organizing that rank order into five categories or quintiles. "Most effective" teachers were defined as those in the highest category (quintile 1); "least effective" teachers were defined as those in the lowest category (quintile 5).
For a technical discussion, see Haycock, 1998.

Adapted from
Sanders, W. L., & Horn, S. P. (1994). The Tennessee value-added assessment system (TVAAS): Mixed-model methodology in educational assessment. *Journal of Personnel Evaluation in Education, 8,* 299–311

Wright, S. P., Horn, S. P., & Sanders, W. L. (1997). Teacher and classroom context effects on student achievement: Implications for teacher evaluation. *Journal of Personnel Evaluation in Education, 11,* 57–67.

Glass, McGaw, & Smith, 1981). That is, a student who scores at the 50th percentile in mathematics in September will score at the 84th percentile on the same test given in May. The findings reported in Figure 8.1 indicate that over a year, students in classes of the most effective teachers will gain much more in achievement than is expected (i.e., 53 percentile points as opposed to 34 percentile points). However, students in the classes of the least effective teachers will gain much less in achievement than is expected (i.e., 14 percentile points as opposed to 34). These findings are even more startling when we consider that some researchers have estimated that students gain about 6 percentage points simply from growing one year older and gleaning new knowledge and information through everyday life (Hattie, 1992; Cahen & Davis, 1977). From this perspective, we might say the least effective teachers add little to students' knowledge over what would be expected from one year of maturation.

If the effect of attending the class of one of the least effective teachers for a year is not debilitating enough, the cumulative effect can be devastating. To illustrate, consider Figure 8.2, which is again based on data from the work of Sanders and his colleagues (as reported by Haycock, 1998).

Figure 8.2 shows a 54-percentile point discrepancy in achievement gains between students with least effective teachers versus those with most effective teachers—29 percentage points versus 83 percentage points respectively over three years. Commenting on this discrepancy, Haycock (1998) notes

> Differences of this magnitude—50 percentile points—are stunning. As all of us know only too well, they can represent the differences between a "remedial" label and placement in the "accelerated" or even "gifted" track. And the difference between entry into a selective college and a lifetime at McDonald's. (p. 4)

Sanders and his colleagues gathered their data from elementary students in Tennessee, yet they are not the only ones to find these differences in achievement. Haycock (1998) reports similar findings from studies conducted in Dallas and Boston.

I have taken a slightly different approach and come to the same conclusions. The studies conducted in Tennessee, Dallas, and Boston were based on data acquired from students over time; I started my calculations with the assumption gathered from my review of research—that schooling accounts for about 20 percent of the variance in student achievement (see the discussion in

---

FIGURE 8.2

Cumulative Effects Over Three Years Between Students with Least Effective Versus Most Effective Teachers

Most effective teacher	83 percentile point gain
Least effective teacher	29 percentile point gain

Chapter 1). However, in my synthesis of the research, I also found that about 67 percent of this effect is due to the effect of individual teachers. That is, about 13 percent of the variance in student achievement in a given subject area is due to what the teacher does and about 7 percent is due to what the school does (Bosker, 1992; Luyten, 1994; Madaus et al., 1979; Marzano, 2000a; Stringfield & Teddlie, 1989). The implications of my analysis are reported in Figure 8.3. For a detailed discussion of how Figure 8.3 was derived, see Technical Note 6, pp. 191–192.

The six scenarios in Figure 8.3 show effects on student achievement of various combinations of school and teacher effectiveness under the assumption that the student enters school achieving at the 50th percentile. If a student begins at the 50th per-

centile in mathematics, for example, and attends an average school and has an average teacher, her achievement will still be at the 50th percentile at the end of about two years (as depicted in the first scenario in Figure 8.3). Now let's consider the second scenario where this student attends a school that is one of the least effective and has a teacher that is classified as one of the least effective. After two years the student has dropped from the 50th percentile to the 3rd percentile. In the third scenario, the student is in a school classified as one of the most effective but has a teacher classified as one of the least effective. Although she enters the class at the 50th percentile, she leaves it two years later at the 37th percentile. In the fourth scenario, the student is in a school that is considered one of the least effective, but she is with

---

FIGURE 8.3

Effects on Student Achievement of School and Teacher Effectiveness with Student Entering School at the 50th Percentile

School and Teacher Scenario	Achievement Percentile After Two Years
Average School and Average Teacher	50th
Least Effective School and Least Effective Teacher	3rd
Most Effective School and Least Effective Teacher	37th
Least Effective School and Most Effective Teacher	63rd
Most Effective School and Most Effective Teacher	96th
Most Effective School and Average Teacher	78th

See Technical Note 6, pp. 191–192, to determine how average, least effective, and most effective schools and teachers were defined.

Adapted from Marzano, R. J. (2000a). A new era of school reform: Going where the research takes us. Aurora, CO: Mid-continent Research for Education and Learning (ERIC Document Reproduction Service No. ED 454255)

a teacher classified as one of the most effective. The student now leaves the class at the 63rd percentile—13 percentile points higher than she entered. The fifth scenario is the most optimistic of all. The student is not only in a school classified as one of the most effective but is with a teacher classified as one of the most effective. She enters the class at the 50th percentile but leaves at the 96th percentile. In the sixth scenario, the student is in a school that is one of the most effective and is with a teacher considered average. After two years the student has risen from the 50th percentile to the 78th percentile.

Regardless of the research basis, it is clear that effective teachers have a profound influence on student achievement and ineffective teachers do not. In fact, ineffective teachers might actually impede the learning of their students. What then are the characteristics of an effective teacher?

Characteristics of an Effective Teacher

I have concluded that the nearly 3,000,000 teachers in this country (National Center for Educational Statistics, 2002) are probably distributed normally in terms of their effectiveness as defined in terms of their impact on student achievement. Consistent with characteristics of the normal or bell curve, most of the teachers are in the middle of the effectiveness distribution or not too far away from the average. There are a few at the extreme positive end and a few at the extreme negative end. This means that most teachers are a little below or a little above average in terms of their impact on student achievement. I

would put teachers at the extreme positive end in the most effective category and teachers at the extreme negative end in the least effective category. A teacher who masters the three factors I have identified would not necessarily be reassigned to the most effective category. Rather, I believe that mastery of the three teacher-level factors will certainly render a teacher at least average (and probably well above average). Yet, teachers who are average in terms of their effectiveness can still have a powerful impact on student achievement as illustrated in the sixth scenario in Figure 8.3.

Specifically, this scenario illustrates that if teachers exhibit average performance and a school is willing to do all that it can to be most effective, then students in that school will demonstrate remarkable gains. Many principals have reported to me that they don't have the freedom or resources to hire the most experienced or most talented teachers. This discussion indicates that such talent and experience are not a prerequisite to effectiveness. If a school is willing to do all that it can at the school level and if all teachers in the school are at least competent in their profession, the school can have a tremendous impact on student achievement.

Teacher-Level Factors: A Comparison Across Researchers

My three teacher-level factors are not the only ways to organize the research on teacher effectiveness. In fact, researchers have identified many variables that correlate with teacher effectiveness. Kathleen Cotton

(1995) has identified more than 150 variables that are components of teacher effectiveness; Barry Fraser and his colleagues (Fraser, Walberg, Welch, & Hattie, 1987) list some 30 variables. These long lists of variables have been organized in a variety of ways. For example, Jere Brophy (1996) uses the following categories:

- instruction,
- classroom management,
- disciplinary interactions, and
- student socialization.

Bert Creemers (1994) uses three categories: curriculum, grouping procedures, and teacher behaviors. Finally, Cotton (1995) uses the following categories to organize the 150 variables she has identified:

- planning,
- setting goals,
- classroom management and organization,
- instruction,
- teacher-student interactions,
- equity, and
- assessment.

As was the case with the school-level factors, my three teacher-level factors are, in most cases, simply a reorganization of the work of other researchers. See Figure 8.4 for a more explicit explanation.

To derive my three factors, I have collapsed two or more categories from another researcher into a single category or placed elements of another researcher's single category into two of my categories. For example, I collapsed three of Cotton's categories into the single category of "classroom management" because Cotton's description of these elements is nearly synonymous with my description of classroom management. For

FIGURE 8.4			
Comparing Teacher-Level Factors Across Researchers			
Marzano (2000a)	Brophy (1996)	Creemers (1994)	Cotton (1995)
Instructional strategies	Instruction	Grouping procedures/teacher behaviors	Planning Setting goals Instruction
Classroom management	Classroom management Disciplinary interventions Student socialization	Teacher behavior	Classroom management and organization Teacher-student interactions Equity
Classroom curriculum design		Curriculum	Assessment

similar reasons, I placed Creemer's category of "teacher behaviors" into my categories "instructional strategies" and "classroom management."

The following three chapters address each of the three teacher-level factors. Chapter 9 explores instructional strategies, Chapter 10 explores classroom management, and Chapter 11 explores classroom curriculum design.

Despite discussing the teacher-level factors in isolation, they are not practiced in isolation. In fact, studies that have attempted to identify the unique or independent effects of instruction versus management versus classroom curricular design have not met with much success (Levy, Wubbels, Brekelmans, & Morganfield, 1997). The act of teaching is a holistic endeavor. Effective teachers employ effective instructional strategies, classroom management techniques, and classroom curricular design in a fluent, seamless fashion. A variety of researchers support this conclusion (Leinhardt & Greens, 1986; Brooks & Hawke, 1985). In his article "In Pursuit of the Expert Pedagogue," David Berliner (1986) likens an expert teacher to a chess master, capable of seeing many things simultaneously and making judgments with seeming ease and fluency.

The interdependence of the three teacher-level factors underscores their difference from the five school-level factors. The school-level factors are ranked in the order of their impact on student achievement, but the teacher-level factors are not. Although there might be research available or in process that allows for this delineation, I have not yet found it.

Summary

This chapter introduces the three teacher-level factors: instructional strategies, classroom management, and classroom curriculum design. Although discussed separately, they cannot be isolated in terms of their classroom application or their impact on student achievement. Additionally, the impact of the individual classroom teacher could have a greater impact on student achievement than the five school-level factors.

INSTRUCTIONAL STRATEGIES

A teacher-level factor that affects student achievement is "instructional strategies." It is perhaps self-evident that more effective teachers use more effective instructional strategies. It is probably also true that effective teachers have more instructional strategies at their disposal.

Since the middle of the 20th century, chess masters have been a subject of fascination for psychologists (deGroot, 1946; Chase & Simon, 1973; Simon, 1980). One general conclusion is that over time they have learned to recognize thousands of possible chess piece arrangements and their associated counter moves. By one estimation, the chess master has acquired 50,000 such chunks of information (see Anderson, 1995). Using David Berliner's analogy (1986), we might reason that the expert teacher has acquired a wide array of instructional strategies along with the knowledge of when these strategies might be the most useful.

What, then, are the instructional strategies that have proven to be effective?

Instructional Strategies That Work

William Bennett, former Secretary of Education, spearheaded one of many attempts to identify instructional strategies that have strong track records of enhancing student achievement. He established the importance of a well-articulated list of research-based strategies in the introduction to his book *What Works: Research About Teaching and Learning* (1986):

> The preparation of this report has been on my mind since the day, a year ago, when I was sworn in as Secretary of Education. In my first statement upon assuming this office, I said, "We must remember that education is not a dismal science. In education research, of course, there is much to find out, but education, despite efforts to make it so, is not essentially mysterious. (p. v)

Bennett quite forcibly makes the point that effective teaching is not as mysterious as some might think. Research can and should provide some clear guidance on the specifics of effective teaching.

Bennett's efforts produced a list of more than 40 research-based practices. Those practices that dealt specifically with classroom instruction included

- use of experiments,
- teacher estimation strategies,
- teacher expectations,
- effort reinforcement,
- classroom time management,
- direct instruction,
- memorization,
- questioning,
- homework, and
- classroom assessment.

Other researchers have produced similar lists. Bert Creemers (1994) identified the following instructional strategies:

- advance organizers,
- evaluation,
- feedback,
- corrective instruction,
- mastery learning,
- ability grouping,
- homework,
- clarity of presentation, and
- questioning.

In his review of the research, John Hattie (1992; also reported in Fraser et al., 1987) provided the list in Figure 9.1.

FIGURE 9.1

Instructional Strategies Identified by John Hattie

Strategy	Number of studies examined	Effect size	Percentile Gain
Individualization	630	0.14	6
Simulation and games	111	0.34	13
Computer-assisted instruction	566	0.31	12
Tutoring	125	0.50	19
Learning hierarchies	25	0.19	8
Mastery learning	104	0.50	19
Homework	110	0.43	17
Instructional media	4421	0.30	12

Source: Hattie, J. A. (1992). Measuring the effects of schooling. *Australian Journal of Education, 36*(1), 5–13.

What separates Hattie's research from that of Bennett and Creemers is that he reports the effect sizes for the various categories of instructional strategies. The effect size reports how many standard deviations the average score in the experimental group (the group that uses the instructional strategy) is above the average score in the control group (the group that did not use the instructional strategy). To illustrate, according to Figure 9.1, tutoring has an average effect size (based on 125 studies examined by Hattie) of .50.

Everything else being equal, the typical student who receives tutoring will obtain achievement scores .50 standard deviation higher than the typical student who does not receive tutoring. This translates into a 19 percentile point gain. (See Technical Note 4, pp. 190–191, for a detailed explanation of effect sizes).

My colleagues and I undertook a similar effort (Marzano, 1998a; Marzano, Gaddy, & Dean, 2000; Marzano, Pickering, & Pollock, 2001). The results are reported in Figure 9.2.

FIGURE 9.2

Categories of Instructional Strategies That Affect Student Achievement

Category	Average Effect Size	Percentile Gain	Number of Effect Sizes	Standard Deviation
Identifying similarities and differences	1.61	45	31	0.31
Summarizing and note taking	1.00	34	179	0.50
Reinforcing effort and providing recognition	0.80	29	21	0.35
Homework and practice	0.77	28	134	0.36
Nonlinguistic representations	0.75	27	246	0.40
Cooperative learning	0.73	27	122	0.40
Setting objectives and providing feedback	0.61	23	408	0.28
Generating and testing hypotheses	0.61	23	63	0.79
Questions, cues, and advance organizers	0.59	22	1,251	0.26

Sources:

Marzano, R. J. (1998a). *A theory-based meta-analysis of research on instruction.* Aurora, CO: Mid-continent Research for Education and Learning. (ERIC Document Reproduction No. ED 427 087)

Marzano, R. J., Gaddy, B. B., & Dean, C. (2000). *What works in classroom instruction?* Aurora, CO: Mid-continent Research for Education and Learning.

Marzano, R. J., Pickering, D. J., & Pollock, J. E. (2001). *Classroom instruction that works: Research-based strategies for increasing student achievement.* Alexandria, VA: Association for Supervision and Curriculum Development.

It is important to comment on the relatively large effect sizes reported in Figure 9.2. The average effect sizes look quite large if you contrast these effect sizes with those commonly reported for the school-level factors. To illustrate, reconsider Scheerens and Bosker's (1997) ranking of the school-level factors, as depicted in Figure 2.1 (p. 17) of this book. The top-ranked factor is time, for which Scheerens and Bosker report an effect size of .39. Yet, the *smallest* effect size in Figure 9.2 is 0.59 for "questions, cues, and advance organizers." Why would the smallest effect size for the instructional strategies reported in Figure 9.2 be greater than the largest effect size reported for the school-level factors? It is because the studies from which the effect sizes in Figure 9.2 were computed generally employed assessments specific to the content being taught while a particular instructional strategy was being used. For example, a study might examine the impact of a particular advance organizer on students' understanding of information presented on the cell. The test used to assess students' achievement was specifically on information about the cell. We might call such assessments "curriculum sensitive."

The studies on school-level factors generally employ standardized tests that are more general in nature than such curriculum-sensitive assessments. When general tests are used as opposed to curriculum-sensitive tests, effect sizes by definition will be much smaller. As George Madaus and colleagues (1979) noted: " . . . what we call curriculum-sensitive measures are precisely that. Compared to conventional standardized tests, they are clearly more dependent on the characteristics of schools and what goes on in them" (pp. 223–224).

Since the publication of *Classroom Instruction That Works: Research-Based Strategies for Increasing Student Achievement* (Marzano, Pickering, & Pollock, 2001), the nine categories of instructional strategies listed in Figure 9.2 have been the basis of study and discussion for thousands of teachers. I have found that the categories are more useful if subdivided into specific behaviors. This makes sense since I created the nine categories by combining strategies with similar characteristics. For example, specific instructional behaviors that involve comparison tasks, classification tasks, metaphors, and analogies were all organized under the general heading "identifying similarities and differences." In all, the nine general instructional categories break down into 34 more specific behaviors as shown in Figure 9.3, p. 82.

Lists of instructional strategies like Figure 9.3 provide useful suggestions for classroom teachers but not much guidance on how to plan for effective instruction. A more useful practice is to organize strategies to provide a framework of effective instructional design. Madeline Hunter (1984) designed the most widely used framework, referred to as "lesson design," although others have been proposed (Reigeluth, 1983; Good & Grouws, 1983). The major components of Hunter's framework are depicted in Figure 9.4 (p. 84).

Historically, lesson design carried the unintended implication that all lessons should contain all components of lesson design. This was never Hunter's intent. In fact, she specifically warned against this inference:

> One of the most typical errors in supervision is that assumption that "all good things must be in every lesson." Each element must

FIGURE 9.3

Instructional Categories Divided into Specific Behaviors

General Instructional Category	Specific Behaviors
Identifying similarities and differences	• assigning in-class and homework tasks that involve comparison and classification • assigning in-class and homework tasks that involve metaphors and analogies
Summarizing and note taking	• asking students to generate verbal summaries • asking students to generate written summaries • asking students to take notes • asking students to revise their notes, correcting errors and adding information
Reinforcing effort and providing recognition	• recognizing and celebrating progress toward learning goals throughout a unit • recognizing and reinforcing the importance of effort • recognizing and celebrating progress toward learning goals at the end of a unit
Homework and practice	• providing specific feedback on all assigned homework • assigning homework for the purpose of students practicing skills and procedures that have been the focus of instruction
Nonlinguistic representations	• asking students to generate mental images representing content • asking students to draw pictures or pictographs representing content • asking students to construct graphic organizers representing content • asking students to act out content • asking students to make physical models of content • asking students to make revisions in their mental images, pictures, pictographs, graphic organizers, and physical models
Cooperative learning	• organizing students in cooperative groups when appropriate • organizing students in ability groups when appropriate
Setting objectives and providing feedback	• setting specific learning goals at the beginning of a unit • asking students to set their own learning goals at the beginning of a unit • providing feedback on learning goals throughout the unit • asking students to keep track of their progress on learning goals • providing summative feedback at the end of a unit • asking students to assess themselves at the end of a unit

FIGURE 9.3 *(continued)*

Instructional Categories Divided into Specific Behaviors

General Instructional Category	Specific Behaviors
Generating and testing hypotheses	• engaging students in projects that involve generating and testing hypotheses through problem solving tasks • engaging students in projects that involve generating and testing hypotheses through decision making tasks • engaging students in projects that involve generating and testing hypotheses through investigation tasks • engaging students in projects that involve generating and testing hypotheses through experimental inquiry tasks • engaging students in projects that involve generating and testing hypotheses through systems analysis tasks • engaging students in projects that involve generating and testing hypotheses through invention tasks
Questions, cues, and advance organizers	• prior to presenting new content, asking questions that help students recall what they might already know about the content • prior to presenting new content, providing students with direct links with what they have studied previously • prior to presenting new content, providing ways for students to organize or think about the content

Source: Marzano, R. J., Pickering, D. J., & Pollock, J. E. (2001). *Classroom instruction that works: Research-based strategies for increasing student achievement.* Alexandria, VA: Association for Supervision and Curriculum Development.

be *thought* about by the teacher and its exclusion is a matter of professional decision making rather than default. . . . As long as that decision is thoughtful and theory based . . . then the teacher is operating as a professional. (p. 176)

In spite of Hunter's warning, her model of lesson design was frequently applied rigidly to hold teachers accountable for the inclusion of all components (Costa, 1984).

To avoid the problem of constraining the flexibility needed for individual lessons, a more robust approach is to organize research-based instructional strategies into a model for unit design. Benjamin Bloom may be the first to validate the "unit" as the basic element of instruction. Bloom (1976) found that during a year of school, students encounter about 150 separate "learning units," each representing about seven hours of schoolwork. Assuming that the school day is divided into five academic courses, students may encounter about 30 learning units within a yearlong course (or about 15 learning units within a semester-long course).

An instructional framework for units, then, represents a viable alternative to lesson design. It guides teachers to the most appropriate use of research-based strategies but does not constrain them as to day-to-day lesson design.

FIGURE 9.4

Elements of Lesson Design

Element	Description
Anticipatory set	A mental set that causes students to focus on what will be learned. It may also give practice in helping students achieve the learning and yield diagnostic data for the teacher. *Example:* "Look at the paragraph on the board. What do you think might be the most important part to remember?"
Objective and purpose	Not only do students *learn* more effectively when they know what they're supposed to be learning and why that learning is important to them, but teachers *teach* more effectively when they have that same information. *Example:* "Frequently people have difficulty in remembering things that are important to them. Sometimes you feel you have studied hard and yet don't remember some of the important parts. Today, we're going to learn ways to identify what's important, and then we'll practice ways we can use to remember important things."
Input	Students must acquire new information about the knowledge, process, or skill they are to achieve. To design the input phase of the lesson so that a successful outcome becomes predictable, the teacher must have analyzed the final objective to identify knowledge and skills that need to be acquired.
Modeling	"Seeing" what is meant is an important adjunct to learning. To avoid stifling creativity, showing several examples of the process or products that students are expected to acquire or produce is helpful.
Checking for understanding	Before students are expected to do something, the teacher should determine that they understand what they are supposed to do and that they have the minimum skills required.
Guided practice	Students practice their new knowledge or skill *under direct teacher supervision.* New learning is like wet cement; it is easily damaged. An error at the beginning of learning can easily "set" so that correcting it later is harder than correcting it immediately.
Independent practice	Independent practice is assigned only after the teacher is reasonably sure that students will not make serious errors. After an initial lesson, students frequently are not ready to practice independently, and the teacher has committed a pedagogical error if unsupervised practice is expected.

Source: Adapted from Hunter, M. (1984). "Knowing, Teaching, and Supervising." In P. Hosford (Ed.), *Using What We Know About Teaching* (pp. 169–192). Alexandria, VA: Association for Supervision and Curriculum Development.

Action Steps

I recommend one action step to successfully implement research-based instructional strategies.

Action Step 1. Provide teachers with an instructional framework for units that employs research-based strategies.

I believe the specific behaviors identified in Figure 9.3 (pp. 82–83) can be organized in a variety of ways to provide teachers with an instructional framework for units. It makes great sense for individual schools to design their own models to allow variations in approach for different types of students and teachers. Indeed, I consistently encourage schools I work with to engage in that very process—constructing their school-specific instructional framework for units. To this end, I have found that schools find the instructional strategies and behaviors presented in Figure 9.3 most useful when they think of general strategies in three categories: (1) those used at regular intervals in a unit; (2) those focusing on input experiences; and (3) those dealing with reviewing, practicing, and applying content.

Regular Unit Intervals

Establish clear goals at the beginning of the unit by identifying clear learning goals and communicating these to students; also by asking students to identify their own learning goals for unit content.

Monitor progress, balance individual work with group work, reinforce effort, and celebrate success throughout the unit by

- having students work individually,
- having students work in cooperative groups,
- having students work in groups based on their knowledge and skill in specific topics,
- giving students periodic feedback on each of the learning goals,
- asking students to keep track of their progress on the learning goals,
- periodically celebrating legitimate progress toward learning goals, and
- pointing out and reinforcing examples of effort.

Assess final goal attainment and celebrate success at the end of the unit by

- providing students with clear evaluations of their progress on each learning goal,
- having students evaluate themselves on each learning goal and comparing their evaluations with the teacher's, and
- recognizing and celebrating the accomplishment of specific goals for specific students.

Input Experiences

Although it is not frequently addressed in the practitioner literature, providing students with input regarding a unit's content is one critical aspect of teaching. John Anderson and colleagues (Anderson, Reder, & Simon, 1995) explain that this is one of the most basic teacher responsibilities. Indeed, Madeline Hunter (1984) included input as a specific component of lesson design (see Figure 9.4, p. 84). Here we consider instructional strategies that can be used to make input effective regardless of the form it takes. These "input-oriented" strategies are organized into strategies to employ directly before an input activity and those to employ during and after an input activity. "Prime" students for the learning experience before an input activity by

- asking questions to help students identify what they already know about the content,
- providing students with direct links between new content and old content, and
- providing students with ways of organizing the new content or thinking about the new content.

During and after the learning experience, students are engaged in synthesizing the knowledge in both linguistic ways (e.g., summarizing, note taking) and nonlinguistic ways (e.g., pictures, symbols). Help students synthesize new information by

- asking students to take notes on the content,
- asking students to construct verbal and written summaries of the content,
- asking students to represent the content as pictures, pictographs, symbols, graphic representations, physical models, or dramatic enactments, and
- asking students to create mental images for the content.

Reviewing, Practicing, and Applying Content
Enable students to make changes, additions, and corrections to their initial understanding of the content as well as to extend their understanding by

- asking students to revise their notes, correcting errors and adding detail,
- asking students to revise their pictures, pictographs, symbols, graphic representations, and physical models, correcting errors and adding detail,
- asking students to revise their mental images, correcting errors and adding detail,
- assigning homework and in-class activities that require students to practice skills and processes,
- assigning homework and in-class activities that require students to compare content,
- assigning homework and in-class activities that require students to classify content,
- assigning homework and in-class activities that require students to create metaphors with content,
- assigning homework and in-class activities that require students to create analogies with content,
- engaging students in projects that require them to generate and test hypotheses through problem-solving tasks,
- engaging students in projects that require them to generate and test hypotheses through decision-making tasks,
- engaging students in projects that require them to generate and test hypotheses through investigation tasks,
- engaging students in projects that require them to generate and test hypotheses through experimental inquiry tasks,
- engaging students in projects that require them to generate and test

hypotheses through systems analysis tasks, and

- engaging students in projects that require them to generate and test hypotheses through invention.

These instructional activities are effective because they help students reanalyze and apply their knowledge.

Summary

The expert teacher has more strategies at her disposal than the ineffective teacher. After presenting lists of instructional strategies, I recommend one action step to successfully implement research-based instructional strategies: to provide teachers with an instructional framework for units that uses research-based strategies.

CLASSROOM MANAGEMENT

Another teacher-level factor is classroom management. It is mentioned in some form in virtually every major study of factors affecting student achievement. Classroom management received its strongest endorsement in a comprehensive study by Margaret Wang, Geneva Haertel, and Herbert Walberg (1993) in which they combined the results of three comprehensive studies. Their content analysis of 86 chapters from annual research reviews, 44 handbook chapters, 20 government and commissioned reports, and 11 journal articles produced a list of 228 variables affecting student achievement. They asked 134 education experts to rate the impact of each variable. The experts concluded from this massive review that classroom management was rated first. This makes intuitive sense—a classroom that is chaotic as a result of poor management not only doesn't enhance achievement, it might even inhibit it.

Although the importance of classroom management is widely recognized, its defini-

tion is elusive. Walter Doyle (1986) defines classroom management as "covering a wide range of teacher duties from distributing resources to students, accounting for student attendance and school property, enforcing compliance with rules and procedures to grouping students for instruction . . ." (p. 394). Daniel Duke (1979) defines classroom management as "the provisions and procedures necessary to establish and maintain an environment in which instruction and learning can occur" (p. xii). Jere Brophy (1996) defines classroom management as ". . . actions taken to create and maintain a learning environment conducive to successful instruction (arranging the physical environment of the classroom, establishing rules and procedures, maintaining attention to lessons and engagement in academic activities" (p. 5).

I define classroom management as the confluence of teacher actions in four distinct areas: (1) establishing and enforcing rules and procedures, (2) carrying out disciplinary actions, (3) maintaining effective teacher and student relationships, and (4) maintaining an appropriate mental set for management. Only when effective practices in these four areas are employed and working in concert is a classroom effectively managed.

Establishing and Enforcing Rules and Procedures

Carolyn Evertson and her colleagues (Evertson, Emmer, Clements, Sanford, & Worsham, 1984) attest to the necessity of establishing and enforcing rules and procedures:

> Rules and procedures vary in different classrooms, but we do not find effectively managed classrooms operating without them. It is simply not possible for a teacher to conduct instruction for children to work productively if they have no guidelines for how to behave, when to move about the room, and where to sit, or if they interrupt the teacher frequently and make whatever amount of noise pleases them. (p. 17)

Although these comments by Evertson and her colleagues are intended for elementary teachers, the comments of Edmund Emmer and his colleagues (Emmer, Evertson, Sanford, Clements, & Worsham, 1984) are intended for secondary teachers and are nearly the same (pp. 17–18). Thus, establishing and enforcing rules and procedures is a prerequisite for effective instruction in all K–12 classrooms.

Rules and procedures both refer to stated expectations regarding behavior. Where a rule identifies general expectations or standards, a procedure communicates expectations for specific behaviors (Evertson et al, 1984;

Emmer et al., 1984). For example, a teacher might establish the rule "respect others and their property." This rule covers a wide range of expected behaviors. This teacher also might establish procedures for collecting assignments, turning in late work, or participating in class discussions. By definition, procedures are fairly specific in nature.

Different classrooms will have different rules and procedures depending on the needs and dispositions of the teacher and the students. However, in general, rules and procedures are commonly established for the following areas:

- general expectations for behavior,
- beginning and ending class,
- transitions and interruptions,
- materials and equipment,
- group work, and
- seatwork and teacher-led activities.

These areas covered under rules and procedures are discussed in more detail in the Action Steps section.

Carrying Out Disciplinary Actions

One of the more hotly debated aspects of classroom management is discipline. Some appear to hold the position that disciplinary actions in almost any form are not only ineffective but counterproductive for student achievement. Alfie Kohn, for example, has articulated this sentiment in a series of works (Kohn 1993, 1996). Consider his comments about the various ways children and students are punished:

How do we punish children? Let us count the ways. We incarcerate them: children are sent to their rooms, teenagers are "grounded" and forbidden to leave the house, students are sent to "detention," and all may be forcibly isolated through "time-out" procedures. (1993, p. 165)

Although Kohn and other like-minded individuals make some useful points (see Wlodkowski, 1982) about inappropriate use of discipline and over-reliance on punishment, the categorical rejection of disciplinary techniques is simply not supported by research. Quite the contrary, the research strongly supports a balanced approach that employs a variety of techniques.

To illustrate, a meta-analysis by Scott Stage and David Quiroz (1997) included more than 99 studies, 200 experimental comparisons, and 5,000 students. Their overall finding was that the "interventions analyzed in this study resulted, on the average, in a reduction of disruptive classroom behavior among 78% of the treated subjects" (p. 356). Four of the categories of disciplinary techniques they identified are particularly relevant: (1) reinforcement, (2) punishment, (3) no immediate consequences, and (4) combined punishment and reinforcement.

Disciplinary techniques that fall into the category **reinforcement** involve some type of recognition or reward for positive behavior or timely cessation of negative behavior. Practices classified as **punishment** involve some type of negative consequences (e.g., loss of privileges, time-out) for inappropriate behavior. Interventions classified as **no immediate consequence** do not involve immediate consequences for inappropriate behavior but

do involve some type of reminder when an inappropriate behavior appears imminent. For example, the teacher might remind a student who typically acts out at recess that she should remember to keep herself under control. Finally, the category of **combined punishment and reinforcement** involves recognition or reward in conjunction with consequences for inappropriate behavior. The effect sizes, means, and related decreases in disruptive behavior for these categories are reported in Figure 10.1. Note that the effective sizes in Figure 10.1 are interpreted as a "decrease" in disruptive behavior, where the effect sizes discussed in previous chapters were interpreted as increases in student achievement. To illustrate, the effect size of .78 reported in Figure 10.1 for punishment means that the average number of disruptive behaviors in classes where punishment is employed is .78 standard deviations and 28 percentile points lower than the average number of disruptive behaviors in classes where punishment is not used.

Three striking aspects of the findings are reported in Figure 10.1. First, the interventions that include no immediate consequence—positive or negative—have the lowest average effective size (0.64). This makes sense. Human beings need feedback to distinguish between those behaviors that are appropriate and those that are not. Second, the interventions that include a combination of both punishment and reinforcement or negative and positive feedback have the highest average effect sizes. This conclusion is also reached by Andy Miller, Eamon Ferguson, and Rachel Simpson (1998) in their review of the research literature: "Clearly, the results

FIGURE 10.1

Effects of Disciplinary Techniques on Classroom Behavior

Disciplinary Technique	Average Effect Size	Number of Effect Sizes	Percentile Decrease in Disruptive Behavior
Reinforcement	0.86	101	31
Punishment	0.78	40	25
No immediate consequence	0.64	70	24
Punishment and reinforcement	0.97	12	33

Source: Stage, S. A., & Quiroz, D. R. (1997). A meta-analysis of interventions to decrease disruptive classroom behavior in public education settings. *School Psychology Review, 26*(3), 333–368.

of these studies should permit schools to strike . . . a 'healthy balance' between rewards and punishments" (p. 56).

Finally, in contrast to those who reject any form of punishment, the average effect size for those interventions that employ punishment is quite respectable (0.78). These findings on punishment should not be interpreted as an indication that any form of punishment is viable. Indeed, in his review of the research, George Bear (1998) strongly warns that the research supports the effectiveness of mild forms of punishment only.

Another striking aspect of the Stage and Quiroz study is depicted in Figure 10.2 (p. 92). The figure reports the overall findings by grade-level intervals. Except for the findings at the upper elementary level, the effect sizes across all levels are quite consistent and quite high. Assuming that the low effect size for the upper elementary level is an anomaly, these findings indicate that disciplinary techniques are useful at every level.

The findings of this meta-analysis speak quite strongly to the efficacy of disciplinary techniques. In fact, these findings lead Stage and Quiroz (1997) to comment

> In summary, this meta-analytic study demonstrates that interventions to reduce disruptive behavior work in public schools. . . . We hope that these findings serve to separate the myth that disruptive classroom behavior cannot be effectively managed from the reality that interventions widely used in our schools do, in fact, reduce disruptive behavior. (pp. 361–362)

Teacher and Student Relationships

The third aspect of effective classroom management is effective teacher and student relationships. An effective relationship may be the keystone that allows the other aspects to work well. If a teacher has a good relationship with students, then students accept her rules, procedures, and disciplinary actions.

FIGURE 10.2

Effects of Discipline Across Grade Levels

Grade Level	Effect Size	Number of Effect Sizes	Percentile Decrease in Disruptive Behavior
Primary	0.91	76	32
Upper Elementary	0.64	85	24
Middle School	0.82	19	29
High School	0.86	17	31

Source: Stage, S. A., & Quiroz, D. R. (1997). A meta-analysis of interventions to decrease disruptive classroom behavior in public education settings. *School Psychology Review, 26*(3), 333–368.

Without the foundation of a good relationship, students commonly contest them. Again, this makes good intuitive sense. What then constitutes an effective relationship between the teacher and students?

Researchers have made attempts to identify general characteristics of teachers that render them more likable and, consequently, more likely to have good relationships with students (Barr, 1958; Good & Brophy, 1995). They have identified characteristics including consideration, buoyancy, and patience, but they have not focused on the dynamics of the teacher and student relationship per se. At least two major research efforts have focused either directly or indirectly on this dynamic.

One effort to identify the dynamics of an effective teacher and student relationship is by Theo Wubbles and his colleagues (Wubbels, Brekelmans, van Tartwijk, & Admiral, 1999; Wubbels & Levy, 1993; Brekelmans, Wubbels, & Creton, 1990). Building on the early work of Timothy Leary (1957), Wubbels (Wubbels & Levy, 1993; Wubbels et al., 1999) articulated two continuums whose interactions define the relationship between teacher and students: high dominance versus high submission and high cooperation versus high opposition.

High dominance is characterized by clarity of purpose and strong guidance. That is, the teacher is clear about his purposes and provides strong academic and behavioral guidance. These are certainly positive characteristics, but high dominance is also characterized by lack of concern for the opinion or needs of students. The other end of this continuum—high submission—is characterized by lack of clarity, purpose, or direction. Neither extreme can be characterized as an optimal teacher and student relationship.

High cooperation is characterized by a concern for the needs and opinions of others and a desire to function as a member of the team. Again, these are positive traits. High cooperation is also characterized by an inability or lack of resolve to lead. The other end of this continuum—high opposition—is characterized by active antagonism toward others and a desire to thwart the goals and desires of others. Again, neither extreme can be characterized as the type of teacher and student relationship conducive to learning. The right combination of moderate dominance (as opposed to high dominance) and moderate cooperation (as opposed to high cooperation) provides the optimal teacher and student relationship for learning. As Wubbels et al. (1999) note

> Briefly, teachers should be effective instructors and lecturers, as well as friendly, helpful, and congenial. They should be able to empathize with students, understand their world, and listen to them. Good teachers are not uncertain, undecided, or confusing in the way they communicate with students. They are not grouchy, gloomy, dissatisfied, aggressive, sarcastic, or quick-tempered. They should be able to set standards and maintain control while still allowing students responsibility and freedom to learn. (p. 167)

Interestingly, when teachers first enter the profession, they readily exhibit behaviors that would be characterized as high in cooperation. Given their lack of experience in leadership positions, they are not very good at exhibiting behaviors that are high in dominance (Wubbels & Levy, 1993). With six to ten years of teaching experience, they become quite competent at dominant behaviors. Unfortunately, they also become less cooperative. As Wubbels and colleagues (1999) put it: "Teachers appear to decline in cooperative behavior and increase in oppositional behavior, a change that negatively affects student attitudes" (p. 166).

A second line of research that addresses the teacher and student relationship regards the needs of different student types. Jere Brophy conducted the most ambitious study to this end, commonly referred to as the Classroom Strategy Study (Brophy, 1996; Brophy & McClasin, 1992). The study involved in-depth interviews with and observations of 98 teachers; some were identified as effective managers and some were not. The heart of the study involved presenting teachers with vignettes regarding specific types of students (e.g., hostile-aggressive students, passive-aggressive students, hyperactive students) in specific situations. Among the many findings, the most effective classroom managers tended to employ different types of strategies with different types of students, whereas ineffective managers did not. Although Brophy did not couch the findings in terms of teacher and student relationships, the link is an obvious one. Effective managers do not treat all students the same, particularly in situations involving behavior problems. Where some students need encouragement, other students need a gentle reminder, and still others might require a firm reprimand. In fact, Brophy (1996) strongly recommended that teachers develop a set of "helping skills" to employ with different types of students.

Maintaining an Appropriate Mental Set

The final aspect important to effective classroom management is an appropriate mental set. The appropriate mental set for a classroom teacher has two essential and distinguishing features: (1) withitness, and (2) emotional objectivity.

The term "withitness" was coined by Jacob Kounin who is generally considered the first researcher to systematically study the characteristics of effective classroom managers. Kounin (1983) carried out his initial research by comparing the behavior of effective and ineffective classroom managers. He concluded that the primary difference was not in how they handled disruptive behavior, but in the disposition of the teacher to quickly and accurately identify problem behavior and act on it. Kounin referred to this disposition as withitness:

> Classroom management is unrelated to how you handle misbehavior and how you handle misbehavior is unrelated to the amount of misbehavior you get. There is one exception. For example, two boys are in the back of the class during an arithmetic lesson. One of them grabs the other's paper and the second one grabs his paper. Then the first one pokes the second in the shoulder jokingly and the other one pokes the first, then they chase each other around the table laughing, then one pulls the shirt off the other and the second pulls his shirt off. Then he unzips the second's fly and he unzips the first guy's fly and the teacher says, "Boys, stop that!" We said that was too late. So it wasn't how she said "stop it" or whether she walked closer or didn't walk closer. Or whether she threatened or didn't threaten. It was whether she demonstrated to the class that she knew what was going on, that she had eyes in the back of her head. It was not whether she came in right away but whether she came in before something spread or became more serious. And we gave that the technical term of withitness. That is the only thing that correlated with management success. (p. 7)

Brophy (1996) describes withitness in more technical and less anecdotal terms:

> Remaining "with it" (aware of what is happening in all parts of the classroom at all times) by continuously scanning the classroom, even when working with small groups or individuals. Also demonstrating this withitness to students by intervening promptly and accurately when inappropriate behavior threatens to become disruptive. This minimizes timing errors (failing to notice and intervene until an incident has already become disruptive) and target errors (mistakes in identifying the students responsible for the problem). (p. 11)

The second distinguishing feature of an appropriate mental set is "emotional objectivity." An effective classroom manager implements and enforces rules and procedures, executes disciplinary actions, and cultivates effective relationships with students without becoming upset if students violate classroom rules and procedures, react negatively to disciplinary actions, or do not respond to the teacher's attempts to forge relationships. As Ron Nelson, Ron Martella, and Benita Galand (1998) note, emotional objectivity allows the teacher to address disciplinary issues in an "unemotional, matter-of-fact" manner (p. 156). Robert and Ruth Soar (1979) also emphasize the importance of emotional objectivity.

Some teachers have reacted negatively, noting that this seems to take the "personal element" out of teacher and student interactions. If the teacher is objective, then she, by definition, is keeping a distance from her students. Although keeping a certain psychological distance from students is useful and perhaps even necessary for effective management, this does not have to translate into aloofness. It simply means carrying out the various aspects of classroom management without becoming emotionally involved or personalizing students' actions. This is very difficult to do since the normal human reaction to student disobedience or lack of response is to feel hurt or even angry. Such high arousal emotional states do not provide a good basis on which to implement rules, execute disciplinary actions, or establish relationships.

Action Steps

I recommend seven action steps to promote effective classroom management. I have categorized each action step under the elements discussed.

Rules and Procedures

Action Step 1. Have teachers articulate and enforce a comprehensive set of classroom rules and procedures.

Both elementary and secondary teachers should have a well-articulated and comprehensive set of rules and procedures. Each category of rules and procedures (listed below) should probably be addressed.

General Classroom Behavior
At the elementary level, rules and procedures for general classroom behavior commonly address the following areas (Doyle, 1986; Evertson et al., 1984; Brophy, 1996):

- being polite and helpful when dealing with others,
- respecting the property of others,
- interrupting the teacher or others, and
- hitting or shoving others.

At the secondary level, rules and procedures commonly address the following areas

(Emmer et al., 1984; Brophy, 1996; Doyle, 1986):

- bringing materials to class,
- being in the assigned seat at the beginning of class,
- respecting and being polite to others,
- talking or not talking at specific times,
- leaving the assigned seat, and
- respecting other people's property.

Beginning of the Day and Class Period
At the elementary level, rules and procedures commonly address the following areas (Evertson et al., 1984; Doyle, 1986; Brophy, 1996):

- beginning the school day with specific social activities (e.g., birthdays, important events in students' lives),
- beginning the day with the Pledge of Allegiance,
- handling administrative activities (e.g., attendance, lunch money),
- ending the day by cleaning the room and individual desks, and
- closing the day by putting away materials.

At the secondary level, rules and procedures commonly address the following areas (Emmer et al., 1984; Doyle, 1986; Brophy, 1996):

- taking attendance,
- addressing students who missed the work from the previous day because of absence,
- dealing with students who are tardy, and
- setting clear expectations for homework.

Transitions and Interruptions

At the elementary level, rules and procedures commonly address the following areas (Evertson et al., 1984; Doyle, 1986; Brophy, 1996):

- leaving the room,
- returning to the room,
- using the bathroom,
- using the library and resource room,
- using the cafeteria,
- using the playground,
- behaving during fire and disaster drills, and
- acting as classroom helpers.

At the secondary level, rules and procedures commonly address the following areas (Emmer et al., 1984; Doyle, 1986; Brophy, 1996):

- leaving the room,
- returning to the room,
- behaving during fire and disaster drills, and
- behaving during split lunch period.

Use of Materials and Equipment

At the elementary level, rules and procedures commonly address the following areas (Evertson, et al., 1984; Doyle, 1986; Brophy, 1996):

- distributing materials;
- collecting materials;
- storing common materials;
- using the teacher's desk and storage areas;
- using students' desks and storage areas; and

- using the drinking fountain, sink, pencil sharpener.

At the secondary level rules and procedures commonly address the following (Emmer, et al., 1984; Doyle, 1986; Brophy, 1996):

- distributing materials,
- collecting materials, and
- storing common materials.

Group Work

At the elementary level, rules and procedures commonly address the following areas (Evertson et al., 1984; Doyle, 1986; Brophy, 1996):

- moving in and out of the group,
- behaving within the group,
- behaving while not in the group, and
- communicating with the teacher.

Rules and procedures at the secondary level commonly address the following areas (Emmer et al., 1984; Doyle, 1986; Brophy, 1996):

- moving in and out of the group,
- acting as group leaders (and other group roles),
- relating as a group to the rest of the class or other groups in the class, and
- communicating with the teacher.

Seatwork and Teacher-Led Activities

Rules and procedures at the elementary level commonly address the following areas (Evertson et al., 1984; Doyle, 1986; Brophy, 1996):

- paying attention during presentations,
- participating,
- talking among students,
- obtaining help,
- behaving while out of seat, and
- behaving when work is completed.

Rules and procedures at the secondary level commonly address the following areas (Emmer et al., 1984; Doyle, 1986; Brophy, 1996):

- paying attention during presentations,
- participating,
- talking among students,
- obtaining help,
- behaving while out of seat, and
- behaving when work is completed.

Disciplinary Interventions

Action Step 2. Have teachers use specific strategies that reinforce appropriate behavior and recognize and provide consequences for inappropriate behavior.

Teachers can use several specific disciplinary strategies to achieve necessary disciplinary interventions. Schools must provide training in the use of these strategies so individual teachers can select those with which they feel most comfortable.

One of the simplest classroom disciplinary procedures is to exhibit **nonverbal disapproval**. This commonly manifests as a simple facial expression directed at the student who has misbehaved. This might also take the form of a physical gesture that has been previously communicated to students as an indication of disapproval. Simple, nonverbal disapproval has been shown to decrease

student misbehavior (Madsen, Becker, & Thomas, 1968).

Token economies involve the use of some type of token (e.g., points, chits) as reinforcement for engaging in appropriate behavior or avoiding inappropriate behavior. The research on token economies was once focused on improving positive behaviors only (O'Leary, Becker, Evans, & Saudargas, 1969). However, research has demonstrated that tokens are most effective if awarded for positive behaviors and taken away for negative behaviors (Kaufman & O'Leary, 1972).

Isolation time-out involves sending the student to a room or location reserved for disruptive students. Although this strategy was originally designed to be used in special education settings for students with severe behavior disorders (Drabman & Spitalnik, 1973), it has been used quite successfully in regular education settings (Zabel, 1986). Isolation time is easily abused if teachers simply wish to get rid of a behavioral problem as opposed to addressing it (Harris, 1985).

Overcorrection is a procedure that is used when a student has misbehaved in such a way as to destroy or alter some physical aspect of the classroom. The student is then required to restore the classroom to the original state and practice the appropriate behavior that would have avoided the damage (Foxx, 1978).

Differential reinforcement requires teachers to first set a limit on the number of particular types of disruptions. Once the limit has been exceeded, some type of negative consequence occurs. Reinforcement can be used to enhance positive behaviors. Again, the teacher establishes a preset goal of positive behaviors (e.g., a student raising his hand before asking a question). When the goal is reached, some form of reward or recognition is provided (Deitz & Repp, 1973; Irvin & Lundervold, 1988).

Group contingency techniques are like token economies except that they apply to a pre-established group of students. **Interdependent group contingency** techniques require every student in the group to meet the group's behavioral criterion to earn credit. **Dependent group contingency** techniques require a specific individual in the group to meet the group's behavioral criterion to earn credit (Litow & Pumroy, 1975).

Finally, **stimulus cueing** relies on providing a cue to students prior to inappropriate behavior (Carr & Durand, 1985; Lobitz, 1974). For example, a teacher might determine that a specific student usually starts talking to students around him before he engages in a more severe disruptive behavior. With this prior condition identified and communicated to the student, the teacher might place a mark on the whiteboard every time the student begins talking to others around him, thus providing a cue to the student that he is about to engage in an activity that will result in negative consequences.

Action Step 3. Institute a schoolwide approach to discipline.

A schoolwide discipline policy does not preclude teachers using some of the individual strategies described in Action Step 2; however, it communicates powerfully to students and parents that teachers speak *with one voice* on how discipline should be addressed. In this section, only one of many useful programs is described (for reviews of other effective schoolwide programs, see Bear, 1998; Brophy, 1996; Nelson, Martella & Galand,

1998). For example, Think Time is a discipline program by Ron Nelson and Beth Carr (1999). The program

- provides for consistent consequences across all teachers in the school when students engage in disruptive behavior,
- provides students with feedback for their disruptive behavior and allows for planning to avoid future incidents of such behavior, and
- enables teachers and students to cut off negative social exchanges and to initiate positive ones.

For a synthesis of the research on Think Time, see Sugai & Colvin, 1996. Execution of Think Time involves the following basic components.

Catching Disruptive Behavior

Teachers immediately note inappropriate student behavior. If the student acknowledges and ceases the behavior, the class continues without further action. However, if the behavior does not cease, the student is sent to the Think Time Classroom or TT Classroom.

Accessing the Think Time Classroom

For most disruptive behaviors, students are asked to move independently to the Think Time Classroom. However, the amount of time it takes students to get to the TT Classroom is tracked. If problems occur, an escort may be sent.

Think Time Debriefing

A written debriefing on the behavior that resulted in assignment to the TT Classroom is critical to the overall process. The teacher in the TT Classroom conducts the debriefing at his convenience. The debriefing usually involves asking students to identify

- their inappropriate behavior,
- what they need to do differently when they return to the classroom (i.e., identify possible replacement behaviors), and
- indicate whether they think they can perform the replacement behaviors.

It is not uncommon to use "pictorial" debriefings with younger students.

Checking the Debriefing Form

The TT classroom teacher examines the debriefing form before a student is dismissed from the TT Classroom. If the form has been correctly filled out, then the student can rejoin the regular classroom.

Rejoining the Regular Classroom

Students rejoining the regular classroom wait by the door. The regular classroom teacher then checks to see if the debriefing form is correct. If the student has missed work, a peer is assigned to help the student catch up.

Think Time is a fairly demanding approach to discipline in that it requires a separate classroom and dedicated teacher for each period of the day, resources not always readily available. In fact, most schoolwide approaches to discipline require similar commitments and resources. However, a schoolwide program communicates a strong sense of solidarity among school staff regarding discipline. Many other programs exist with established research bases, including Assertive Discipline (Canter & Canter, 1976, 1992); Skillstreaming (Goldstein, Sprafkin, Gershaw, & Klein, 1980); the Improving Social

Awareness and Social Problem-Solving Project (Elias & Clabby, 1989; Elias & Tobian, 1996); the Social Problem-Solving Program (Weissberg, Jackson, & Shriver, 1993); the Interpersonal Cognitive Problem-Solving Program (Shure, 1992); and Cooperative Discipline (Albert, 1989).

Teacher and Student Relationships

Action Step 4. Help teachers develop a balance of moderate dominance and moderate cooperation in their dealings with students.

The core of effective teacher and student relationships is a healthy balance between dominance and cooperation. One thing that makes such a balance difficult is that students rely primarily on teacher behaviors to indicate whether the teacher is providing guidance or is cooperative. As Theo Wubbels, Mieke Brekelmans, Jan van Tartwijk, and Wilfred Admiral (1999) explain

> We consider every behavior that someone displays in the presence of someone else as a communication and therefore we assume that in the presence of someone else one cannot *not* [original emphasis] communicate. . . . Whatever someone's intentions are, the other persons in the communication will infer meaning from that someone's behavior. If, for example, teachers ignore students' questions, perhaps they do not hear them, then students may not only get this inattention but also infer that the teacher is too busy or thinks that the students are too dull to understand or that the questions are unimportant. The message that students take from the teacher's negation can be different from the teacher's intention. . . . (p. 154)

Thus, teachers must identify those behaviors they engage in that communicate a proper level of dominance balanced by a proper level of cooperation.

Behaviors that convey appropriate levels of dominance include many of the instructional techniques addressed in Chapter 9, particularly those dealing with establishing clear instructional goals. For example, a teacher conveys the impression of appropriate dominance when she

- establishes the learning goals at the beginning of a unit of instruction,
- provides feedback on those goals,
- continually and systematically revisits the goals, and
- provides summative feedback regarding the goals.

Appropriate dominance is also exhibited by providing students with clear understanding of performance levels for specific learning goals. To this end, rubrics are an excellent tool. Assume that the teacher has identified "understanding and utilizing fractions" as one of the learning goals for a unit. The teacher might present students with the following rubric as a guide to performance expectations:

4 You understand the characteristics of fractions along with the different types. You can accurately describe how fractions are related to decimals and percentages. You can convert fractions to decimals and can explain the process.

3 You understand the basic characteristics of fractions. You know how fractions are related to decimals and percentages. You can convert fractions to decimals.

2 You have a basic understanding of the following, but have some small misunderstandings with one or more of the following: the characteristics of fractions, the relationship between fractions, decimals, and percentages, how to convert fractions to decimals.

1 You have some major problems or misunderstandings with one or more of the following: the characteristics of fractions, the relationship between fractions, decimals, and percentages, how to convert fractions to decimals.

Behaviors regarding learning goals can also convey appropriate levels of cooperation. Allowing students to set some of their own learning goals at the beginning of a unit or asking students what they might like to learn conveys a sense of cooperation. Demonstrating personal interest in each student in class also conveys cooperation (McCombs & Whisler, 1997; Combs, 1982). Behaviors that communicate this include

- talking informally with students before, during, and after class about their interests;
- greeting students outside of school such as at extracurricular events or at stores;
- singling out a few students each day in the lunchroom and talking to them;
- being aware of and commenting on important events in students' lives, such as participation in sports, drama, or other extracurricular activities;
- complimenting students on important achievements in and outside of school;
- including students in the process of planning classroom activities, soliciting their ideas and considering their interests; and

- meeting students at the door as they come into class and saying hello to each child, making sure to use each student's name.

Engaging in equitable and positive classroom behaviors also communicates appropriate levels of cooperation (Kerman, Kimball, & Martin, 1980; Sadker & Sadker, 1994; Grayson & Martin, 1985). Such behaviors include

- making eye contact with each student in the room by moving about freely and scanning the room as you speak;
- deliberately moving toward and being close to each student;
- attributing ideas to the students who initiated them (for instance, "Dennis has just added to Mary's idea by saying that . . . ");
- allowing and encouraging all students to be part of class discussions and interactions; and
- providing appropriate "wait time" for all students, regardless of their past performance or your perception of their abilities.

A final behavior that conveys appropriate levels of cooperation is the manner in which teachers respond to incorrect responses or lack of response (Hunter, 1969). Useful behaviors in these situations include

- emphasizing what was right about an incorrect response;
- encouraging collaboration among students;

- restating the question and allowing time for students to think before you expect a response;
- rephrasing the question to give students a better understanding;
- offering hints or cues;
- providing the answer and asking for elaboration (asking the student to say it in his own words or provide another example of the answer); and
- respecting the student's option to pass, when appropriate.

Action Step 5. Provide teachers with an awareness of the needs of different types of students and ways of alleviating those needs.

Effective classroom managers are aware of important differences among students. Identifying the differences helps the teacher to better understand individual students and leads students to believe that the teacher has a personal interest in them. Jere Brophy (1996) and Brenda Freeman (1994) have identified categories of various types of students and their related needs. In an attempt to make the research and theory of others more applicable to the classroom, Marzano and Marzano (in preparation) have consolidated this research, identifying five general types of students and the actions that are most useful with each type. For example, Figure 10. 3 (pp. 103–105) defines the source of student misbehavior, provides general personality characteristics of misbehaving students, and offers suggestions on improving teacher-and-student relationships.

Appropriate Mental Set for Management

Action Step 6. Have teachers employ specific strategies to maintain or heighten their awareness regarding the actions of students in their classes ("withitness").

Withitness might appear to be a characteristic that does not lend itself to development. You are either a with-it teacher, or you're not. In fact, there is at least one aspect of this disposition that can be practiced and cultivated. Almost all examples of withitness explicitly note that with-it teachers frequently scan the classroom, particularly when working with a small group of students or an individual (Berliner, 1986; Brophy, 1996; Kounin, 1983). If anything inappropriate is occurring, they turn attention to it immediately. Teachers who do not have a high awareness of their students' actions can practice the simple behavior of looking around the room frequently and periodically for indications of disruption.

Some aspects of withitness are far more subtle. Experienced teachers who have developed these subtle dispositions to a high degree might visit the classrooms of teachers who have not. After class, the mentor teacher might point out behavioral incidents that should have been recognized and acknowledged. The less experienced teacher might also visit the classroom of the mentor teacher to identify behaviors associated with withitness.

Action Step 7. Have teachers employ specific strategies that help them maintain a healthy emotional objectivity with their students.

Maintaining a healthy emotional objectivity with students might also appear to be resistant to behavioral strategies. However, even something as simple as trying to understand the reasons for misbehavior can help teachers establish and maintain healthy objectivity. Student misbehavior usually has nothing to do with a specific teacher (Dreikurs, 1968; Dreikurs, Grunwald, & Pepper, 1982). Once a teacher realizes this, she has a better chance of treating student misbehavior as impersonal. When a specific student misbehaves, a teacher can explicitly identify reasons why the student might have misbehaved that do not imply disrespect for or aggression toward the teacher. This strategy is a simple variation of a time-honored strategy from clinical psychology sometimes referred to as "reframing" (Ellis, 1977; Meichenbaum, 1977).

Teachers might also monitor their own attitudes about specific students (Good, 1982; Rosenshine, 1983; Rosenthal & Jacobson, 1968). Most teachers are aware that when their attitudes toward specific students are positive, they can operate in an objective manner with those students. However, many teachers are unaware of the extent to which their negative attitudes toward specific students interfere with their objectivity toward those students. The following process has been recommended to counteract this bias (Marzano, Pickering, Arredondo, Blackburn, Brandt, Moffett, Paynter, Pollock & Whisler, 1997):

- mentally review your students before class, noting those with whom you anticipate having problems (either academic or behavioral);

FIGURE 10.3
Student Types, Characteristics, and Behavior Actions

Brophy	Freeman	Marzano & Marzano		Definitions & Source	Characteristics	Suggestions
shy/withdrawn	invisible	passive	fear of relationships	Behavior that is structured to avoid the domination of others or the pain of negative experiences. The child attempts to protect self from criticism, ridicule, or rejection. Is a possible reaction to abuse and neglect. Can have a biochemical basis such as anxiety.	Avoids connection with others, is shy, doesn't initiate conversations, attempts to be invisible, has negative self-talk.	Provide safe adult and peer interactions and give protection from aggressive people. Give assertiveness and positive self-talk training. Reward small successes quickly. Withhold criticism.
failure syndrome	low achiever conformer		fear of failure		Gives up easily, is convinced he can't succeed, is easily frustrated, has negative self-talk.	
underachiever/ alienated						
low achiever						
hostile-aggressive	alienated disengagers	aggressive	hostile	Behavior that is structured to overpower, dominate, harm, or control others without regard for their well-being. Few true success experiences have occurred. The child has often role modeled other aggressive people. Has had minimal or ineffective limits set on them. Is a possible reaction to abuse and neglect. Can have a biochemical basis such as depression.	Rages, threatens, or intimidates others. Can be verbally or physically abusive to people, animals, or objects.	Describe the student's behavior clearly. Contract with them to reward corrected behavior and give them consequences for uncorrected behavior. Be consistent and provide immediate rewards and consequences. Encourage and acknowledge extracurricular activities in and out of school. Give student responsibilities to help teacher or other students to allow for success experiences.
defiant			oppositional		Does opposite of what is asked. Demands that others agree or give in. Resists verbally or nonverbally.	
passive-aggressive			covert		Appears to agree, then does the opposite of what is asked. Often acts innocent while setting up problems for others.	*(continued)*

FIGURE 10.3 *(continued)*

Student Types, Characteristics, and Behavior Actions

Brophy	Freeman	Marzano & Marzano		Definitions & Source	Characteristics	Suggestions
hyperactive		attention problems	hyperactive	Behavior that demonstrates either motor or attentional difficulties resulting from a neurological disorder. The child's symptoms may be exacerbated by family or social stressors or other biochemical conditions such as anxiety, depression, or bipolar disorders.	Has difficulty with motor control, both physically and verbally. Fidgets, leaves seat frequently, interrupts, talks excessively.	Contract with the student to manage behaviors. Teach basic concentration, study, and thinking skills. Separate student in a quiet work area. Help them list each step of a task. Reward successes, assign peer tutor.
distractible			inattentive		Has difficulty staying focused and following through on projects. Has difficulty with listening, remembering, and organizing.	
perfectionist	perfectionist	perfectionist		Behavior that is geared toward avoiding the embarrassment and assumed shame of making mistakes. The child fears what will happen if errors are discovered. Has unrealistically high expectations of self. Has possibly received criticism or lack of acceptance while making mistakes during the process of learning.	Over focuses on small details of project. Will avoid projects if unsure of outcome. Focuses on results and not relationships. Is self-critical.	Ask the student to make mistakes on purpose, then show acceptance. Have them tutor other students.

(continued)

FIGURE 10.3 *(continued)*

Student Types, Characteristics, and Behavior Actions

Brophy	Freeman	Marzano & Marzano	Definitions & Source	Characteristics	Suggestions
peer rejected		socially rejected	Behavior that is based on the misinterpretation of nonverbal signals of others. The child misunderstands facial expressions and body language. Hasn't received adequate training in these areas and has poor role modeling.	Attempts to make friends but is inept and unsuccessful. Is forced to be alone. Is often teased for unusual behaviors, appearances, or lack of social skills.	Teach the student to keep the appropriate physical distance from others. Teach the meaning of facial expressions such as anger and hurt. Give instructions regarding appropriate voice intonation and volume. Make suggestions regarding hygiene, dress, mannerisms, and posture.

Sources:
Brophy, J. E. (1996). *Teaching problem students*. New York: Guilford.
Freeman, B. (1994). Power motivation and youth: An analysis of troubled students and student leaders. *Journal of Counseling and Development, 72*(6), 661–671.
Marzano, R. J., & Marzano, J. S. (in preparation). *Classroom management that works*.

- imagine these "problem" students succeeding or engaging in positive classroom behavior; and
- keep in mind your positive expectations when interacting with these students.

Summary

Although classroom management is on nearly every list of factors associated with student achievement, it is not a simple construct. Four integrated aspects of this factor were identified: establishing and enforcing a comprehensive list of rules and procedures, using disciplinary interventions that strike a balance between positive reinforcement for appropriate behavior and negative consequences for inappropriate behavior, establishing relationships with students that involve appropriate levels of dominance and cooperation, and developing the mental dispositions of withitness and an emotional objectivity toward students. I recommended seven action steps to address these four aspects of classroom management.

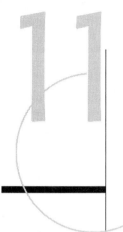

CLASSROOM CURRICULUM DESIGN

The third teacher-level factor is "classroom curriculum design." It may be the least addressed teacher-level factor. This lack of attention is unfortunate for two reasons. First, there is a strong and extensive research base that can be readily translated into practical suggestions and protocols for the construction of classroom curriculum. Second, many breakdowns in student learning may be a function of poor classroom curriculum design.

Before discussing the specifics of classroom curriculum design, let's briefly address the nature of curriculum in general. The following definitions are a representative sample of those used throughout the 20th century:

> Curriculum is all of the experiences children have under the guidance of the teacher. (Caswell & Campbell, 1935, p. 7)

> Curriculum encompasses all learning opportunities provided by the school. (Saylor & Alexander, 1974, p. 25)

> Curriculum [is] a plan or program for experiences which the learner encounters under the direction of the school. (Oliva, 1982)

As these examples illustrate, the term is used so broadly in some cases that it is difficult to converge on a meaning. In fact, Larry Cuban (1992) notes: "Over 1,100 curriculum books have been written since the turn of the [20th] century, each with a different version of what 'curriculum' means" (p. 221). I define *classroom* curriculum design as the sequencing and pacing of content along with the experiences students have with that content. My use of the qualifier *classroom* is important. By definition, I am considering those decisions regarding sequencing, pacing, and experiences that are the purview of the classroom teacher. Some aspects of curricular design are addressed at the school level if, in fact, a school has a guaranteed and viable curriculum. Regardless of the direction provided by the school (or district), individual teachers still need to make decisions regarding curricular design at the classroom level given the unique characteristics of their students. Indeed, in a meta-analysis involving 22 studies, Ellen Whitener (1989) found a strong relationship between a student's knowledge and experience with content and the type of sequencing and pacing necessary to learn that content.

Unfortunately, teachers frequently do not make the decisions about how to sequence and pace content within their lessons and units. Rather, they rely on the design of textbooks for guidance. Roger Farr and his colleagues note that this is common at both the elementary and secondary levels (Farr, Tulley, & Rayford, 1984). One of the major findings from the Third International Mathematics and Science Study (TIMSS) was that teachers in the United States exhibit an overreliance on textbooks for decisions about content and pacing (Stevenson & Stigler, 1992; Stigler & Hiebert, 1999). If textbooks were organized in ways consistent with known principles of learning, this wouldn't be so bad. Unfortunately, this does not seem to be the case (Venesky, 1992). For example, science textbooks have been described as well-illustrated dictionaries as opposed to effective vehicles for student learning (Rothmann, 1988). It is clear that classroom teachers must make decisions about sequencing and presentation of content. What are the principles that should guide those decisions? To begin answering this question, let's consider two current movements in education that can, if implemented incorrectly, work against effective classroom curriculum design. These movements are loosely referred to as "constructivism" and "brain-based education."

Multiple books and reports published within the last decade sought to apply the theory of constructivism and the research on the brain to K–12 education (Berman, 2001; Brandt, 1998; Brooks & Brooks, 1999, 2001; Caine & Caine, 1991, 1997; Sousa, 2001; Sylwester, 2000; Sylwester & Margulies, 1998; Wolfe, 2001). My comments should not be interpreted as a criticism of researchers' intent or scholarship. In some cases, however, K–12 educators have misapplied their suggestions or, more seriously, discarded proven practices in the name of constructivism or brain-based education. Although these two fields offer great insight into the dynamics of teaching and learning, they should be used with caution and not overly applied in lieu of time-honored and well-researched practices. These cautions are detailed in the writings of both John Bruer (Bruer, 1993, 1997) and John Anderson and his colleagues (Anderson, Reder, & Simon, 1995, 1996; Anderson, Greeno, Reder, & Simon, 2000). I draw from their work heavily in this discussion.

According to Anderson and his colleagues (1995), the constructivist vision of learning is captured nicely by the following quotation from Paul Cobb and his colleagues (Cobb, Yackel, & Wood, 1992) regarding the subject of mathematics:

> . . . learning would be viewed as an active, constructive process in which students attempt to resolve problems that arise as they participate in the mathematical practices of the classroom. Such a view emphasizes that the learning-teaching process is interactive in nature and involves the implicit and explicit negotiation of mathematical meanings. In the course of these negotiations, the teacher and students elaborate the taken-as-shared mathematical reality that

constitutes the basis for their ongoing communication. (p. 5)

Cobb and colleagues (Cobb, Wood, Yackel, Nicholls, Wheatley, Trigatti, & Perlwitz, 1991) exemplify this position by describing an effort to teach 2nd graders to count by tens. Instead of teaching students the principle, the teacher provides objects bundled in groups of ten. Invariably, students discover that counting by tens is more efficient than counting by ones. Of course, there are many laudable aspects of this example. Anderson, Reder, & Simon (1995) note "One can readily agree with one part of the constructivist claim: that learning must be an active process (p. 11)." Anderson and colleagues warn that this principle is frequently overgeneralized to mean that teachers should rarely (if ever) teach content to students.

The same concern about overgeneralization has been articulated on brain research. John Bruer (1997) asserts that the brain research is not yet conclusive enough to provide specific guidance for K–12 educators:

> However, we should be wary of claims that neuroscience has much to tell us about education, particularly if those claims derive from the neuroscience and education argument. The neuroscience and education argument attempts to link learning, particularly early childhood learning, with what neuroscience has discovered about neural development and synaptic change. Neuroscience has discovered a great deal about neurons and synapses but not nearly enough to guide educational practice. Currently, the span between brain and learning cannot support much of a load. Too many people marching in step across it could be dangerous. (p. 15)

The confusion created by well-intended applications (and, in some cases, misapplications) of constructivism and brain research are substantive enough to make the suggestions in this chapter difficult to defend. It is helpful to identify some basic principles about the nature of learning and the nature of content (and their interactions), and to compare and contrast these principles with educational applications of constructivism and brain research. These principles are derived primarily from the world of cognitive psychology—the most fertile soil for educational reform at the present time. As Bruer explains, when the brain research does reach the point at which it can guide educational practice, it will use the well-established principles of cognitive psychology:

> There is a well-established bridge, now nearly 50 years old, between education and cognitive psychology. There is a second bridge, only around 10 years old, between cognitive psychology and neuroscience. This newer bridge is allowing us to see how mental functions map onto brain structures. When neuroscience does begin to provide useful insights about instruction and educational practice, those insights will be the result of extensive traffic over this second bridge. Cognitive psychology provides the only firm ground we have to anchor these bridges. It is the only way to go if we eventually want to move between education and the brain. (p. 4)

Three principles from cognitive psychology form the basis for my recommended action steps to implement effective classroom curriculum design.

Principle 1. Learning is enhanced when a teacher identifies specific types of knowledge that are the focus of a unit or lesson.

One of the common themes in constructivist and brain-based models of instruction is that the content to be learned is a flexible and sometimes negotiated commodity. Such sentiments are commonly expressed as "student autonomy" (Brooks & Brooks, 2001), "alternate curriculums" (Sylwester, 2000), or "invitational learning" (Barrell, 2001). These are useful ideas, but can be detrimental to effective instruction if interpreted to mean that teachers should not have clear learning goals, communicate these goals to students, and design instruction around them. Even when a teacher has clear learning goals, students might not obtain the targeted knowledge and skill. Graham Nuthall dramatically illustrated this rather disturbing phenomenon (Nuthall, 1999; Nuthall & Alton-Lee, 1993, 1995). He traced the experiences of elementary students in integrated science and social studies units on the topic of Antarctica. In general, all students were involved in the same basic learning experiences. However, after three weeks, the content recalled and understood was quite different from student to student. The same was true after one year. For example, where some students had detailed and accurate recollections of a specific incident that occurred on Mt. Erebus in Antarctica, other students had incorrect recollections or none at all. Reasons included differences in levels of engagement, differences in the number of tasks completed, and differences in the types of optional activities students selected.

A direct implication of Nuthall's work is that teachers must identify specific aspects of content to be addressed and plan the learning experiences accordingly. This is not quite as simple as it sounds because most content has many potential elements that might be the focus of instruction. For example, possible focuses for instruction in fractions include

- the relationship between fractions and whole numbers,
- the relationship between fractions and decimals,
- the relationship between fractions and percents,
- the process of converting fractions to decimals, and
- the different categories or types of fractions.

The complex nature of seemingly straightforward instructional topics is well recognized in the research and theoretical literature (Kintsch, 1974, 1979; van Dijk, 1977, 1980; van Dijk & Kintsvh, 1983). Some of the more salient aspects of an instructional topic that might be the focus of instruction are listed in Figure 11.1 (pp. 110–111).

Principle 2. Learning requires engagement in tasks that are structured or are sufficiently similar to allow for effective transfer of knowledge.

Virtually all discussions of constructivism or brain-based education emphasize the need for students to generate their own unique meaning regarding the content being learned. However, some of the discussions of constructivism and brain-based approaches do not recognize the need for teachers to structure classroom tasks to facilitate the construction of meaning. Some even suggest that

FIGURE 11.1

Aspects of an Instructional Topic to Focus Instruction

Aspect of Topic	Explanation or Example
Category	The topic of non-constitutional governments belongs to the category of unlimited governments whereas the topic of constitutional governments belongs to category of limited governments.
Subcategories	Subcategories of mathematical functions include step functions, linear functions, and curvilinear functions.
Examples	Within the topic of constitutional governments are the following contemporary examples: Canada, Australia, New Zealand, and the United States.
Associated comparisons	To fully understand ratios, it is important for students to know how they compare with fractions, decimals, and percentages.
Associated characteristics	Characteristics are important when the topic involves types of persons, places, living and nonliving things, events, and abstractions: • Types of persons: "It takes at least two years of training to become a firefighter." • Types of places: "Large cities commonly have high crime rates." • Types of living things: "Golden retrievers are usually good hunting dogs." • Types of nonliving things: "Firearms are the subject of heated debate." • Types of events: "Football games involve two teams of 11 players each." • Types of abstractions: "Fear is one of the most powerful of human emotions."
Associated cause-and-effect or correlational relationships	Cause-and-effect relationships identify a cause or causes for a specific outcome (e.g., "Tuberculosis is caused by the turbercle bacillus."). When this type of relationship is singled out for emphasis, students are usually expected to understand the specific elements within the cause-and-effect relationship and how they interact. That is, to understand the cause-and-effect relationship regarding tuberculosis, students would have to understand the sequence of events that occur, the elements involved, and the type and strength of relationships between those elements. Correlational relationships are not causal in nature. Rather, a change in one element is associated with a change in another (e.g., "The number of caribou in the Arctic habitat is directly proportional to the number of lemmings in any given year."). Again, when this type of relationship is singled out, students are commonly expected to know the elements involved.
Associated episodes	Episodes include (1) a setting (e.g. a particular time and place), (2) specific participants, (3) a particular duration, (4) a specific sequence of events, and (5) specific cause-and-effect relationships. For example, students should be aware of the specifics surrounding the invasion of Kuwait by Iraq.
Associated facts	Facts are important when a topic involves a specific person, place, living thing, or nonliving thing: • Specific person: "One of Charles Dickens's most respected books was *A Tale of Two Cities.*" • Specific place: "Denver is the state capitol of Colorado." • Specific living thing: "The race horse Seattle Slew was one of the few horses ever to win the triple crown of horse racing." • Specific nonliving thing: "The Empire State Building is more than 100 stories high."

FIGURE 11.1 (continued)

Aspects of an Instructional Topic to Focus Instruction

Aspect of Topic	Explanation or Example
Associated terms	The terms *numerator* and *denominator* are important to understanding the topic of fractions.
Associated skills	Skills are procedures that involve specific steps commonly executed in a specific sequence. The skill of converting fractions to decimals is important to understanding the topic of fractions. When students learn the skill, they can execute the steps with relative fluency.
Associated processes	Processes are procedures that involve steps that are not performed in a specific sequence. The order of the steps changes given the situation in which the process is used. Using the computer program Word Perfect involves a process. Although there are steps involved, they are used differently depending on the nature of the writing task.

Source: Workshop materials. Copyright © 2001 R. J. Marzano.

---

structure inhibits learning. Leslie Hart was one of the early champions of this perspective. His sentiments are captured in the following quotation from his book *Human Brain and Human Learning* (1983):

> Since the brain is indisputably a multipath, multimodal apparatus, the notion of mandatory sequences, or even any fixed sequences, is unsupportable. Each of us learns in a personal, highly individual, mainly random way, always adding to, sorting out, and revising all the input—from teachers or elsewhere—that we have had up to that point. That being the case, *any group instruction that has been tightly, logically planned will have been wrongly planned for most of the group,* [original emphasis] and will inevitably inhibit, prevent or distort learning. (p. 55)

The tendency to underestimate the importance of a logical progression of content and tasks is evident in some brain-based practices such as "orchestrated immersion" (Caine & Caine, 1991). Although orchestrated immersion does have merit, it has overstepped its utility when it is interpreted to mean that structured learning is not necessary.

The need for structure becomes obvious when we consider the primacy of the psychological principle of "sameness." The importance of sameness in learning was recognized more than 100 years ago by William James in his book *Principles of Psychology* (1890; cited in Campbell, 1986): " . . . the mind makes continual use of sameness, and if deprived of it, would have a different structure from what is has" (p. 60). The importance of sameness is also prominent in discussions of transfer of learning. In their book *Learning, Remembering, Believing: Enhancing Human Performance*, Daniel Druckman and Robert Bjork (1994) note: "A general principle of transfer seems to be that identical elements are necessary" (p. 36). Finally, the importance of sameness has been consistently demonstrated by the research of Douglas Carnine and Edward Kameenui (Carnine, 1992; Kameenui, 1992; Carnine & Kameenui, 1992). Carnine (1992) notes

If sameness is the psychological key for organizing curriculum, the content itself must be the lock. The mechanism that allows the lock to function is the organization of the content in ways that highlight important sameness. (p. 12)

According to James Flavell (1971), the very definition of structured learning involves presenting tasks that are similar. He explains

To apply the term "structure" correctly, it appears that there must be, at a minimum, an ensemble of two or more elements together with one or more relationships interlinking these elements. (p. 443)

In short, learning is enhanced when students are presented with tasks that are similar enough for them to ascertain their sameness. By definition, this requires a teacher to structure the learning experiences of students.

Principle 3. Learning requires multiple exposure to and complex interactions with knowledge.

It would certainly be handy if one exposure to content was sufficient for students to learn it. We know this is not the case. For example, Piaget (1971) described two types of learning: one in which new knowledge is integrated into the learner's existing knowledge base (assimilation) and another in which existing knowledge structures are changed (accommodation). Multiple exposures to knowledge over time are necessary for assimilation, however, complex interaction with knowledge over time allows for the more powerful, second type of learning—accommodation.

Schema theory provides another perspective on the importance of multiple exposures to and interactions with content. Schemata

are the basic packets in which knowledge is stored in permanent memory (Anderson, 1994). Schema development, then, is synonymous with knowledge development. Three types of schema development exist: (1) accretion, (2) tuning, and (3) restructuring (Rumelhart & Norman, 1981).

Accretion and **tuning** describe the gradual accumulation or addition of knowledge over time and the expression of that knowledge in more parsimonious ways. **Restructuring** involves reorganizing knowledge so that it can produce new insights. Accretion and tuning require multiple exposures to content while restructuring requires multiple exposures and complex interaction with content.

The clear picture provided by Piaget's learning theory and by schema theory is that multiple exposures to knowledge are required to integrate and retain knowledge in permanent memory. Complex interaction with knowledge is required for new knowledge to change our basic understandings. Graham Nuthall's research provides guidance as to how this might play out in a classroom setting.

Building on the research of Carolyn Rovee-Collier (1995), Nuthall (1999) found that students require about four exposures to content to adequately integrate it into their existing knowledge base. Nuthall notes that these exposures should be no more than two days apart:

We found that it took a minimum of three to four exposures with no more than a two-day gap or 'time window' (Rovee-Collier, 1995) between each one, for these experiences to become integrated as a new knowledge construct. (p. 305)

The types of experiences students have with content should be varied from exposure to exposure. In fact, it seems to be the case that some types of experiences produce more effective learning than others. To illustrate, consider Figure 11.2. The most striking aspect of the findings reported in Figure 11.2 is the impact of dramatic instruction. It has an effect size of 1.12 immediately after instruction and an effect size of .80 twelve months after instruction. The other two types of experiences, although effective, do not approach this level. Verbal instruction involves telling students about content or having them read about it; visual instruction involves using pictures and other forms of visual representations. Dramatic instruction involves students being engaged in or observing some dramatic representation of the content. In its simplest form, the "story" dramatizes the information but does not require extensive preparation. About the use of stories, Nuthall (1999) notes:

> Our studies suggest that narratives provide powerful structures for organization and storage of curriculum content in memory. . . . Stories often contain a rich variety of supplemental information and connect to personal experiences, as well as being integrated and held together by a familiar structure. (p. 337)

Other researchers have reported similar conclusions about the instructional potential of stories (Barrell, 2001; Hicks, 1993; Schank, 1990).

Figure 11.3 (p. 114) provides another perspective on the effects of different types of instructional activities. The findings are from the research of Barbara Guzzetti, Tonja Snyder, and Gene Glass (Guzzetti, Snyder, & Glass, 1993). They compared the effectiveness of various learning experiences on correcting students' misconceptions about content. As Figure 11.3 illustrates, simply activating prior knowledge—asking students what they know about a topic or what they remember about a topic—produces very little conceptual change.

FIGURE 11.2
Effects of Different Types of Learning Experiences

Type of Experience	Effect Size Immediately After Instruction	Effect Size After 12 Months
Verbal Instruction	0.74	0.64
Visual Instruction	0.90	0.74
Dramatic Instruction	1.12	0.80

Sources:
Nuthall, G. (1999). The way students learn: Acquiring knowledge from an integrated science and social studies unit. *The Elementary School Journal, 99*(4), 303–341.

Nuthall, G., & Alton-Lee, A. (1995). Assessing classroom learning: How students use their knowledge and experience to answer classroom achievement test questions in science and social studies. *American Educational Research Journal, 32*(1), 185–223.

Indeed, the average effect size for this type of experience in the 14 studies examined by Guzzetti and her colleagues was only .08. Having students discuss what they know about the topic produces substantially more conceptual change by infusing new perspectives and new ideas. It has an average effect size of .51. The biggest conceptual change is obtained from students engaging in argumentation— taking a position regarding the content and providing evidence for that position. It has an average effect size of .80.

When we consider the research in its totality, a logical picture starts to emerge. When students are first exposed to content, learning should ideally involve the use of stories or other forms of dramatization along with the use of visual representations of information. In subsequent exposures, learning experiences should involve discussion and (ideally) tasks that require students to make and defend judgments.

Cognitive psychologists frequently make a distinction between two types of knowledge— declarative and procedural (Anderson, 1982, 1983; Fitts & Posner, 1967). Where declarative knowledge is more information based, procedural knowledge is more skill or process based. For example, knowledge of the characteristics of Antarctica or significant events that occurred on Mt. Erebus is declarative because it involves information. In contrast, knowledge of how to do long division or the steps involved in a specific type of proof is procedural because it involves processes.

The distinction between the two is important because they develop in different ways. To be used effectively, procedural knowledge must be learned to a level of **automaticity** or **controlled processing**—with little or no conscious thought. To illustrate, procedures for decoding words are commonly learned to a level of automaticity (Laberge & Samuels, 1974). We don't think about the process; we do it with no conscious thought or perceived effort. Other procedures, like those we might use to balance an algebraic equation, are not learned to the level of automaticity but are learned to the level of controlled processing (Shiffrin & Schneider,

---

FIGURE 11.3

Effects of Different Types of Learning Experiences in Correcting Students' Misconceptions About Content

Category	Number of Effect Sizes	Average Effect Size
Activate Prior Student Knowledge	14	0.08
Student Discussion	11	0.51
Student Argumentation	3	0.80

Source: Guzzetti, B. J., Snyder, T. E., & Glass, G. V. (1993). Promoting conceptual change in science: A comparative meta-analysis of instructional interventions from reading education and science education. *Reading Research Quarterly, 28*(2), 117–155.

1977). We must think about which action we might perform next, but all possible steps are already known to us.

Regardless of the level to which procedural knowledge is learned, practice is a necessary ingredient. Without practice, the chances of reaching the requisite levels of learning are small indeed. As Anderson, Reder, and Simon (1995) explain: "In denying the critical role of practice one is denying children the very thing they need to achieve real competence" (p. 7). Yet the critically important role of practice has been ignored and even negated by some. To illustrate, consider the following recommendation from the National Council of Teachers of Mathematics (NCTM) as articulated in their standards document, *Principles and Standards for School Mathematics* (2000):

> Classroom discourse and social interaction can be used to promote the recognition of connections among ideas and reorganization of knowledge. . . . By having students talk about their informal strategies, teachers can help them become aware of, and build on, their implicit informal knowledge. . . . Moreover, in such settings, *procedural fluency* and conceptual understanding *can be developed through problem solving, reasoning, and argumentation* [emphasis added]. (p. 21)

Part of this recommendation is definitely in keeping with the research in cognitive psychology. However, if students *only* discussed and argued about their personal routines for the procedure of multiplication, for example, and did not engage in any form of practice, the chances of them being able to perform multiplication at the level of automaticity or controlled processing would be quite small. Aren't the scholars who drafted the NCTM

standards familiar with the research on learning procedural knowledge? Of course they are. A probable reason for their recommendation is that the framers never intended much of the procedural knowledge listed in the standards to be learned to the level of automaticity or controlled processing. This is evidenced by a statement in the standards document:

> Moreover, as judgments change about the facts or procedures that are essential in an increasingly technological world, conceptual understanding becomes even more important. For example, most of the arithmetic and algebraic procedures long viewed as the heart of the school mathematics curriculum can now be performed with handheld calculators. Thus, more attention can be given to understanding the number concepts and the modeling procedures used in problem solving. (p. 20)

Those who downplay the importance of practice do not necessarily argue that practice is an unnecessary ingredient. Rather, they simply believe that few procedures must be learned to the level of automaticity or controlled processing given the technological help that is now available. Before handheld calculators, students had to learn multiplication and division to the level of automaticity. Today, this might not be the case. Which, if any, procedures should be learned to the level of automaticity or controlled processing is certainly a matter for subject matter specialists. However, if a procedure is one that students should learn to the level of automaticity or controlled processing, then practice is an absolute necessity.

Effective practice is not an unthinking execution of a set of steps or rote memorization. Effective practice involves a "shaping" of the process as originally learned (Anderson, 1982, 1983; Fitts & Posner, 1967). This requires a great deal of reasoning about the process and even trial and error to determine process modifications. In short, practice is not the pariah that some apparently think it to be. It is a necessary part of procedural learning and involves complex levels of higher order thought.

Action Steps

I recommend five action steps to translate the five principles into effective classroom curriculum design.

Action Step 1. Have teachers identify the important declarative and procedural knowledge in the topics that are to be the focus of instruction.

To this end, Charles Reigeluth and Faith Stein (1983) recommend the following steps:

> (1) selecting one type of content as the organizing content (concepts, principles, or procedures); (2) listing all of the organizing content that is to be taught in the course; (3) selecting a few organizing content ideas that are the most basic, simple, and/or fundamental; and (4) presenting those ideas at the application level rather than the more superficial and abstract memorization level. (p. 344)

This action might not be as straightforward for teachers as it appears because most of the topics that are the focus of a unit of instruction contain both declarative and procedural knowledge. For example, declarative aspects of fractions, such as the relationship between fractions and decimals, might be the focus of instruction.

Or procedural aspects of fractions, such as converting fractions to decimals, might be the focus. Figure 11.4 presents a useful set of questions that a teacher might ask about a topic to distinguish between the two types of knowledge. These are derived from the aspects of a topic depicted in Figure 11.1 (pp. 110–111).

Action Step 2. Have teachers present new content multiple times using a variety of input modes.

It appears that at least four experiences spread no more than two days apart are required to learn declarative knowledge at an adequate level (Nuthall, 1999; Rovee-Collier, 1995). It also appears that these exposures should involve a variety of input modes.

A useful way of conceptualizing input modes is to think in terms of direct versus indirect experiences.

Direct experiences involve real or simulated physical activity. For example, a direct experience for the topic of democracy would be one that involves students in a democratic activity such as using the democratic process to make all classroom decisions during a two-week period. Another form of direct experience is through simulation such as students learning how to drive using computer software.

Indirect experiences are those in which students are not physically involved. Demonstrations, films, readings, and lectures are all indirect experiences. Indirect ways of learning about hibernation could include observing a classroom pet that goes into hibernation for the winter, watching a film on hibernation, reading about hibernation, or listening to an oral presentation about

---

FIGURE 11.4

Planning Questions to Identify Important Knowledge Within a Topic

Topic _____

About the declarative aspects of this topic, is it important for students to know the

- Category?

- Subcategories?

- Examples?

- Associated comparisons?

- Associated characteristics?

- Associated cause-and-effect relationships?

- Associated correlational relationships?

- Associated episodes?

- Associated facts (specific persons, places, living and nonliving things)?

- Associated terms?

About the procedural aspects of this topic, is it important for students to know the skills or processes? Is it

- A specific skill or process?

- The specific steps or phases of a skill or process?

---

hibernation. Indirect experiences vary in terms of whether the information is presented in a narrative or expository fashion.

Demonstrations, films, readings, and lectures can be in either form. Hence, classroom curriculum design involves determining whether learning experiences will be direct or indirect and whether the information will be presented in narrative or expository form.

Action Step 3. Have teachers make a distinction between those skills and processes students are to master versus those they are not.

In educational terms, reaching the level of automaticity or controlled processing is sometimes referred to as "mastery." If mastery is expected of any procedure at any grade level, students should engage in adequate amounts of practice.

Probably the most detailed work on attaining mastery through practice has been done in the field of "precision teaching" developed by Ogden Lindsley (1972). Lindsley's techniques have been used in virtually every academic discipline. Highly behavioristic in nature, precision teaching involves periodically measuring students' speed and accuracy in performing a skill or process and then checking each measurement on a standard behavior chart.

Precision teaching is detailed and powerful but is probably far too time consuming and labor intensive for most teachers. Some aspects of precision teaching, however, can be readily adapted to classroom instruction such as practicing with specific goals of speed and accuracy in mind. A teacher in San Diego once explained to me how she emphasized speed and accuracy when her students practiced a new skill. She periodically provided students with sample problems in dividing fractions, which they performed independently in a set period of time. They then charted their accuracy and speed. Over two weeks, students would do this four to seven times. Thus, their charts provided a visual record of their progress. Again, it is important to note that some mathematics educators might determine that dividing by fractions is a procedure that students need not master—in which case, extensive practice would not be required.

Action Step 4. Have teachers present content in groups or categories that demonstrate the critical features of the content.

Teachers must structure content in such a way as to highlight its "sameness." Douglas Carnine (1992) provides some clear examples of such organization. To illustrate, consider the following set of formulas:

Rectangular Prism: $l \times w \times h = v$
Wedge: $1/2 \times l \times w \times h = v$
Triangular Pyramid: $1/6 \times l \times w \times h = v$
Cylinder: $pi \times r^2 \times h = v$
Rectangular Pyramid: $1/3 \times l \times w \times h = v$
Cone: $1/3 \times pi \times r^2 \times h = v$
Sphere: $4/3 \times pi \times r^3 = v$

Although all those formulas represent volume, they provide little insight into the nature of volume when presented in isolation. Carnine notes that an insightful teacher can organize these into categories that highlight the central feature for all formulas for

volume, that is, volume equals base times height ($V = b \times h$):

Rectangular Prism $b \times h$	Wedge $b \times h$	Cylinder $b \times h$
Rectangular Pyramid $b \times 1/3 \times h$	Triangular Pyramid $b \times 1/3 \times h$	Cone $b \times 1/3 \times h$
Sphere $b \times 2/3 \times h$		

For the regular figures—rectangular prism, wedge, and cylinder—the volume is the product of the base and the height. For figures that come to a point—rectangular pyramid, triangular pyramid, and cone—the volume is 1/3 times the product of the base and height. The sphere is a special case in which the volume is 2/3 times the product of the base and height. As Carnine notes: "The sameness analysis makes explicit the core concept that volume equals base times height. This core concept is obscured in math textbooks that present seven different formulas" (p. 14).

Diane Kinder and William Bursuck (1992) provide an example in social studies. They explain that the inherent sameness in many historical events can be highlighted by use of what they refer to as the "problem-solution-effect analysis."

We propose that people and governments are reacting to problems, that the causes of those problems are small in number, and that there are a few common solutions to those problems. The outcomes or effects of these solutions, though not always clearly stated in textbooks, might, in fact, result in other problems. This problem-solution-effect analysis seems to provide a frame or schema for many historical events. (p. 29)

They illustrate how a teacher might cluster a set of historical events together in a way that highlights critical features similar to all these events. For example, World War I, World War II, and the War on Terrorism might be presented together to highlight the impact of sudden, surprise attacks or invasions.

Action Step 5. Have teachers engage students in complex tasks that require addressing content in unique ways.

Tasks that involve problem solving, decision making, systems analysis, creating metaphors, creating analogies, and the like are complex in nature. Being involved in such tasks certainly enhances students' understanding of content. However, it is the act of explaining and justifying one's conclusions that facilitates deep conceptual changes (Guzzetti, Snyder, & Glass, 1993). James Kinneavy (1991) has detailed the powerful impact of students defending and justifying their conclusions. Historically, formal arguments contain grounds, warrants, backing, and qualifiers (Toulmin, Rieke, & Janik, 1981). These important and useful elements are described in Figure 11.5. Students might simply be asked to include the following elements when justifying their conclusions:

FIGURE 11.5

Formal Elements of an Argument

Element	Description
1. Grounds	Once a claim is made, it is usually supported by grounds. Depending on the type of claim made, grounds may be composed of • matters of common knowledge, • expert opinion, • previously established information, • experimental observation, and • other information considered "factual."
2. Warrants	Warrants specify or interpret the information in the grounds. That is, where grounds specify the source of support for a claim and the general nature of the support, warrants provide a detailed analysis of the information highlighted by grounds.
3. Backing	Backing establishes the validity of warrants. That is, warrants in and of themselves might not be wholly trusted. Consequently, it is often appropriate for some discussion of the validity or general acceptance of the warrants used.
4. Qualifiers	Not all warrants lead to their claims with the same degree of certainty. Consequently, qualifiers articulate the degree of certainty for the claim and/or qualifiers to the claim.

Source: Toulmin, S., Rieke, R., & Janik, A. (1981). *An introduction to reasoning.* New York: Macmillan.

- the basic claim,
- the evidence supporting their claim,
- a discussion regarding why their evidence should be considered valid, and
- statements identifying any limitations on their claims, evidence or the validity of their evidence.

Consider the following decision-making task that might be assigned to junior high students.

> Select an influential person from the 15th or 16th century whose actions had important consequences. Determine the factors this person had to consider before taking those important actions. What alternatives were available to this person? Determine the goals that motivated the person in deciding to take the actions and the criteria the person probably applied in making the decision. What were the possible trade-offs in selecting one alternative over another? What were the risks and rewards, and how could either be measured? Without the benefit of hindsight, would you have made the same choice? Explain why or why not. As you study this decision, reflect on the kinds of history-making decisions that are made today. You can present your findings in oral or written form.

Thus students would be asked to articulate their basic claim or conclusion, provide evidence for their conclusion, explain why their evidence is valid, and describe any qualifications regarding the information they have presented.

Summary

This chapter presented three principles from cognitive psychology to explain some misconceptions and misrepresentations of constructivism and brain-based education. These principles were then translated into five recommended action steps that addressed teachers' needs to identify and articulate the specifics of content, to ensure that students have multiple exposures to content, to identify procedures to be mastered, to structure content and tasks using the principle of sameness, and to engage students in complex tasks that require them to address content in unique ways.

Section III

STUDENT-LEVEL FACTORS

List of Figures in Section III

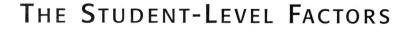

THE STUDENT-LEVEL FACTORS

One of the perceived truisms in education has been that student background characteristics are the most important determinants of student achievement. Indeed, as discussed in Chapter 1, this was one of the primary conclusions of the studies by Coleman and colleagues (1966) and by Jencks and colleagues (1972). It has also been assumed that, implicitly or explicitly, these background characteristics are largely impervious to change. Popular books such as *Bias in Mental Testing* by Arthur Jensen (1980) and *The Bell Curve* by Richard Heurnstein and Charles Murray (1994) have made elaborate statistical cases that background characteristics, particularly intelligence, are genetically based and can be changed little by schooling. In contrast, I believe that the research clearly shows that even some of most negative aspects of a student's background can be mediated by school-based interventions.

In Chapter 1, I supplied evidence that schools generally account for only 20 percent of the variance in student achievement and that student background characteristics account for the other 80 percent. But what if a school could do something about those background characteristics? In the next three chapters, we explore which student background factors schools can address and what they might do about them. What, then, are the student background characteristics that influence academic achievement?

Student-Level Factors: A Comparison Across Researchers

Many different lists of student-level factors exist. For example, in *Human Characteristics and School Learning*, Benjamin Bloom (1976) identifies two basic student background characteristics: (1) cognitive characteristics and (2) affective characteristics. In *A Psychological Theory of Educational Productivity*, Herbert Walberg (1980) identifies three salient background characteristics: (1) ability or prior achievement, (2) development as indexed by age or stage of maturation, and (3) motivation or self-concept. Barry Fraser, Herbert Walberg, Wayne Welch and John Hattie (1987) identify three factors: (1) ability, (2) motivation, and (3) home environment. In my own synthesis of the research in *A New Era of School Reform: Going Where the Research Takes Us* (Marzano, 2000a), I identify four factors: (1) home atmosphere, (2) prior knowledge, (3) aptitude, and (4) interest.

I have combined my previous work with that of others to construct the model presented in this book. Three student-level factors are addressed in this section:

1. Home environment
2. Learned intelligence and background knowledge
3. Motivation

How these relate to my previous work and the work of others is depicted in Figure 12.1.

The figure shows that I have collapsed my previous terms "aptitude" and "prior knowledge" into a single category called "learned intelligence/background knowledge." The "learned intelligence" aspect of this category title might sound like an oxymoron, but it is not. Also, I have renamed "interest" as the more robust "motivation."

Although they use different names, previous researchers generally identify the same student-level factors as those used in this book. The lack of reference by Bloom (1976) and Walberg (1980) to home environment is simply an artifact of their categorization schemes. Both, in fact, note that home environment plays a critical role in student achievement.

The next three chapters in this section address each of the student-level factors. Chapter 13 addresses home environment, Chapter 14 addresses learned intelligence and background knowledge, and Chapter 15 addresses motivation.

FIGURE 12.1

Comparing Student-Level Factors Across Researchers

Student-Level Factors	Bloom (1976)	Walberg (1980)	Fraser et al. (1987)	Marzano (2000a)
Home environment			Home environment	Home environment
Learned intelligence or Background knowledge	Cognitive characteristics	Ability or prior achievement, or Development	Ability	Aptitude Prior knowledge
Motivation	Affective characteristics	Motivation or self-concept	Motivation	Interest

Summary

Both research and theory indicate that student-level factors account for the lion's share of variance in student achievement. However, the negative effects of these factors can be overcome. Three student-level factors were identified: home environment, learned intelligence and background knowledge, and motivation.

HOME ENVIRONMENT

For decades, educational researchers, educational practitioners, and the public at large have assumed that socioeconomic status (SES) is one of the best predictors of academic achievement. The Coleman report supported that theory. As explained by Karl White (1982), the Coleman report confirmed for educators what they thought they already knew: "that a strong relationship exists between all kinds of achievement variables and what has come to be known as socioeconomic status (SES)" (p. 46). White also notes that the belief in the strong relationship between SES and student achievement is so pervasive that it has rarely been questioned. To illustrate, consider the following quotes:

> The family characteristic that is the most powerful predictor of school performance is socioeconomic status (SES): the higher the SES of the student's family, the higher his academic achievement. This relationship has been documented in countless studies and seems to hold no matter what measure of status is used (occupation of principal breadwinner, family income, parents' education, or some combination of these). (Boocock, 1972, p. 32)

> To categorize youth according to the social class position of their parents is to order them on the extent of their participation and degree of success in the American Educational System. This has been so consistently confirmed by research that it can now be regarded as an empirical law. . . . SES predicts grades, achievement and intelligence test scores, retentions at grade level, course failures, truancy, suspensions from school, high school dropouts, plans for college attendance, and total amount of formal schooling. (Charters, 1963, pp. 739–740)

> The positive association between school completion, family socioeconomic status, and measured ability is well known. (Welch, 1974, p. 32)

In spite of previous testimonials to the strength of relationship between SES and student achievement, the actual research findings vary widely. Specifically, White notes correlations between SES and student achievement that are as high as 0.80 and as low as 0.10.

White conducted a meta-analysis of 101 reports that yielded 636 correlations. He found that, depending on how SES was defined, the correlation between SES and student achievement could vary widely, as depicted in Figure 13.1.

The figure reports the strength of relationship between four elements commonly associated with SES and student achievement: The income of the adults (e.g., parents) in the home, the education of the adults in the home, the occupation of the adults in the home, and the atmosphere in the home. Figure 13.1 shows that home atmosphere has the strongest relationship with student achievement. This is an important finding. As White explains:

> More striking, however, is the fact that measures of home atmosphere correlated much

higher with academic achievement than did any single or combined group of the traditional indicators of SES. Recalling the comments by Jencks et al. (1972) cited earlier, there are many differences among families that can potentially affect the academic achievement of the children in addition to differences in education, occupational level, and income of the parents. It is not at all implausible that some low-SES parents (defined in terms of income, education, and/or occupational level) are very good at creating a home atmosphere that fosters learning (e.g., read to their children, help them with their homework, encourage them to go to college, and take them to the library and to cultural events), whereas other low-SES parents are not. (p. 471)

As White illustrates, the effects of SES have historically been thought of as extremely large and impervious to change. However, White provides for great hope given that the most important aspect of SES is the effect of home environment, as opposed to factors such as

FIGURE 13.1

Effects of Various Aspects of Socioeconomic Status on Achievement

SES Indicator	Correlation	Effect Size	Percentile Gain	Percentage of Variance Explained
Income	.32	.67	25	9.92
Education	.19	.38	24	3.24
Occupation	.20	.42	26	4.04
Home atmosphere only	.58	1.42	42	33.29

Note: For a discussion of correlation, effect size, percentile gain, and percentage of variance explained and their relationships, see Technical Notes 1 & 4 (pp. 187–188, 190–191).

Source: White, K. R. (1982). The relationship between socioeconomic status and academic achievement. *Psychological Bulletin, 91*(3), 461–481.

parental income and education. Where a school cannot change the income, education, or occupation of adults in the home, it can have a potential impact on the atmosphere in the home. Thus, a home environment structured in specific ways can positively affect achievement. What characteristics, then, of a home environment can have a positive impact on student achievement?

Xitao Fan and Michael Chen (2001) conducted a meta-analysis that involved more than 90 correlations. They found that the average correlation between home environment and student achievement was 0.33, indicating that, on the average, the home environment accounts for 10.89 percent of the variance in student achievement. However, home environment is not a unidimensional construct. Rather, it is composed of three basic elements: (1) communication about school, (2) supervision, and (3) parental expectations and parenting styles.

Communication About School

Communication about school refers to parents' interest in and communication about the schoolwork of their children. This element of home environment has been described as "the structure of the environment and how the environment can be manipulated to encourage and support children's academic learning" (Christenson, Rounds, & Gorney, 1992, pp.183–184). In their analysis of 10 studies involving 26,493 families, Fan and Chen found the average correlation between this element and academic achievement to be 0.17. Many other

researchers have reported the importance of this factor to student learning (Bradshaw & Amundson, 1985; Chavkin & Williams, 1985; Cooper, 1989; Gonzalez & Blanco, 1991; Leler, 1983; Peng & Wright, 1994; Radencich & Schumm, 1988; Yap & Enoki, 1995). Although many aspects of communication interact in complex ways, those commonly mentioned include

- parents having frequent and systematic discussions with their children regarding schoolwork,
- parents encouraging their children regarding schoolwork, and
- parents providing resources to help their children do schoolwork.

Supervision

Supervision generally refers to the extent to which parents monitor and control their children's behavior to optimize academic achievement. In their review of 12 studies involving 69,137 families, Chen and Fan found the average correlation between this aspect of home environment and academic achievement to be 0.13. This is the lowest correlation among the three home environment factors. However, Chen and Fan caution against concluding that parental supervision is not important. The seemingly low correlation might simply mean that tight supervision is done more in families where students are not performing well. As Chen and Fan (2001) note

The findings above, however, should not be interpreted simplistically as indicating that home supervision has little to offer in enhancing children's education. One potential reason for the weak relationship between home supervision and students' academic achievement as observed here is that closer parental supervision is implemented at home because students are not doing well academically in school in the first place. If this is the case, close parental supervision in many homes may be the result of poor academic performance of the students. Consequently, parental supervision may have a weak or even negative [statistical] relationship with students' academic achievement. (pp. 13–14)

Specific behaviors commonly associated with effective home supervision include monitoring the time spent doing homework (Fehrmann, Keith, & Reimers, 1987; Peng & Wright, 1994), monitoring when students return home from school and what they do after school (Ho Sui-Chu & Willms, 1993), and monitoring the extent to which students watch television (Park, 1995).

Several researchers have sought to determine the relationship between television viewing and academic achievement (Neuman, 1980; Williams, Haertel, Haertel, & Walberg, 1982). In general, these studies indicate that television viewing negatively impacts achievement. However, Sandra Christensen, Theresa Rounds, and Deborah Gorney (1992) explain that the relationship is not a straightforward one and must be interpreted with caution, particularly for members of different SES categories:

In middle- and lower-class families, a moderate amount of television viewing (2–4 hours per day) correlates with a relative increase in achievement. . . In general, students who view a great deal of television (more than 6 hours of television per day) have significantly lower achievement scores in reading, writing, and mathematics than children who watch less than 6 hours per day . . . and small amounts of viewing (2–3 hours per day) may increase achievement for disadvantaged children. (p. 186)

We might then conclude that television viewing should be limited to a moderate amount of time and closely monitored by parents. Eliminating television viewing altogether does not seem warranted.

Parental Expectations and Parenting Style

Parental expectations and parenting styles is the third and most important element of home environment. In their analysis of 10 studies involving 24,826 families, Fan and Chen (2001) found the average correlation to be 0.39—the largest correlation among the three elements. Fan and Chen focus on the manner and extent to which parents communicate their academic aspirations to their children. The relationship between this dynamic and student achievement is fairly straightforward—high expectations communicated to students are associated with enhanced achievement (Boersma & Chapman, 1982; Cohen, 1987; Marjoribanks, 1988; Scott-Jones, 1984). Student perceptions of parental expectations are also correlated with achievement (Gigliotti & Brookover, 1975; Johnson, Brookover, & Farnell, 1989). In fact, student perceptions of parental expectations may be more important than the actual expectations themselves. As Christenson et al. (1992) note: ". . . it is not clear whether it is the children's own beliefs and expectations or actual parent expectations that influence achievement" (p. 182).

The parenting style used to communicate expectations appears critical. Indeed, many of the studies Fan and Chen include in their discussion of parental expectations focus on parenting styles (Hess, Holloway, Dickson, & Price, 1984; Peng & Wright, 1994; Voekl, 1993).

In general, parenting styles can be organized into three categories: authoritarian, permissive, and authoritative. These categories were originally referred to as disciplinary styles (Baumrind, 1978) but then later were referred to as parenting styles (Baumrind, 1991) when researchers realized the embedded role of communication. The first two of these styles have little relationship with achievement, whereas the third is purported to have a relatively strong positive relationship (Christenson et al., 1992).

An **authoritarian** style is one in which the parents establish and implement all household rules with little or no discussion with children. Rules are absolute and their transgression is punctuated by swift punishment often accompanied by negative emotions from parents. Parents make the majority of decisions for their children across a wide spectrum of activities such as the sports children pursue, the friends they are allowed to have, and the types of entertainment they are allowed to engage in. The authoritarian parenting style is not so much defined by the restrictions placed on these activities as the fact that these restrictions are imposed with little discussion or input from the children.

The **permissive** style is the antithesis of the authoritarian style. Parents establish few if any household rules and rarely punish inappropriate behavior. Children are left to develop their own rules for conduct and, for the most part, are left to their own devices when it comes to day-to-day decisions. There are few, if any, restrictions regarding sports, friends, or entertainment. Although it might seem that this approach fosters independence and autonomy, which in turn enhance academic achievement, there is no evidence of this. In fact, the evidence suggests that the permissive parenting style can be harmful to academic achievement. As Christenson and colleagues (1992) note: "it is better to err on the side of too much parent control since granting autonomy too early appears to correlate negatively with school accomplishments" (p. 189).

The preferred style is the **authoritative** style. Jennifer Rosenau (1998) explains that authoritative parenting is characterized by "parental warmth, inductive discipline, non-punitive punishment practices, and consistency in child rearing . . ." (p. 12). Although the household has rules, they are commonly established with input from the children. And, transgressions are met with consequences, but are not punitive in nature and executed with little or no negative emotion. Finally, parents with an authoritative style communicate interest in the day-to-day lives of their children.

Action Steps

The three elements of home environment do not lend themselves to direct intervention by the school. The school cannot (and should not) go into homes and recommend specific techniques for communicating about school, for supervising students, or for parental expectations and parenting style. The school can provide information and training on establishing a home environment conducive to academic success. Indeed, the second standard of the National Standards for Parent/Family Involvement Programs (Parent Teacher Association, 1997) urges that parenting skills be promoted and supported by the school. Given that schools are somewhat limited in their ability to establish a supportive home environment, I recommend only one action step for this factor.

Action Step 1. Provide training and support to parents to enhance their communication with their children about school, their supervision of their children, and their ability to communicate expectations to their children within the context of an effective parenting style.

This usually manifests as a training program or programs provided by the school. When approached systematically and thoughtfully, such programs can effect a change in the home environment (Onikama, Hammond, & Koki, 1998; Tangri & Moles, 1987) that translates into improved academic performance. A meta-analysis of 29 controlled studies over a 10-year period indicated that the academic achievement of students in 91 percent of the groups where parents were involved in training programs was superior to that of students in the control groups (Graue, Weinstein, & Walberg, 1983).

Some schools and districts build training into their reform efforts. Beth Antunez (2000) notes that the San Francisco Unified School District (SFUSD) has established a policy that each school site—preschool through high school—must develop a long-range parent involvement plan. Among other features, the SFUSD model recommends that schools establish development opportunities to parents through school-sponsored training.

Some parent training programs are embedded in large-scale school improvement efforts that involve multiple schools and multiple districts. The Teacher-Parent Partnership for the Enhancement of School Success (Swick, 1991) is a training-based program that seeks to develop parents' self-confidence in establishing a home environment conducive to learning. Implemented in rural South Carolina, the project was a collaborative effort between the University of South Carolina and 18 rural school districts. It not only includes training sessions for parents but also sessions for teachers to facilitate parent involvement in the school. Another program, Even Start, has the expressed purpose "to improve the educational opportunities for children and their parents" (Center for Community Education, 1989). The project emphasizes that effective parenting requires training and support in parents' roles as communicators, leaders, advisors, and advocates.

Although there is no established format for parent training programs, features associated with effective programs include the following (Filipczak, Lordeman, & Friedman, 1977; Goodson & Hess, 1975; Graue, Weinstein, & Walberg, 1983; Tangri & Moles, 1987):

- sessions are offered from one to two hours at night,
- parents attend sessions free of charge,
- sessions are offered on a weekly basis although one-time sessions may also be employed,

- sessions focus on specific behaviors parents might use, and
- sessions are used as a vehicle to involve parents in other aspects of school.

Schools wishing to address all aspects of home environment might establish a series of mini-courses for parents. One mini-course would address parental interest in schoolwork and how to communicate to enhance academic achievement. A second mini-course might address activities that should be supervised and supervision techniques. A third mini-course could address parenting styles and techniques for communicating expectations. The strong message to parents would be that the home environment has a profound impact on the academic achievement of their children and that they have the power to alter the environment of their household.

Summary

Home environment is distinguished from socioeconomic status as a specific, alterable set of behaviors that have a much stronger relationship with student achievement than do household income, occupation, and education. Three aspects of home environment were discussed: communication about school, supervision, and parental expectations and parenting style. I recommended one action step—a series of courses or trainings offered to parents, free of charge.

LEARNED INTELLIGENCE AND BACKGROUND KNOWLEDGE

earned intelligence might strike some as an oxymoron. The coupling of this phrase with the factor of *background knowledge* is certainly not common. However, at least one type of intelligence is learned; this type of intelligence is, for all practical purposes, the same as background knowledge.

Intelligence: The Two Types

I preface the examination of the research on intelligence by noting that some discussions make a distinction between intelligence and aptitude (Anastasi, 1982; Snow & Lohman, 1989). However useful, the distinction is a fairly technical one and does not serve the purposes of this chapter. Consequently, throughout this chapter and the remainder of the book, the terms intelligence and aptitude are used interchangeably.

The assertion that intelligence and academic achievement have a strong relationship has an intuitively valid ring. The more intelligence we have, the easier it is to learn, and

school is certainly about learning. Indeed, numerous studies have documented the strength of this relationship. The findings from some of these studies are summarized in Figure 14.1, p. 134. Given that correlations of .50 or higher (and their related effect sizes) are rare in the social sciences (Cohen, 1988), the findings reported are impressive.

Researchers Arthur Jensen (1980), Richard Heurnstein, and Charles Murray (1994), assert that intelligence is a fixed, immutable characteristic. An examination of the nature of aptitude, however, provides a different perspective, especially if the two types of intelligence are made distinct.

A basic distinction was first proposed by Raymond Cattell (1971/1987) and further developed by Phillip Ackerman (1996). Within this theory, intelligence is thought of as consisting of two constructs: intelligence as knowledge (*crystallized intelligence*) and intelligence as cognitive processes (*fluid intelligence*). Crystallized intelligence is exemplified by knowledge of facts, generalizations,

FIGURE 14.1

Correlation Between Intelligence and Achievement

Research Study	Correlation	Effect Size	Percentile Gain	Percentage of Variance Explained
Fraser et al. (1987)	0.40	0.88	31	16
Walberg (1984)	0.71	2.02	48	50
Bloom (1984)	0.60	1.50	43	36
Dochy, Segers, & Buehl (1999)	0.43	0.95	33	19
Bloom (1976)	0.63	1.62	45	40
Steinkamp & Maehr (1983)	0.33	0.70	36	11
Boulanger (1981)	0.49	1.13	37	24

Note: For a discussion of correlation, effect size, percentile gain, and percentage of variance explained, and their relationships see Technical Notes 1 & 4, pp. 187–188, 190–191.

and principles. Mental procedures and faculties such as abstract reasoning, working memory capacity, and working memory efficiency exemplify fluid intelligence. Where fluid intelligence is assumed to be innate and not subject to alteration from environment factors, crystallized intelligence is thought to be learned. It is also assumed that fluid intelligence is instrumental in the development of crystallized intelligence. Thus, the more fluid intelligence we have, the more easily we acquire crystallized intelligence as we interact with the world.

Which type of intelligence—crystallized or fluid—is more strongly related to academic achievement? Eric Rolfhus and Phillip Ackerman (1999) administered intelligence tests to 141 adults, along with knowledge tests in 20 different subject matter areas.

They then examined the relationship between subject matter test scores and fluid versus crystallized intelligence. Little relationship was found between academic knowledge and fluid intelligence, but a strong relationship was found between academic knowledge and crystallized intelligence. As stated by Rolfhus and Ackerman (1999), these findings suggest that academic "knowledge is more highly associated with [crystallized] abilities than with [fluid] abilities" (p. 520).

Background Knowledge

The strong correlation between crystallized intelligence and academic achievement helps to explain the strong relationship between background knowledge (or "prior knowledge" in some studies) and achievement. This research is as ubiquitous as the finding that aptitude is strongly correlated with academic achievement. Figure 14.2 reports findings from some of these studies. Again, the correlations (and their related effect sizes) reported here are quite impressive in terms of their size.

Filip Dochy, Mien Segers, and Michelle Buehl (1999) conducted one of the most extensive investigations of the relationship between background knowledge and academic achievement. In their analysis of 183 studies, they found that 91.5 percent of the studies demonstrated positive effects of background knowledge on learning; those that did not demonstrate positive effects measured background knowledge in ways that were indirect, questionable, or even invalid. For example, in some of these studies, subjects were simply asked if they were familiar with content as opposed to actually being assessed on their content knowledge.

Some clear generalizations emerge. First, the research supports the notion that crystallized intelligence, as opposed to fluid or innate intelligence, is the stronger correlate of academic achievement. Second, crystallized intelligence and background knowledge, for all practical purposes, can be considered identical as far as academic achievement is concerned.

FIGURE 14.2

Correlation Between Background Knowledge and Achievement

Research Study	Correlation	Effect Size	Percentile Gain	Percentage of Variance Explained
Bloom (1976)	0.74	2.20[a]	48	55
Dochy (1992) (in Dochy, Segers, & Buehl, 1999)	0.65	1.71	46	42
Tobias (1994)	0.66	1.76[a]	46	44
Alexander, Kulikowich, & Schulze (1994)	0.46	1.04[a]	35	21
Dochy et al. (1999)	0.66	1.76[a]	46	44
Schiefele & Krapp (1996)	0.21	0.43	16	4
Tamir (1996)	0.64	1.67	45	41
Boulanger (1981)	0.46	1.04	35	21

[a] = estimated from reported data

Note: For a discussion of correlation, effect size, percentile gain, and percentage of variance explained, and their relationships see Technical Notes 1 & 4, pp. 187–188, 190–191.

Crystallized intelligence is learned knowledge about the world; background knowledge is learned knowledge about a specific domain. Enhancing a student's background knowledge is akin to enhancing his crystallized intelligence, which is one of the strongest determiners of academic achievement.

Low crystallized intelligence can be produced by a variety of situations. It is certainly true that students who have high fluid intelligence **and** access to a variety of experiences will quite naturally acquire substantial crystallized intelligence. A student with low fluid intelligence in the same experience-rich environment will have lower crystallized intelligence. It is not the case, however, that low crystallized intelligence is necessarily a function of low fluid intelligence. Indeed, a person with high fluid intelligence without access to a variety of experiences will also have low crystallized intelligence simply because of lack of opportunity to acquire it. The person with low fluid intelligence **and** limited access to a wide experiential base is in a double bind, suffering not only from reduced ability to acquire crystallized intelligence but also without access to the experiential base to build it.

Only the confluence of high fluid intelligence and a rich experiential base is conducive to high crystallized intelligence. Engaging in activities aimed at enhancing the background knowledge of students, then, provides benefits for a wide range of students. Schools might take two basic approaches—direct approaches and indirect approaches.

Direct Approaches to Enhancing Crystallized Intelligence: Mentoring

By definition, a direct approach means increasing the variety and depth of out-of-class experiences such as field trips to museums and art galleries or school-sponsored travel and exchange programs. Despite the power of these experiences, schools are usually limited financially as to the number and type of such experiences they can provide.

A viable alternative is to establish mentoring relationships with members of the community. Broadly defined, mentoring is a one-to-one relationship between a caring adult and a youth who needs support. Although mentoring relationships can develop quite naturally between students and teachers, relatives, or coaches, planned mentoring relationships are those in which a student is matched with a mentor through a structured program (Brewster & Fager, 1998).

The apparent key to establishing effective mentoring relationships is to establish trust between two strangers from different age groups (Sipe, 1999). Trust is key, but not easily established between partners from different SES groups or ethnic groups. Although there is no script for an effective mentor and mentee relationship, effective mentors are likely to engage in the following practices (Sipe, 1999):

- maintain a steady and consistent presence in the student's life,
- take responsibility for keeping the relationship alive and realize that it will probably be one-sided,

- involve the youth in decisions about how time will be spent and respect the youth's viewpoint,
- recognize the youth's need for "fun," and
- become acquainted with the youth's family.

Jean Grossman and Amy Johnson (2002) describe the findings from evaluations of two popular mentoring programs: Big Brothers Big Sisters (BBBS) and Philadelphia Futures' Sponsor-A-Scholar (SAS). BBBS pairs an unrelated adult volunteer with a student from a single-parent household. The volunteer and student agree to meet two to four times per month for at least one year, with meetings lasting two to four hours. Grossman and Johnson note that "BBBS is not designed to ameliorate specific problems or reach specific goals, but rather to provide a youth with an adult friend who promotes general youth development objectives" (p. 8).

SAS has more specific goals. Its primary objective is to help students from Philadelphia's public schools "make it" to college. According to Grossman and Johnson: "This goal is sought through a range of support services chief among which are the provision of long-term mentoring and financial help with college-related expenses" (p. 8). Students and mentors work together for five years, from 9th grade through the first year of college. Mentors monitor students' academic progress and help them with the college application process.

Although Grossman and Johnson report the findings in terms of specific aspects of the mentor and mentee relationships (e.g., length of relationship, frequency of relationship), general findings for participating versus nonparticipating students include

- higher GPA in high school,
- higher likelihood to enroll in college, and
- higher likelihood to persist in college.

Indirect Approaches to Enhancing Crystallized Intelligence: Vocabulary

Permanent memory is the repository for everything learned—all knowledge and skill. We might say that it is the place in which crystallized intelligence resides. A common model for the manner in which information is represented in permanent memory is that it is organized in modular form. John Anderson (1995) refers to these modules as memory "records." Alan Paivio (1990) has further expanded our understanding of permanent memory with his "dual coding" theory. He hypothesizes two primary components to these memory records—linguistic representations and imagery representations. What is perhaps most interesting about these dual-coded memory records is that they are accompanied by a tag or label. For example, the word *house* is the tag or label for a specific record of images with accompanying linguistic information. As students have new experiences, they store these experiences as memory records. Fully formed memory records have an associated tag or label. The more records we have with their accompanying tags, the more crystallized intelligence we have. Our vocabulary knowledge, then, is a good indication of our crystallized intelligence.

Although crystallized intelligence is certainly not synonymous with vocabulary development, vocabulary is commonly considered a good general measure of intelligence (Chall,

1987). Indeed, Coleman and colleagues (1966) used verbal ability as their primary dependent measure (see Madaus et al., 1979, for a discussion). Not surprisingly, the relationship between vocabulary knowledge and academic achievement is also well established. For example, as early as 1941, researchers estimated that for students in grades 4 through 12, there was about a 6,000-word gap between students at the 25th and 50th percentiles on standardized tests (Nagy & Herman, 1984). Using a more advanced method of calculating vocabulary size, William Nagy and Patricia Herman (1984) estimated the difference to be anywhere between 4,500 and 5,400 words for low- versus high-achieving students.

Research also supports the relationship between vocabulary development and access to a wide variety of experiences. For example, Nagy and Herman (1984) found a consistent difference in vocabulary development between groups at different socioeconomic status (SES) levels. They estimated a 4,700-word difference in vocabulary knowledge between high- and low-SES students. Similarly, they estimated that mid-SES 1st graders know about 50 percent more words than do low-SES 1st graders. Michael Graves and Wayne Slater (1987) found that 1st graders from higher-income backgrounds had about double the vocabulary size of those from lower-income backgrounds. Although different researchers use slightly different estimates, all seem to agree that huge variations in vocabulary size exist between students from different backgrounds. Those students with high access to a variety of experiences (generally) have large vocabularies; those with low access (generally) do not.

The Debate Over Vocabulary Instruction

How, then can a school help increase the vocabulary of students? Two somewhat competing approaches currently exist: (1) wide reading, and (2) direct vocabulary instruction.

Wide Reading

Reading widely to enhance vocabulary makes good intuitive sense; the more students read, the more new labels they acquire for the experiences they read about. In fact, some theorists assert that wide reading is the only viable way of enhancing vocabulary. One strong argument for wide reading versus direct vocabulary instruction is that there are just too many words to teach individually. To illustrate, William Nagy and Richard Anderson (1984) estimated that the number of words in "printed school English" (i.e., those words K–12 students encounter in print) is about 85,000. Obviously, it would be impossible to teach this many words one at a time. Steven Stahl and Marilyn Fairbanks (1986) summarize this position in the following way:

> Since vocabulary-teaching programs typically teach 10 to 12 words a week or about 400 words per year, of which perhaps 75% or 300 are learned, vocabulary instruction is not adequate to cope with the volume of new words that children need to learn and do learn without instruction. (p. 100)

Nagy and Herman (1987) provide the following logic for wide reading as the sole vehicle for developing vocabulary:

> If students were to spend 25 minutes a day reading at a rate of 200 words per minute for 200 days out of the year, they would

encounter a million words of text annually. According to our estimates, with this amount of reading, children would encounter between 15,000 and 30,000 unfamiliar words. If one in 20 of these is learned, the yearly gain in vocabulary will be between 750 and 1,500 words. (p. 26)

Thus, if one takes the previous discussion at face value, direct vocabulary instruction may not only be inadvisable but downright foolish. Indeed, providing opportunities for students to read widely as a part of their regular schooling makes good sense.

Programs that facilitate wide reading for students have been in place for decades (Hunt, 1970). Many of those programs use the name of Sustained Silent Reading (SSR) or similar variants such as Free Voluntary Reading (FVR), Uninterrupted Sustained Silent Reading (USSR), and Positive Outcomes While Enjoying Reading (POWER). A simple Sustained Silent Reading program is one in which students (and quite often teachers) read silently for about 10 to 20 minutes from books of their choice. As we have seen, the logic underlying this approach is that it incidentally increases vocabulary. Another rationale for this approach is that if students are ever to become proficient independent readers, they must break from the heavily scaffolded and structured reading activities commonly used in their class work.

The research on SSR has produced ambiguous results on its effectiveness in improving reading comprehension (National Institute of Child Health and Human Development, 2000; Holt & O'Tuel, 1989; Pilgreen & Krashen, 1993). One explanation might be that teachers and schools have

employed so many variations that the defining characteristics have been lost (Nagy, Campenni, & Shaw, 2000). Wide reading has also been shown to have a positive impact on vocabulary development, but, again, the findings are inconsistent (Elley, 1989; Morrow, Pressley, Smith, & Smith, 1997; Pressley, 1998; Robbins & Ehri, 1994; Rosenhouse, Feitelson, Kita, & Goldstein, 1997).

Where wide reading certainly is critical to vocabulary development, research over the decades simply does not support the position that it is sufficient in and of itself to ensure proper vocabulary development. As Isabel Beck and Margaret McKeown (1991) explain: "research spanning several decades has failed to uncover evidence that word meanings are routinely acquired from context" (p. 799).

A study by Joseph Jenkins, Marcy Stein, and Katherine Wysocki (1984) dramatically demonstrates this point. They found that to *adequately* learn a new word in context (without instruction), students must be exposed to it about six times before they have enough experience with it to ascertain and remember its meaning. Beyond six exposures, the increase in learning was negligible. These findings are consistent with Stahl and Fairbanks (1986) who reported that multiple exposures to words produced a better understanding of meaning (although Stahl and Fairbanks do not identify an optimum number of exposures).

These conclusions seriously undermine the logic of the "wide reading" approach to vocabulary development *as the sole vehicle for vocabulary development*. Again, the working principle underlying the wide reading approach to vocabulary development is that students will figure out the meaning of and remember a portion of the new words they encounter in their reading. However, this argument fails to acknowledge the fact that students will encounter the vast majority of new words only a few times. Indeed, word frequency studies indicate that most words appear very infrequently in written material. More than 90 percent of the words students encounter while reading occur less than once in a million words of text; about half occur less than once in a billion words (Nagy & Anderson, 1984). Thus, the encounters students have with new words in their reading are, for the most part, isolated, single encounters that will not produce enough exposure to learn the new words.

Direct Vocabulary Instruction

Direct instruction does not imply rote memorization of definitions. One of the critical elements of direct vocabulary instruction is that students should elaborate on the meaning of new words they encounter. This simply means that the student "expands on" the information initially presented about a word (Pressley, 1998). This is the antithesis of memorizing definitions.

As the work of Allan Paivio suggests, one of the best ways to elaborate on a newly learned vocabulary term is to generate imagery representations of its meaning. The research on the impact of generating images to learn and remember new words is quite strong. In an analysis of 11 controlled studies, Glen Powell (1980) found that instructional techniques using imagery produced achievement gains in word knowledge that were 34 percentile points higher than techniques that did not.

A distinct difference exists between the effects of instruction in words from generalized vocabulary lists and words specific to a given topic. Many vocabulary development programs use vocabulary lists of high-frequency words—words that commonly appear in the written language (Carroll, Davies, & Richman, 1971; Harris & Jacobson, 1972). These high-frequency lists typically do not focus on the vocabulary from academic subject areas. Yet these are the words that should be the focus of instruction in a vocabulary development program designed to enhance academic achievement. In a meta-analysis, Stahl and Fairbanks (1986) found that instruction in general words like those found in high-frequency word lists enhanced students' ability to understand new content by 12 percentage points. However, when the words are selected because they are critical to academic content, the effect is a 33 percentage point gain. The dramatic difference indicates that direct instruction in words specific to academic content can have a profound effect on students' abilities to learn that content.

Considered together, the research on wide reading and direct vocabulary instruction paint a fairly clear picture of what a comprehensive program of vocabulary development might look like. For example,

- students are engaged in wide reading about subject matter content and content of their choice;
- students receive direct instruction on words and phrases that are critical to their understanding of academic content;
- students are exposed to new words multiple times; and

- students are encouraged to elaborate on their understanding of new words using mental images, pictures, and symbols.

Action Steps

I recommend three action steps to promote the acquisition of learned intelligence and background knowledge.

Action Step 1. Involve students in programs that directly increase the number and quality of life experiences students have.

Ways to accomplish this might include trips to art galleries, museums, companies, and different areas of the city. If resources are limited, a viable alternative is to provide mentoring designed specifically to enhance life experiences. This is particularly important for those students who do not come from experience-rich environments. Reilly (1992) cites several sources for volunteer mentors including

- major businesses,
- other school volunteer programs,
- service organizations and clubs,
- postsecondary education institutions,
- media (newspaper, TV, or radio) announcements,
- chambers of commerce,
- volunteer referral services, and
- local religious and cultural organizations.

In addition to many fine mentoring programs like BBBS and SAS, Gregory Clinton (2002) notes the schools can also design their own school-based programs. As a guide, Clinton

recommends the steps articulated by Jay Smink, Director of the National Dropout Prevention Center:

- secure the commitment of the district leadership,
- identify and select program staff,
- establish program goals and objectives (i.e., enhance the life experiences of students),
- prescribe activities and procedures,
- identify students,
- promote the program and recruit mentors,
- train mentors and students,
- match mentors and students,
- monitor the program, and
- evaluate ongoing and terminated cases.

Action Step 2. Involve students in a program of wide reading that emphasizes vocabulary development.

There is no single way to design a wide reading program at the school level. (For a discussion of how to organize and manage an SSR program see *The SSR Handbook: How to Organize and Manage a Sustained Silent Reading Program* by Janice Pilgreen, 2000). Guidelines that are commonly observed in a wide reading program include

- A period of time (e.g., 10 to 20 minutes) is set aside during the school day for all students to engage in silent reading.
- Students are expected to bring their own (appropriate) choice of book and read silently.
- Reading materials are selected outside of the reading time unless the teacher takes

the class to the library to select reading material.

- Teachers are encouraged to set aside a secure location in their room for students to leave books.
- Students are not allowed to sleep or do homework during reading time.
- Reading time should not create extra work for teachers in terms of grading or record keeping.

Two additions should be made to the typical SSR approach: (1) ask students to identify interesting words and try to determine their meanings, and (2) encourage students to keep track of these words in a personal vocabulary notebook. Using what is known about learning words during reading (Pressley, 1998), you might provide students with a process like the following for learning words from context:

- As you are engaged in silent reading in class or at home, identify new words you find interesting.
- Write these words on a small piece of paper and mark the page using the slip of paper.
- When you finish reading, go back and try to figure out the meaning of these words using the information and clues surrounding the word. If you are not sure, make your best guess.
- Write the word and your guess in your vocabulary notebook.

Then, integrate these student-selected words with words directly taught to students.

Action Step 3. Provide direct instruction in vocabulary terms and phrases that are important to specific subject matter content.

A sustained silent reading program with a vocabulary emphasis is only half of a comprehensive intervention to indirectly enhance learned intelligence. The other is direct instruction in terms and phrases selected because of their importance to academic content.

Researchers at Mid-continent Research for Education and Learning (McREL) have identified 6,700 terms that are critical to the understanding of 14 different subject areas (Marzano, Kendall, & Gaddy, 1999). Consider a few mathematics terms and phrases within the general category of probability that are appropriate for students in grades 6–8:

- experiment,
- odds,
- theoretical probability,
- tree diagram,
- simulation, and
- experimental probability.

Two significant aspects are revealed in the McREL academic vocabulary list. First, the number of terms is small enough to make direct instruction feasible. If students were to receive instruction in about 18 words per week over the course of their K–12 schooling, they would be exposed to all 6,700 terms covering 14 subject areas. Of course, the number of terms directly taught can be reduced if only selected subjects are targeted. Second, by definition, these terms are the ones students are most likely to encounter in their subject matter classes. Lists of subject matter terms, then, provide a new foundation for vocabulary development—one that has the potential of enhancing students' academic background knowledge.

Given that a viable list of subject matter terms is being used, teachers can systematically teach these terms as a regular part of classroom instruction and students add these words to their vocabulary notebooks. Coordination of effort from teacher to teacher and grade level to grade level is important. To ensure that students receive instruction in all the critical terms at appropriate times, teachers must do cross-grade planning.

The research implies that a sequential process is best for learning these academic terms:

1. Students are presented with a brief, informal explanation, description, or demonstration of the term and asked to describe this information in their own words.
2. Students are presented with an imagery-based representation of the new term.
3. Students are asked to create their own imagery-based representations for the term.
4. Students are asked to elaborate on the term by making connections with other words.
5. Over time, students are asked to add new information to their understanding of terms and delete or alter erroneous information.

Summary

Between crystallized and fluid intelligence, crystallized intelligence has the stronger relationship with academic achievement. Background knowledge and crystallized intelligence are, for all practical purposes, identical, particularly as they relate to academic achievement. A strong link is established between crystallized intelligence and vocabulary knowledge. This theory base implies that academic or learned intelligence can be directly enhanced by deepening the experiential base of students and indirectly enhanced by a combined program of wide reading and direct vocabulary instruction. I recommended three action steps to promote the acquisition of learned intelligence and background knowledge.

STUDENT MOTIVATION

The link between student motivation and achievement is straightforward. If students are motivated to learn the content in a given subject, their achievement in that subject will most likely be good. If students are not motivated to learn the content, their achievement will likely be limited. The validity of this relationship is supported by a fair amount of research, some of which is summarized in Figure 15.1. Except for that reported by Steinkamp and Maehr (1983), the correlations (and their related effect sizes) reported in Figure 15.1 are relatively large attesting to the impact of motivation on learning.

Although the link between motivation and achievement is established, the dynamics of motivation are not. Let's consider the research and theory on the nature of those dynamics.

Research and Theory

At risk of oversimplifying a complex phenomenon, I address five lines of research and

theory that converge to provide a fairly consistent picture of the nature of motivation: (1) drive theory, (2) attribution theory, (3) self-worth theory, (4) emotions, and (5) self-system. (For detailed discussions of the theory and research underlying motivation, see Bandura, 1997; Covington, 1992; Harter, 1999). At a very general level, the study of motivation addresses the reasons why we do things. As Martin Covington (1992) explains

Simply put, motivation deals with the *why* of behavior: *Why* for example, do individuals choose to work on certain tasks and not on others: *why* do they exhibit more or less energy in the pursuit of these tasks and *why* do some people persist until the task is completed, whereas others give up before they really start, or in some cases pursue more elegant solutions long after perfectly sensible answers have presented themselves? (pp. 12–13)

Drive Theory

Much of the current research and theory on classroom motivation has roots in the work of

FIGURE 15.1

...on and Achievement

	Correlation	Effect Size	Percentile Gain	Percentage of Variance Explained
	0.30	0.63	24	9
	0.35	0.75	27	12
	0.42	0.93	32	18
Tobias (1994)	0.45	1.01	34	20
Bloom (1976)	0.30	0.63	24	9
Steinkamp & Maehr (1983)	0.19	0.39	15	4
Willingham, Pollack, & Lewis (2002)	0.63	1.62	45	37

Note: For a discussion of correlations, effect size, percentile gain, and percentage of variances explained and their relationships, see Technical Notes 1 and 4, pp. 187–188, 190–191.

John Atkinson (Atkinson, 1957, 1964, 1987; Atkinson & Raynor, 1974). Atkinson's early work was expanded and applied by David McClelland (1965). One of Atkinson's premises was that the dynamics of motivation can be described in terms of two competing forces or *drives*—the striving for success and the fear of failure. Both drives operate simultaneously. Over time, people develop strong tendencies to be either success oriented or failure avoidant. When these tendencies become habituated, they commonly manifest as an emotional backdrop to any new task.

Students who are success oriented are generally motivated to engage in new tasks because of anticipated emotional rewards. Students who are failure avoidant are not motivated to engage in new tasks because failing incurs negative affect. This makes classroom motivation quite difficult, particularly where the teacher is trying to establish high standards. Students who are success oriented are generally motivated by challenges; students who are failure avoidant are generally not. In fact, those students who are failure avoidant might develop self-handicapping strategies that ensure they fail for reasons other than lack of ability. These self-handicapping strategies include procrastination (Rothblum, Solomon, & Murakami, 1986; Solomon & Rothblum, 1984), setting excessively high unattainable goals (Snyder, 1984), and admitting to small weaknesses or handicaps to establish an excuse for failing (establishing an "academic wooden leg") (Covington, 1992; Covington, Omelich, & Schwarzer, 1986).

Although many aspects of drive theory can be found in modern theories of motivation, current theories have been significantly influenced by attribution theory.

Attribution Theory

As articulated by Bernard Weiner (Weiner, 1972, 1974; Weiner, Frieze, Kulka, Reed, Rest, & Rosenbaum, 1971), attribution theory postulates that how students perceive the causes of their prior successes and failures is a better determinant of motivation and persistence than is a learned success or failure avoidance orientation. In general, there are four causes individuals attribute to their success: ability, effort, luck, and task difficulty. Of these, effort is the most useful because a strong belief in effort as the cause of success can translate into a willingness to engage in complex tasks and persist over time. Covington (1992) explains

> One of the most important features of attribution theory is its focus on the role of effort in achievement. This emphasis is justified for several reasons. For one thing, if students believe their failures occur for a lack of trying, then they are more likely to remain optimistic about succeeding in the future. For another thing, trying hard is known to increase pride in success and to offset feelings of guilt at having failed. And, perhaps, most important of all, the emphasis on the role of effort in achievement is justified because it is widely believed that student effort is modifiable through the actions of teachers. (p. 16)

Attribution theory provided motivation theory with a new and potentially powerful perspective. From an attribution perspective, motivation is not a fixed drive. We can even change our motivation by understanding our attributions, according to the work of Martin Seligman (Seligman, 1975; Seligman, Maier, & Geer, 1968; Seligman, Maier, & Solomon, 1971). Seligman postulates that the way individuals explain their success or failure is a learned trait. Probably most famous for his concept of "explanatory style," Seligman, like Weiner, posits that individuals learn to explain success or failure in certain ways. However, they also have the power to change a negative explanatory style (referred to as "learned helplessness") to a more success-oriented style ("learned optimism").

Self-Worth Theory

Self-worth theory is based on the premise that the search for self-acceptance is one of the highest human priorities (Covington, 1984, 1985, 1987; Covington & Berry, 1976). Self-acceptance usually manifests as acceptance of status in one's immediate or peer culture. This dynamic makes the classroom a threatening place to some students. As Covington (1992) explains

> In our society there is a pervasive tendency to equate accomplishment with human value, or put simply, individuals are thought to be only as worthy as their achievements. Because of this, it is understandable that students often confuse ability with worth. For those students who are already insecure, tying a sense of worth to ability is a risky step because schools can threaten their ability. This is true because schools typically provide insufficient rewards for all students to strive for success. Instead, too many children must struggle simply to avoid failure. (p. 74)

Self-worth theory adds still another perspective to classroom motivation. If the criterion for self-acceptance in the classroom is high academic accomplishment relative to others, then by definition, only a few high-performing students can obtain a sense of self-worth.

Emotions

In the last two decades, several researchers have discussed the importance of emotions in human motivation (Gazzaniga, 1992; LeDoux, 1994, 1996; Pinker, 1997; Restak, 1994; Sylwester, 1995). In *The Emotional Brain: The Mysterious Underpinnings of Emotional Life*, Joseph LeDoux (1996) makes a strong case that emotions play a prominent role in motivation. He explains that human beings have relatively little control over their emotions:

> Anyone who has tried to fake an emotion, or who has been the recipient of a faked one, knows all too well the futility of the attempt. While conscious control of emotions is weak, emotions can flood consciousness. This is so because the wiring of the brain at this point in our evolutionary history is such that connections from the emotional systems to the cognitive systems are stronger than connections from the cognitive systems to the emotional systems. (p. 19)

Regarding the power of emotions once they occur, LeDoux explains

> They chart the course of moment-to-moment action as well as set the sails toward long-term achievements. But our emotions can also get us into trouble. When fear becomes anxiety, desire gives way to greed, or annoyance turns to anger, anger to hatred, friendship to envy, love to obsession, or pleasure to addiction, our emotions start working against us. Mental health is maintained by emotional hygiene, and mental

problems to a large extent reflect breakdown of emotional order. Emotions can have both useful and pathological consequences. (pp. 19–20)

For LeDoux, then, emotions are primary motivators that often override an individual's system of values and beliefs relative to their influence on human behavior. Nisbett and Wilson (1977) found that people are often mistaken about internal causes for feelings. They concluded that people always find causes for their emotions, but when rational and plausible reasons are not available, people make up reasons and believe them.

Self-System

In general, the self-system contains a network of interrelated goals (Markus & Ruvulo, 1990; Harter, 1980) that help us decide whether to engage in a new task. In effect, many of the dynamics described in the previous theories fit into the description of the self-system or "the self." As Mihaly Csikszentmihalyi (1990) explains

> The self is no ordinary piece of information ... In fact, it contains [almost] everything ... that passes through consciousness: all the memories, actions, desires, pleasures, and pains are included in it. And more than anything else, the self represents the hierarchy of goals that we have built up, bit by bit over the years. ... At any given time we are usually aware of only a tiny part of it ... (p. 34)

The critical feature of the self-system is that it houses our deeply seeded needs and aspirations organized in somewhat of a hierarchical structure. It is this structure that provides a new and powerful perspective on classroom motivation.

Abraham Maslow (1968, 1971) was the first psychologist to popularize the notion of a hierarchical structure to human needs. He postulated five levels of needs/aspirations:

1. basic needs that include food and water,
2. the need for personal safety,
3. social needs including the need to belong,
4. esteem needs that include feelings of self-respect and the respect of others, and
5. self-actualization or the need for a sense of personal fulfillment.

Although Maslow's hierarchy has been criticized for being unscientific and unsubstantiated (Wahba, & Bridwell, 1976), it still provides us with powerful insights into the nature of human motivation. As Covington (1992) explains, "it provides a useful way of thinking about the factors that activate normal human beings" (p. 19).

Maslow's highest level of need—self-actualization—adds an aspect to motivation not present in the previous discussions. That is, drive theory, self-worth theory, attribution theory, and the impact of emotions on motivation all fit somewhere within the first four levels of Maslow's hierarchy. These theories do not explain human motivation at Maslow's fifth level. Covington (1992) describes this type of motivation as the need for evidence that "one is achieving fully what he or she is capable of becoming" (p. 19).

Maslow's work suggests that human beings harbor aspirations that in some way define them as whole human beings. These aspirations seemingly differ from individual to individual. Where one person might have aspirations for some noteworthy physical accomplishment such as running a marathon,

another might harbor aspirations for a significant intellectual accomplishment such as writing a best-selling book. Exactly where these aspirations come from is a subject of speculation only. They may be products of a combination of factors such as the general culture we live in, our home environment, the influence of our peers, or the influence of the media.

Although the source of self-actualizing aspirations is not well understood, how to foster such aspirations is (Klausner, 1965). Csikszentmihalyi (1990) has even identified four factors critical to successful completion of self-actualizing experiences that he refers to as "flow experiences":

1. the freedom to set clear goals that are highly meaningful to the individual,
2. having the resources to carry out the goals and becoming immersed in the act of trying to accomplish them,
3. paying attention to what is happening and making changes when necessary, and
4. enjoying immediate short-term successes while keeping an eye on the ultimate goal.

What can be learned from the vast research and theory on motivation that might be used by schools to motivate students? It seems clear that students develop drives for success or failure avoidance and that these drives affect their willingness to engage in classroom tasks. For some students, challenging tasks present no obstacle because of their strong drive for success; for others, even simple tasks are quite threatening because of their strong drive to avoid failure. Compounding the issue is the role of emotions and the innate need for a sense of self-worth that render the failure avoidant student very difficult to motivate. However, these drives and tendencies are not cast in stone. They are at least partially a function of how a student explains success and failure in his world. An understanding of personal explanatory style and the importance of that style in willingness to engage in challenging tasks can provide a student with some control over his motivation. Finally, students whose aspirations are met gain a sense of fulfillment and personal accomplishment that is second to none. Their success requires a high level of freedom in setting related goals and then working toward them.

Action Steps

I recommend four action steps that a school or individual teacher can take to enhance individual student motivation.

Action Step 1. Provide students with feedback on their knowledge gain.

When success in the classroom is defined in terms of competitive status with others, only a few students can be successful. However, when individual growth is the criterion for success, then all students can experience success regardless of their comparative status. To accomplish this, two elements are required: (1) an assessment of the achievement level at which students enter a class or a unit of instruction, and (2) an assessment of the achievement level at which students exit the class or unit of instruction. With these elements in hand, individual students' knowledge gain can be determined.

Some teachers accomplish this comparison by giving a pretest at the beginning of class and then administering a test at the end. Typically, these tests are scored on a 100-point scale. I prefer to use pretest and post-study rubrics like the one depicted in Figure 15.2 (p. 150). It is the generic form of the rubric presented in Chapter 10. The rubric in Figure 15.2 might be used to keep track of performance on different class topics. For example, a 5th grade mathematics teacher might address the topics of probability, distributions, and data analysis in a unit. The teacher could assess each student's status on each topic using the rubric in Figure 15.2 at the beginning and the end of the class or unit. The difference in rubric scores would indicate individual student learning.

Of course there are other ways to honor and highlight knowledge gain and, consequently, provide all students with opportunities to experience success. For example, I once worked with teachers from a school with the traditional honor roll. In addition, they instituted a quarterly "on-a-roll" that recognized students for their personal academic growth.

Action Step 2. Provide students with tasks and activities that are inherently engaging.

Thomas Malone (1981a, 1981b) explains that the dynamics of human motivation imply that some tasks are inherently engaging. Such tasks have three characteristics. First, they present **manageable challenges** for students. As Covington (1992) explains: "Tasks are engaging to the degree they challenge the individual's present capacity, yet permit some control over the level of challenge faced" (p. 160). Second, inherently

---

FIGURE 15.2

Generic Rubrics for Topics Addressed in Class

4 The student has a complete and detailed understanding of the information important to the topic AND the student can perform the skills and processes important to the topic fluently and without error.

3 The student has an understanding of the information important to the topic but not in great detail AND the student can perform the skills or processes important to the topic without significant error.

2 The student has some misconceptions or is missing some information important to the topic but still has a general understanding of the topic AND/OR the student makes significant errors when performing the skills or processes important to the topic but still performs a rough approximation of these skills and processes.

1 The student has major misunderstandings or is missing critical information about the topic AND/OR the student cannot perform even a rough approximation of the skills and processes important to the topic.

---

engaging tasks **arouse curiosity**. This is accomplished by "providing sufficient complexity so that outcomes are not always certain" (Covington, 1992, p. 160). Finally, inherently engaging tasks involve **fantasy arousal**. Again, Covington (1992) explains that fantasy arousal is not "merely unbridled wish fulfillment or fairy tales, but rather the creation of imaginary circumstances that permit the free and unfettered use of one's growing abilities" (p. 160).

Covington (1992) provides examples of a variety of such tasks, all of which are conducted in a game-like environment. One such game is Global Gambit. To play, the class is organized into teams representing different nations. The setting is a conference to discuss possible solutions to imminent global warming. Before engaging in the game, the teacher presents students with information about the possible effects of global warming such as rising oceans drowning London and drought triggering riots in Los Angeles. The object is to negotiate a plan to deal with these and other eventualities. Countries can construct plans to protect their local interests or can band together to seek broader regional or worldwide solutions. Whatever plans are devised, countries must consider the impact on other countries.

Instructional games like these are not only intrinsically motivating to students, but apparently develop self-reflection skills, effective group behaviors, and critical inquiry skills (Engle & Ochoa, 1988).

Action Step 3. Provide opportunities for students to construct and work on long-term projects of their own design.

To truly elicit the motivation that comes with what Csikszentmihalyi refers to as a flow experience, we must engage in tasks that address Maslow's fifth category—self-actualization. These tasks might elicit a type of motivation superior to any others (Deci & Ryna, 1980; 1985). Covington (1992) explains that these tasks elicit "the desire to become more effective as a person or to perform actions for their own sake" (p. 157). These tasks are a cut above the "inherently engaging" tasks described in Action Step 2.

They are intensely personal to students and commonly have to do with long-term aspirations. Allowing students to work on long-term projects of their own choosing encourages motivation.

I introduced the notion of engaging students in long-term projects of their own design in the book *A Different Kind of Classroom* (Marzano, 1992). At that time I was struck by a personal example of a young man who changed his entire academic profile by setting a personal goal that addressed self-actualization. That young man is my son Todd. In 1992, I described this process as depicted in Figure 15.3 (p. 152). Todd's story was published in *A Different Kind of Classroom*. Since then the story has changed considerably. Todd completed officer candidate school in 1992 and received his "wings of gold." He was assigned to fly F/A-18s and served his country in Desert Fox over Iraq and Operation Enduring Freedom over Afghanistan for which he received two combat air medals. However, the biggest thrill for Todd came when he graduated from the Navy's Top Gun training program in 1999. For him, the movie became a reality.

Since the publication of *A Different Kind of Classroom*, I have encountered a few programs that engage students in projects that allow them to pursue their deeply held passions. For example, the Pathfinder Project (www.Pathfinderusa.com) seeks to awaken these passions by presenting students with actual stories like Todd's. Stimulated by these inspirational stories, students identify long-term goals of their own design and are provided support in the attainment of these goals. A program like the Pathfinder Project can easily be instituted at the school level.

After completing their projects, students present their accomplishments and what they learned about themselves.

Action Step 4. Teach students about the dynamics of motivation and how those dynamics affect them.

This last action step is perhaps the most direct in enhancing student motivation because it provides students with an understanding of the dynamics of motivation at both the general and personal levels. Attempts to do this apparently have met with success. For example, Gregory Andrews and Ray Debus (1978) worked with 6th graders to help them understand the impact of their negative attributions on their motivation and behavior. Students were randomly assigned to experimental and control groups; those in the experimental group received training about the nature of attributions and reinforcement when they attributed their failures to effort (instead of ability). Students who had been described as demoralized persisted longer in their school tasks than they did previously. Students also displayed an increased effectiveness in their thinking strategies. Other studies have reported similar findings (Chapin & Dyck, 1976; Dweck, 1975; Wilson & Linville, 1985; Zoeller, Mahoney, & Weiner, 1983).

The work of Martin Seligman (1975, 1991) is also relevant. Seligman's model of personal explanatory style notes that "optimists" differ from "pessimists" in how they explain success and failure in their lives (see Chapter 18 for more information). Thus, knowing our unique dispositions can give us power over our own motivation. Although Seligman's work is geared toward adults,

---

FIGURE 15.3

Todd's Story

Although not a terribly poor high school student, Todd was certainly not at the top of his class. He took as few academic courses as possible, and his 3.00 GPA was essentially the result of A's in metal shop and phys ed and C's in mathematics and science. In the middle of his junior year, he announced that he was not going to go to college. His logic was that he was not academically oriented (which was true), did not like school (also true), and was talented in auto mechanics (true again). Being the second son of Italian immigrants who stressed education as the way to a better life, I was extremely upset. Of course, I gave many unsolicited speeches about the importance of going to college and the probable effect that not going would have on his life.

At some point during this traumatic period, Todd went to see *Top Gun*, a movie about a modern-day navy aviator. Immediately after seeing the movie, he announced that he wanted to be a fighter pilot. This discouraged me because I believed my son was setting unrealistic goals. A happy turn of events (from my perspective) occurred when my son announced that he was going to college, because "you have to have a college degree to be a fighter pilot." I thought that if I could get him into college under any pretense he would soon abandon the foolishness of trying to be a fighter pilot, given the academic rigors involved. Since Todd had not distinguished himself in science and mathematics in high school, how could he possibly master the advanced mathematics and science he'd need to be a fighter pilot?

To my utter amazement, Todd attacked the science and mathematics courses in college with a fervor I had previously not witnessed in him. He made detailed plans about how to transfer from an open-enrollment community college (the only one he could get into) to one of the best engineering schools in the country. He managed his time and money at a level of detail that bordered on obsession. He strove for accuracy in all his academic classes and surely worked at the edge rather than the center of his competence every day. As I write this book, I can proudly report that Todd is about to graduate magna cum laude with a degree in aerospace engineering from the third best engineering school in the country. Recently, he was inducted into a prestigious engineering fraternity. And along the way he obtained his private pilot's license, receiving a score of 100 on the examination given by the Federal Aviation Administration (the first time in fifteen years anyone from our region received such a high score). Finally (and most important to Todd), he was one of only two candidates from the state accepted into the Aviator's Officer Candidate School of the United States Navy, which is the navy's first and biggest step to becoming a fighter pilot. (pp. 140–141)

Source: Marzano, R. J. (1992). *A different kind of classroom: Teaching with Dimensions of Learning.* Alexandria, VA: Association for Supervision and Curriculum Development.

---

there is nothing prohibiting its adoption with students at the secondary level.

Summary

The theory and research regarding student motivation was briefly reviewed as a complex set of dynamics interacting to dispose students to be motivated or highly resistant to motivation. These dynamics include the student's drive for success or failure avoidance, the student's attributions, the student's need for a sense of self-worth, the student's emotional dynamics, and the workings of the student's self-system. The four action steps include altering the competitive nature of classroom success, engaging students in long-term projects that tap into their deeply held passions, and providing students with information about motivation and training in techniques to control their motivation.

Section IV

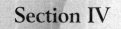MPLEMENTATION

List of Figures in Section IV

16

IMPLEMENTING THE MODEL

Ultimately, the validity of the model described in this book depends on the extent to which schools can and do use it to enhance student achievement. This is in keeping with the long tradition of school effectiveness research. As David Reynolds and his colleagues (Reynolds, Teddlie, Hopkins, & Stringfield, 2000) explain: "The 'founding fathers' of effective schools research in the United States, Edmonds and Brookover . . . had an explicit commitment to the work being utilized to improve schools" (p. 206). In this last section, I lay out specific steps for schools to identify those elements of the model that are most applicable to them, identify specific actions to take, implement those actions, and determine their effects. This section is about the process of school reform.

The Changing Nature of School Reform

Anyone familiar with the history of education in the United States is well aware that it is replete with reform efforts. The particular type of reform addressed in this book has historical roots in the 1960s. As described by Reynolds and colleagues (2000), this was the time of the first phase of the school improvement movement. The emphasis in this phase was on the adoption of curriculum materials. The materials were generally high quality, presumably because they were well funded and produced by teams of psychologists and subject matter specialists.

The second phase, the era of documentation, took place in the early 1970s. As discussed in Chapter 2, great efforts were made to determine the exact impact (or lack thereof) schools had on student achievement and the factors that contributed to it.

The third phase spanned the 1970s and 1980s and brought the implementation of a wide variety of models and projects born in the second phase. Although this period saw some noteworthy successes, it was fraught with problems. In general, the projects did not produce the results promised or implied by the research. This was not due to poor quality or validity, but to a lack of understanding of the change process. Michael Fullan (1982) notes that clear descriptions of what a successful school looks like do not provide guidance as to how a school should acquire that look. Fullan (1993) further exhorts that an understanding of the nature of change is paramount to implementing the school effectiveness research.

The fourth phase is still emerging. I sometimes refer to it as the new era of school reform. What makes this era new? What is to stop this era from following the disturbing path of previous eras? (For a discussion of the failures of previous efforts, see Cuban, 1990.)

The New Era of School Reform

I believe that the new era of school reform is based on three principles that make it very different from its predecessors.

Principle 1. The new era of school reform is based on the realization that reform is a highly contextualized phenomenon.

Reform efforts will and should look substantively different from school to school (Hallinger & Murphy, 1985; Owens, 1987; Teddlie, Stringfield, Wimpelberg, & Kirby, 1989). J. Douglas Willms (1992) makes the same point: "I doubt whether another two decades of research will . . . help us specify a *model for all seasons* [original emphasis]—a model that would apply to all schools in all communities at all times" (p. 65). Context-

ualized reform should be interpreted cautiously from school to school. Just because the research indicates that a particular school-level factor is important to student achievement doesn't mean that it is important in a given school. As Reynolds and colleagues (2000) note

> Sometimes the adoption of ideas from research has been somewhat uncritical; for example, the numerous attempts to apply findings from one specific context to another entirely different context when research has increasingly demonstrated significant contextual differences. (p. 216)

The world of schooling doesn't follow the general world of (particularly synthesized) research as closely as researchers would like. Therefore, in the new era of reform, schools will look carefully at the research, but then determine which factors apply to their particular context.

Principle 2. The new era of school reform is characterized by a heavy emphasis on data.

Indeed, one of the defining characteristics of schools producing unprecedented gains in student achievement (particularly with students whose backgrounds are not conducive to such gains), is that they rely on data to identify probable successful interventions (Hopkins & Ainskow, 1993). They also rely on data to determine how effective those interventions are when implemented (Barth et al., 1999; Schmoker, 2001). Regarding the Oak Park School District in Detroit, Mike Schmoker (2001) notes

If there is anything we can learn from districts like Oak Park, it is that successful organizations do not just *collect data*, they *revere it* [original emphasis]. They aren't satisfied with data until data have life and meaning for every teacher, every pertinent party. They use data to create and to ensure an objective, commonly held reality . . . The use of data allows for organized, *simplified* [original emphasis] discussions that merge to create focused priorities and productive action. (p. 51)

Principle 3. In the new era of school reform, change is approached on an incremental basis.

As Michael Fullan (1982) explains

. . . most change theorists and practitioners agree that significant changes should be attempted, but they should be carried out in a more incremental, development way. . . . Large plans and vague ideas make a lethal combination. . . . Significant change can be accomplished by taking a developmental approach, building in more and more components of the change over time. Complex changes can be pursued incrementally by developing one or two steps at a time. (p. 102)

To illustrate incremental change, Reynolds, Teddlie, Hopkins, and Stringfield (2000) describe the process one school—Barclay— used to adopt the programs and procedures employed by another school—Calvert. They note: "Barclay did not attempt to implement the whole Calvert curriculum and instructional programme all at once, but gradually, grade by grade level. In this way it was possible to prepare teachers for the next grade level using a cascade model" (p. 223). Although the benefits of an incremental approach were certainly known in the early days of U.S. school reform, this approach frequently was not taken. Thus, administrators and classroom teachers are often overwhelmed by the sheer amount of change attempted and the work involved.

This final section of this book contains two chapters. Chapter 17 addresses the specific sequence of steps recommended to use the model presented in this book. Chapter 18 addresses the critical role of leadership throughout the reform process.

Summary

This chapter has introduced the fourth and final section of the book dealing with implementing the model. A case was made that the school reform movement in this country has entered a new phase or new era that builds on previous phases. Three principles that define that new era were articulated.

USING THE MODEL

In Chapter 16, I outlined three principles for a new era of school reform. When followed, these principles have the potential of making this wave of reform more significant than any previous effort. In this chapter, I outline the process a school might use to apply those principles using the model described in the previous chapters. The process can be characterized as involving four phases: (1) taking the pulse of a school, (2) identifying and implementing an intervention, (3) examining the effect on achievement, and (4) moving to the next issue.

Phase I: Take the Pulse of Your School

The first step is to examine the school's practices relative to the school-level, teacher-level, and student-level factors. To this end, I have developed and field-tested a questionnaire that can be found in its entirety in the Appendix (pp. 179–186). For discussion purposes, the first 21 items (showing the five school-level factors) are listed in Figure 17.1. The questionnaire in the Appendix has similar items for the teacher-level and student-level factors.

The questionnaire is for all personnel involved in the reform effort (generally all administrators and teachers). It provides the first important set of data a school will use. Of course, the data gathered from this instrument is perceptual in nature, that is, respondents answer based on how they *perceive* a situation. The reality may be different. Schools that have used the questionnaire, however, report that it provides them with an efficient way of obtaining a snapshot of their performance on the three factor levels. Most report that the data have enough validity to provide the basis for initiating a comprehensive reform effort.

The questionnaire has 66 items. Each item involves three questions:

1. To what extent do we engage in this behavior or address this issue?

FIGURE 17.1

Survey Items for School-Level Factors

Excerpt from Snapshot Survey (see Appendix)	Question 1 — To what extent do we engage in this behavior or address this issue?				Question 2 — How much will a change in our practices on this item increase the academic achievement of our students?				Question 3 — How much effort will it take to significantly change our practices regarding this issue?			
	Not at all			To a great extent	Not at all			To a great extent	Not much		A lot, but possible to do	Too much to do
In my school . . .	1	2	3	4	1	2	3	4	1	2	3	4
Guaranteed and Viable Curriculum 1. The content considered essential for all students to learn versus the content considered supplemental has been identified and communicated to teachers.												
2. The amount of essential content that has been identified can be addressed in the instructional time available to teachers.												
3. The essential content is organized and sequenced in a way that students have ample opportunity to learn it.												
4. Someone checks to ensure that teachers address the essential content.												
5. The instructional time available to teachers is protected by minimizing interruptions and scheduled noninstructional activities.												
Challenging Goals and Effective Feedback 6. An assessment system is used that provides for timely feedback (e.g., at least every nine weeks) on specific knowledge and skills for individual students.												
7. Specific achievement goals are set for the school as a whole.												
8. Specific achievement goals are set for individual students.												
9. Performance on schoolwide and individual student goals is used to plan for future actions.												
Parent and Community Involvement 10. Effective vehicles are in place to communicate to parents and community.												
11. Effective vehicles are in place for parents and community to communicate to the school.												

FIGURE 17.1 (continued)											
Survey Items for School-Level Factors											
Excerpt from Snapshot Survey (see Appendix)	Question 1 — To what extent do we engage in this behavior or address this issue?				Question 2 — How much will a change in our practices on this item increase the academic achievement of our students?				Question 3 — How much effort will it take to significantly change our practices regarding this issue?			
	Not at all			To a great extent	Not at all			To a great extent	Not much		A lot, but possible to do	Too much to do
	1	2	3	4	1	2	3	4	1	2	3	4
12. Opportunities are provided for parents and community to be involved in the day-to-day operations of the school.												
13. Vehicles are in place for parents and community to be involved in the governance of the school.												
Safe and Orderly Environment 14. The physical environment and school routines have been structured in such a way as to avoid chaos and promote good behavior.												
15. Clear rules and procedures pertaining to schoolwide behavior have been established.												
16. Appropriate consequences for violations of schoolwide rules and procedures have been established and implemented.												
17. A program that teaches and reinforces student self-discipline and responsibility has been implemented.												
18. A system for early detection of students who are prone to violence and extreme behavior has been implemented.												
Collegiality and Professionalism 19. Norms for conduct among professional staff and administrators that foster collegiality and professionalism have been established.												
20. Governance structures that allow for teacher involvement in schoolwide decisions and policies have been established.												
21. Teachers are engaged in staff development activities that address specific content area issues and allow for "hands on" trial and evaluation of specific techniques.												

2. How much will a change in our practices on this item increase the academic achievement of our students?
3. How much effort will it take to significantly change our practices regarding this issue?

Question 1 focuses on how well the school is doing in a specific aspect of a school-level, teacher-level, or student-level factor. To illustrate, consider item 4 in the questionnaire: "In my school someone checks to ensure that teachers address the essential content." Scores near the low end of the scale (1) indicate that the school does not engage in this behavior; scores near the high end of the scale (4) indicate that the school is addressing this issue well (or at least how the school is perceived to address this issue).

Answers to question 2 provide perceptual data about the extent to which current practices relative to this issue will actually enhance student achievement. These answers qualify the answers to question 1 and provide guidance on whether a school should consider this issue as a focus for reform. For example, the responses to question 1 might indicate that the school does not perform well on item 4—checking to ensure that teachers address the essential content. Looking at this response in isolation might lead to the conclusion that this issue or practice is a good focus of a school reform effort. However, the response to question 2 might indicate that those who completed the questionnaire believe that changing behavior here would not significantly enhance student achievement.

It is important to remember that all factors and their elements do not apply to all schools. Consequently, a school might not perform well relative to a specific factor or a specific aspect of that factor (e.g., "checking on whether teachers address the essential content" within the school-level factor of "a guaranteed and viable curriculum"). However, the school might do other things that compensate for its failure to follow recommended practice (e.g., teachers may informally monitor their coverage of the content). Although the staff might believe they are not addressing a particular behavior or practice well, they might also believe that better performance in this practice will not have a significant effect on student achievement.

Answers to question 3 provide perceptual data regarding how much effort it will take to change current practice. Scores near 1 indicate that changes would be relatively easy to make; scores near 4 indicate that changes would be too difficult. Recall that change should be incremental, meaning that schools should address practices that they believe they have the time, resources, and energy to address. Addressing an issue that is perceived as important but for which time, resources, and energy are lacking is a formula for failure.

When a school considers the responses to all three questions for each item, it can identify the issues on which teachers and administrators perceive (1) they are not doing well, **and** (2) changes in their practices can enhance student achievement, **and** (3) the effort it will take to make substantive change is not too great. Issues that have all three characteristics are the starting place of effective school reform.

To illustrate how schools have used the questionnaire, consider Figure 17.2 (p. 164).

FIGURE 17.2

Responses to Five Items with Lowest Average Ratings for Question 1

Item No.	Item	Question 1		Question 2		Question 3	
		Average	Mode	Average	Mode	Average	Mode
14	The physical environment and school routines have been structured in such a way as to avoid chaos and promote good behavior.	1.92	2	2.34	2	2.24	2
1	The content considered essential for all students to learn versus the content considered supplemental has been identified and communicated to teachers.	1.72	2	3.11	3	3.14	3
8	Specific achievement goals are set for individual students.	1.52	2	2.13	2	2.47	2
2	The amount of essential content that has been identified can be addressed in the instructional time available.	1.44	1	3.52	4	3.21	3
6	An assessment system is used that provides for timely feedback (e.g., at least every nine weeks) on specific knowledge and skills for individual students.	1.36	1	3.81	4	3.74	4

Figure 17.2 depicts results similar to those obtained at one middle school that administered the entire questionnaire (i.e., the pattern of scores is identical to that of the middle school even though the specific means reported in Figure 17.2 are not). Only those five items that had the lowest average score on question 1 are listed. Note that for each item the average score and the modal (most common) score are reported. The item with the lowest average score is item 6, the next lowest score is item 2. At face value, these results indicate that developing an assessment system that provides timely feedback (e.g., at least every nine weeks) is the first issue the school should address. Item 6 has a very high average score on question 2, indicating that student achievement will be enhanced if the school addresses this issue. The responses to question 2, then, continue to support the development of an assessment system that provides timely feedback as the initial focus of school reform. However, the average response to question 3 changes the picture dramatically. The average score is 3.74 and the modal score is 4. This indicates respondents believed that addressing this issue would require more energy and resources than they are willing to expend. For this reason, the school decided not to address

the design of a new assessment system as the initial focus of school reform. Rather, they opted to focus on something that did not pose such a monumental effort. They finally settled on item 1—identifying essential versus supplemental content. The average score of 1.72 on question 1 (mode = 2) indicates that teachers and administrators generally did not perceive the school as doing particularly well on this issue. The average score of 3.11 in question 2 (mode = 3) indicates that teachers and administrators believed that enhanced performance here would raise student achievement. The key factor was the response to question 3. Its average score of 3.14 (mode = 3) indicates that teachers and administrators believed that this issue would certainly require some hard work but not so much as to be prohibitive. In summary, by using the questionnaire in the Appendix, this middle school was able to identify a focus for their school reform efforts that had a broad base of support.

Phase II: Identify and Implement an Intervention

The second phase of a school reform effort is to identify and implement a specific intervention that addresses the issue identified in phase I. Of course there are many ways to address any particular issue. For some issues, existing programs and practices can be purchased. For example, relative to item 6 (an assessment system), the Northwest Evaluation Association located in Portland, Oregon, has developed assessments that are keyed to state tests. It also regularly contracts with schools and districts to develop custom

tests. For other issues, formal programs and practices are not as available. To my knowledge, no specific programs address item 14, for example (physical environment and perceptions of safety and order). A school would have to make its own determinations as to which aspects of the school's physical environment and routines should be changed and then design those changes themselves.

Once a specific intervention is identified, it must be thoroughly implemented if a school is to expect it to impact student achievement. This might sound obvious, but the work of Eugene Hall, Shirley Hord, Susan Loucks, and their colleagues (Hall & Hord, 1987; Hall & Loucks, 1978; Hall, Loucks, Rutherford, & Newlove, 1975; Hord, Rutherford, Huling-Austin, & Hall, 1987) has shown that there are many stages of implementation. Just because a school has provided training in a new intervention does not mean that staff members are actually using it. Sadly, many, if not most, interventions are not fully implemented. In fact, it is not uncommon for an intervention to be considered ineffective or marginally effective when, in fact, the intervention was improperly or only partially implemented (Loucks, 1975; Hall & Hord, 1987).

Thomas Guskey (2000) recommends that schools gather data to determine if an intervention has been implemented widely and properly. (Although Guskey's comments are about staff development interventions in particular, his suggestions apply well to all aspects of school reform.) One approach is to use Hall and Hord's (1987) "Levels of Use" scale that describes six levels of implementation. These levels range from nonuse by staff members (e.g., staff members have no involvement in the intervention and are doing nothing to be involved) to renewal (staff members have progressed past deliberate use of the intervention and are seeking modifications in it to improve its impact). Levels of Use instruments have been developed that are easily employed and can be used to track the developing implementation.

Several less formal methods allow schools to collect data on the extent of an intervention's implementation. Among these, Guskey lists direct observation, participant interviews, and questionnaires.

Direct observation is the simplest and most immediate method of gathering evidence. It involves an individual or individuals making observations based on the critical indicators of the intervention. **Participant interviews** use some form of sampling. For example, a representative sample of staff members might be selected for interviewing. To save time, the interview might be recorded and played later to find evidence of the defining features of the intervention. **Questionnaires** are the most popular method for gathering informal evidence. Guskey notes that they can be used to gather data on almost every aspect of an organization's functioning. However, Guskey warns

> In interpreting questionnaire results, it is also important to keep in mind that responses to questionnaire items reflect *individuals' perceptions* [original emphasis] of organization support and change. As such, they are indirect measures—not direct evidence. Although individuals' perceptions are clearly important, sometimes they are based on limited knowledge or experience. As a result, they may represent a biased perspective. At the same time, questionnaire results

> represent a valuable source of evidence that, when thoughtfully analyzed, can help inform many important evaluation decisions. (p. 168)

Guskey's cautions should be kept in mind when administering and interpreting the results from the questionnaire in the Appendix. Although it provides useful information about the functioning of a school and possible future direction, it is perceptual information only.

Phase III: Examine the Effect on Achievement

The goal of any intervention is to positively impact student achievement. Therefore, *not* collecting data on student achievement (once there is some evidence that the intervention has been implemented) is a major mistake—one that can ultimately kill a school reform effort. Collecting this data, however, is frequently viewed as so problematic that it is rarely done.

I believe this is because K–12 educators are constrained by unrealistic expectations regarding the nature of evidence. Most administrators and teachers have taken graduate level courses in research design or evaluation methodology. The rules for evidence are quite stringent within those fields of endeavor (as they should be). However, just because a school cannot meet the stringent criteria doesn't mean that it is better not to gather evidence at all. Again, Guskey provides a useful perspective on the issue:

> In most cases you simply cannot get ironclad proof [regarding the impact of an interven-

tion on student achievement]. To do so, you would need to eliminate or control for all other factors that could have caused the change. This requires the random assignment of educators and students to experimental and control groups. The experimental group would take part in the [intervention], and the control group would not. Comparable measures would then be gathered from each and the difference tested. . . . The problem, of course, is that nearly all [interventions] take place in real-world settings, where such experimental conditions are impossible to meet. (p. 87)

I believe there are many ways that schools can collect evidence regarding the impact of interventions on student achievement. Here I present one possibility. It is an approach that can be easily used by schools and provides *adequate* information about student achievement with which to make an informal determination on an intervention's effectiveness.

One of the first things a school must do is to identify the type of achievement data that it will use as evidence. Educators and noneducators alike have a natural tendency to dismiss any type of achievement data other than state tests or standardized tests. Although these forms of assessment certainly have their place, they are not the best vehicles for evaluating the effectiveness of a specific intervention or set of interventions. Several reasons exist for this, not the least of which is that these are typically once-a-year only assessments.

Another reason why state tests and standardized tests are probably not the best assessment devices is that they are not specific to the content being taught. This shortcoming has been highlighted by many researchers including Alfie Kohn (2000),

James McMillan (1997), and James Popham (2001). George Madaus and his colleagues (Madaus, Kelleghan, Rakow, & King, 1979) conducted the seminal study on this issue. In a study involving 52 schools, they found that a significantly different picture of student learning was obtained when "curriculum-specific" tests (those measuring specific course content) were used instead of standardized tests. They warned that attempts to judge the effectiveness of a school (or, in this context, the effectiveness of an intervention) using standardized tests could produce fallacious conclusions:

> When we consider the tradition of American research on school effectiveness over the past decade, we find that the procedures used militated in several ways against any significant effects of schools. First, standardized tests were used as measures of student performance. There are very good reasons for this: they were readily available, thought to be objective, had been popular for over fifty years, and were useful for making comparisons across schools. Their disadvantages, however, did not receive adequate attention. (p. 225)

Given the inadequacies of state tests and standardized tests, a viable option for informal evaluation purposes is to use teacher-made assessments. By definition such tests are curriculum specific, because teachers will naturally design their tests to assess the content they have actually taught.

If a school decides to use data from teacher-made tests, it must then address how to analyze that data, or (more technically) the type of data analysis design it will use. Guskey's comments illustrate that the most powerful types of designs contrast a group of students who are involved in the intervention with a group of students who are not. In the real world, this is not usually possible. An alternative is to contrast the scores for students before the intervention and after. Educators sometimes reject these types of "gain score" designs because they are not true experimental designs favored within the research and evaluation literature. However, their utility and validity are severely underrated, and they are legitimate ways of determining student learning (Rogosa, Brandt, & Zimowsky, 1982; Willett, 1985, 1988).

To employ this approach, teachers would administer comprehensive pretests and post-tests on the content they cover across an entire quarter. They would score those assessments using a common scale such as percentage scores. For example, 5th grade math teachers would administer a pretest at the beginning of the first quarter on the content to be addressed that quarter and a post-test at the end of the quarter. They could probably use the same assessment for the pretest and the post-test given how quickly students forget the answers to specific items (Wilson & Putnam, 1982). This type of gain score data would be collected prior to, during, and after the implementation of the intervention. To illustrate the outcome of such an endeavor, consider Figure 17.3, which contains hypothetical data for six subject areas.

The intervention illustrated in Figure 17.3 was being implemented during the first two quarters of the year. For example, the school might have taken the first two quarters of the year to identify the essential versus supplemental content and then communicate this to teachers. Of course, the typical school would probably have more classes and sub-

jects than depicted, but for ease of discussion, I have kept the example small.

With these data, the school is in a position to determine if the gains in learning after the full implementation of the intervention are greater than the gains prior to the full implementation. The gain scores during the second semester, then, represent student learning after the intervention. If we were conducting a formal evaluation, we would perform a test to determine if the gains in the second semester are significantly different from the gains in the first semester. However, the school is not bound by the same conventions as those for a formal evaluation or a formal study. In this case, the school could simply compare the differences in gain scores graphically, as shown in Figure 17.4 (p. 170). The figure depicts plots of the average gain scores for the first semester compared to the average gain scores for the second semester. Obviously, something has changed from the first to second semester. The gains in the second semester are greater than those in the first. If the school could assume that gains would be about the same from quarter to quarter, then the profile depicted in Figure 17.4 could be interpreted as evidence that the intervention had an impact on student learning. If the school did not expect gain scores to be the same from quarter to quarter but had a good idea as to the pattern for any differences, it could still determine if the pattern after the intervention was different from before the intervention. A different pattern of scores after the intervention would indicate that the intervention had an effect on student achievement. Examining patterns of scores before and after an intervention is part of a long and honored tradition in research. In

		FIGURE 17.3			
		Gain Scores by Quarters for Various Subjects			
Grade	Subject	1st Quarter	2nd Quarter	3rd Quarter	4th Quarter
6	Mathematics	12.2	9.3	13.1	14.2
	Science	9.3	8.3	12.4	11.3
	Language Arts	12.5	12.1	13.2	12.8
	History/Geography	10.3	11.4	12.1	13.1
	Art	7.5	12.5	13.5	14.2
	Civics	10.3	11.2	12.2	13.1
	Average	10.35	10.80	12.75	13.12
7	Mathematics	8.4	10.1	12.3	14.1
	Science	10.2	9.4	11.4	12.5
	Language Arts	8.5	9.7	10.9	11.2
	History/Geography	10.5	12.1	12.4	13.4
	Art	10.7	11.4	14.5	12.5
	Civics	9.3	9.2	12.4	13.5
	Average	9.60	10.32	12.32	12.87
8	Mathematics	7.5	9.2	9.7	13.2
	Science	8.7	8.0	10.1	9.8
	Language Arts	9.2	9.4	12.9	11.4
	History/Geography	10.1	9.7	12.4	12.2
	Art	7.8	8.4	11.4	9.8
	Civics	11.3	10.9	11.7	12.3
	Average	9.10	9.27	11.37	11.45
	Status of Intervention	Being Implemented		Fully Implemented	

fact, if enough data points are available, these patterns can be submitted to statistical tests of significance (Glass, Willson, & Gottman, 1975; Mayer & Lewis, 1979).

This discussion should not be taken as an argument against experimental design, the use of significance tests, or the use of formal assessments as opposed to teacher-made tests. Rather, the discussion is intended to support the point that a school should gather the best available achievement data and analyze it in the most comprehensive and rigorous way possible to help determine if an intervention or interventions actually impact student

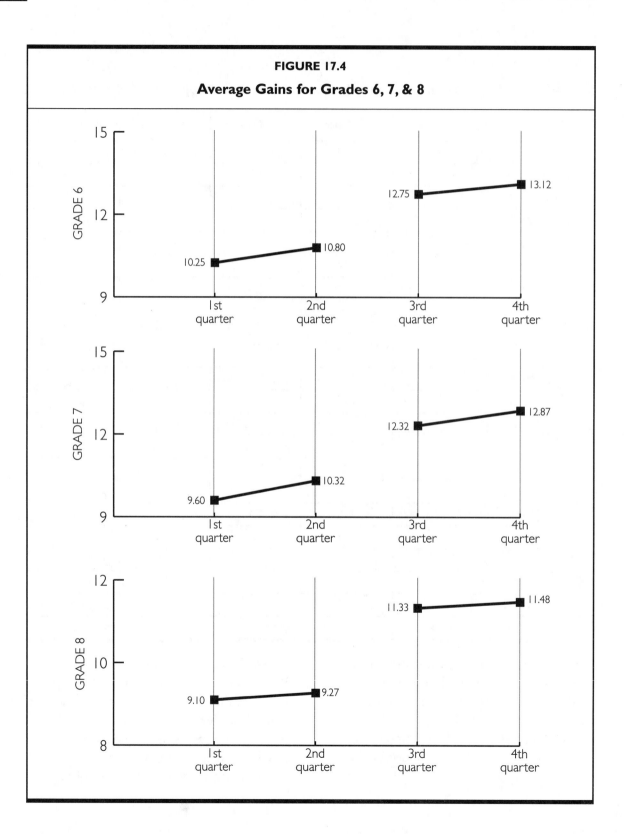

FIGURE 17.4

Average Gains for Grades 6, 7, & 8

achievement. However, even in the absence of formal tests, experimental design, and statistical hypothesis testing, a school can still collect data that provides valuable evidence on the impact of their efforts.

Phase IV: Move to the Next Issue

Once an intervention has been implemented and evaluated, the school should address the next issue and its accompanying intervention. Given some evidence for the positive impact of its first intervention, the staff might be inspired to take on a more difficult issue. Using the example from Figure 17.2 (p. 164), the school might now be ready to tackle the issue of designing a more effective assessment system (see item 6).

School reform in the new era, then, is a continuous process. A school is always seeking to address the next issue that can enhance student achievement. It is this process of continuously striving for improvement that breeds excellence (Fullan, 1982; Joyce, Wolf, & Calhoun, 1993; Hord, Rutherford, Huling-Austin, & Hall, 1987).

Summary

This chapter has described four phases a school might experience when using the model of school-level, teacher-level, and student-level factors. These are collecting perceptual data on the specific elements of the factors; identifying and implementing an intervention; examining the impact of the intervention on student achievement; and moving to the next issue. A case was made that even without the use of formal research or evaluation techniques, a school can and should carry out these phases.

THE CRITICAL ROLE
OF LEADERSHIP

In Chapter 2, I alluded to the fact that leadership was purposely omitted from my model of factors associated with student achievement. This is not because leadership is unimportant. On the contrary, leadership could be considered the single most important aspect of effective school reform. It is frequently mentioned in the early research on school effectiveness (Brookover et al., 1978, 1979; Edmonds, 1979a, 1979b, 1979c, 1981a, 1981b; Purkey & Smith, 1982, 1983; Rutter et al., 1979) and continues to be a staple in the research (Scheerens & Bosker, 1997; Teddlie & Reynolds, 2000).

The strongest reason for separating leadership from the model of factors is that it influences virtually every aspect of the model presented in this book. Leadership is a necessary condition for effective reform relative to the school-level, the teacher-level, and the student-level factors. To illustrate, research indicates that leadership has a strong relationship with (among others)

- the extent to which a school has a clear mission and goals (Bamburg & Andrews, 1990; Duke, 1982),
- the overall climate of the school and the climate in individual classrooms (Griffith, 2000; Villani, 1996; Brookover et al., 1978, 1979; Brookover & Lezotte, 1979),
- the attitudes of teachers (Brookover & Lezotte, 1979; Oakes, 1989; Purkey & Smith, 1983; Rutter et al., 1979),
- the classroom practices of teachers (Brookover et al., 1978; Brookover & Lezotte, 1979; McDill, Rigsby, & Myers, 1969; Miller & Sayre, 1986),
- the organization of curriculum and instruction (Bossert et al., 1982; Cohen & Miller, 1980; Eberts & Stone, 1988; Glasman & Binianimou, 1981; Oakes, 1989), and
- students' opportunity to learn (Duke & Canady, 1991; Dwyer, 1986; Murphy & Hallinger, 1989).

172

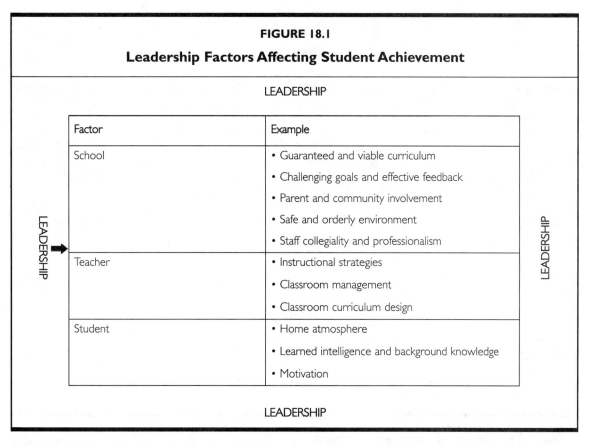

FIGURE 18.1

Leadership Factors Affecting Student Achievement

LEADERSHIP

Factor	Example
School	• Guaranteed and viable curriculum • Challenging goals and effective feedback • Parent and community involvement • Safe and orderly environment • Staff collegiality and professionalism
Teacher	• Instructional strategies • Classroom management • Classroom curriculum design
Student	• Home atmosphere • Learned intelligence and background knowledge • Motivation

LEADERSHIP

Since leadership is apparently the foundation for change at all levels, a complete representation of the model used in this book might be that in Figure 18.1.

Leadership for Change

Given its importance to the process of school reform, let's consider the characteristics of effective leadership. I should caution that my treatment is necessarily a brief and shallow one. Those interested in more thorough discussions should consult one or more of the many fine books on the topic (Blase & Kirby, 2000; Blase & Blase, 2001; Blumberg & Greenfield, 1986; Fullan, 1982; Hoy, Tarter, & Kottkamp, 1991; Lipham, 1981; Sergiovanni, 1992).

So many characteristics have been identified that a comprehensive list is unwieldy. To illustrate how diverse a comprehensive list might be, consider Figure 18.2 (p. 174), which provides an overview of leadership characteristics from just five studies.

Rather than attempt to add to this list, I have identified three principles of leadership for change that relate specifically to the use of the model presented in this book. Although these principles are research based, their primary source is my experience in working with schools across the country over the last three decades.

FIGURE 18.2

Overview of Characteristics Associated with Effective Leaders

Blum, Butler & Olson (1987)	Hallinger & Murphy (1987)	Neufeld & Freeman (1992)	Levine & Lezotte (1990)	Sammons, Hillman & Mortimore (1995)
• has clear vision • communicates to staff • establishes safe environment • knows quality instruction • monitors school performance	• frames goals • communicates goals • evaluates instruction • coordinates curriculum • monitors progress • protects instructional time • maintains high visibility • provides incentives for teachers • selects and participates in professional development activities • establishes explicit academic goals	• trusts and treats teachers as professionals • creates nonrestrictive work environment • is neither dogmatic nor autocratic • invites divergent points of view • gives teachers a clear voice in decisions	• supervises instructional practices • supports teachers • has high energy • vigorously selects and replaces teachers • has "maverick" orientation • monitors school activities • acquires necessary resources	• viewed as the leading professional • uses a participatory management approach • is firm • is purposeful

---

Principle 1. Leadership for change is most effective when carried out by a small group of educators with the principal functioning as a strong cohesive force.

One of the common misconceptions about leadership at the school level is that it should reside with a single individual—namely the principal (Hallinger, Bickman, & Davis, 1996). This belief is apparently so pervasive that it crosses the boundaries of nations and cultures (Caldwell, 1992; Cheng, 1994; Eckholm, 1992; Heck, 1993; Murphy & Hallinger, 1992). Although it is certainly true that strong leadership from the principal can be a powerful force toward school reform, the notion that an individual can effect

change by sheer will and personality is simply not supported by the research. In fact, the evidence supports the assertion that a substantive change initiative must be supported both by administrators and by teachers (Conley & Bacharach, 1990; Glickman, 1993, 1998; Maeroff, 1988; Schlechty, 1990). As described by Joseph Blase and Peggy Kirby (2000), those who work with students on a day-to-day basis—namely the teachers—must be involved in substantive decisions regarding changes that affect their day-to-day lives.

The principal's role is important. Reform requires a titular and conceptual leader. In fact, a great deal of research indicates that no one other than the school administrator can easily assume the role of visible head of a reform effort. Unfortunately, this is because of the egalitarian culture of schools in which all teachers are considered equal regardless of their expertise or performance. Attempts by a teacher or group of teachers to lead a reform effort are often met with resistance (Feiman-Nemser & Floden, 1986; Little, 1990; Lortie, 1975; Rosenholtz, 1989). Noah Friedkin and Michael Slater (1994) describe this phenomenon:

> Teachers' physical isolation in pursuing instructional activities and their norms of professional autonomy, privacy, and equity serve to inhibit the emergence of strong informal leaders from their ranks. (p. 14)

We are left with the intuitively appealing option of a strong leadership *team;* the principal and other administrators operating as key players and working with a dedicated group of classroom teachers.

Principle 2. The leadership team must operate in such a way as to provide strong guidance while demonstrating respect for those not on the team.

The existence of a strong leadership team does not imply a lack of involvement from teachers (or administrators) who are not on the team. Indeed, the leadership team operates best by ensuring that the views and concerns of all members of the school faculty are represented in its deliberations.

One critical function of the leadership team is to send the message to nonteam members that they are valued and respected as professionals. This means that the principal and leadership team should not try to micromanage the running of the school. Noah

Friedkin and Michael Slater (1994) demonstrated this in a study of 17 elementary schools in California. They identified the characteristics of principals that were statistically associated with effective leadership compared to those that were not. One of the more interesting features of their study was that effective leadership was defined in terms of students' academic performance over a four-year period. Unfortunately, it is somewhat rare in the research on leadership to find student achievement as the criterion for effectiveness. Some of the results of their study are reported in Figure 18.3 (p. 176).

The findings in Figure 18.3 imply that the effective principal does not try to play a *direct* role in the day-to-day lives of the teachers. When leadership is defined in terms of student achievement, behaviors such as commenting on specific lessons or solving specific instructional problems are not predictors of effective leadership. Rather, the effective principal engages in behaviors that are more *indirect* in the day-to-day lives of teachers. These behaviors are focused on the efficient running of the school, but they are not intrusive in the routines and practices of individual classroom teachers (although effective principals do communicate an interest in these routines and practices). Philip Hallinger, Leonard Bickman, and Ken Davis (1996) explain this dynamic:

> More robust conceptualizations of principal leadership suggest that the effects of principal leadership are most likely to occur *indirectly* [emphasis added] through the principal's efforts to influence those who come into direct contact with students in the instructional setting. (p. 532)

FIGURE 18.3

Leadership Behaviors of Effective Versus Ineffective Principals

Behaviors associated with an effective leader	Behaviors not associated with an effective leader
• Makes formal observations • Is accessible to discuss ideas • Seeks teacher input for key decisions • Portrays confidence in teachers • Monitors the continuity of the curriculum	• Has frequent staff meetings • Uses formal rewards for good teaching • Reviews teachers' lesson plans • Helps solve specific instructional problems • Gives feedback on specific lessons

Source: Friedkin, N. E., & Slater, M. R. (1994). School leadership and performance: A social network approach. *Sociology of Education, 67*, 139–157.

In the final analysis, Friedkin and Slater (1994) concluded that the effective leader has two primary traits:

> Our evidence suggests that two key dimensions of principals' [effectiveness] are: (1) accessibility and attentiveness to matters of concern to teachers and (2) collaborative problem solving and decision making on instructional issues in the context of mutual respect. The frequency of transactions between principals and teachers is not a key dimension of [effectiveness]. Intrusive forms of governance are negatively associated with [principal effectiveness] and with school performance. (p. 151)

The applications of these findings are fairly straightforward. The leadership team should be attentive to the concerns of teachers, easily accessible, and should engage in collaborative decision making and problem solving with teachers who are not members of the team. The leadership team should not be intrusive in the daily lives of teachers. All of this should be done in an atmosphere of mutual respect.

Principle 3. Effective leadership for change is characterized by specific behaviors that enhance interpersonal relationships.

Although effective leadership does not involve a specific type of personality, it is true that effective leaders, whether they are administrators or teacher-members of the leadership team, display specific behaviors when interacting with their colleagues. It is these behaviors that help establish personal relationships that are critical to the success of any reform effort. As a result of their survey involving more than 1,200 K–12 teachers, Blase and Kirby (2000) identified three leader characteristics as critical to building personal relationships that are conducive to effective reform efforts: (1) optimism, (2) honesty, and (3) consideration.

Optimism

Optimism is a leadership trait that is critical to effective reform because it provides hope during the difficult times that inevitably accompany substantive change. Despite the term being used to mean many things in everyday usage, research is fairly specific about its defining features. Martin Seligman (1991) has defined optimism as the power of nonnegative thinking. The optimist avoids "catastrophizing" during times of adversity. That is, he does not portray obstacles as insurmountable. Seligman notes that optimists can be contrasted with pessimists on three dimensions as depicted in Figure 18.4.

Blase and Kirby assert that the effect of optimistic leadership on teachers is increased self-esteem and motivation. Consider the following quote from one of the teachers in their study commenting on the impact of an administrator who was particularly optimistic:

She has a very positive feeling about our school. She enjoys her job and it is reflected to the rest of the teachers . . . She faces every day as a new day with new challenges. I try to do the same. I don't mind coming to school this year. When the alarm goes off, I'm "up and at them" this year. (p. 108)

Honesty

Honesty is characterized by truthfulness and consistency between words and actions. In addition to the study by Blase and Kirby (2000), many other studies have identified honesty as critical to effective leadership (Andrews in Brandt, 1987; Friedkin & Slater, 1994; Villani, 1996). A quote from a teacher in Blase and Kirby's study illustrates the impact of honesty on teachers:

FIGURE 18.4	
Characteristics of Optimists	
Dimension	**Optimist versus Pessimist**
External versus internal	Optimists tend to explain adversity as a function of causes external to the school (e.g., there isn't enough money to fund this project); pessimists tend to explain adversity as a function of causes that are endemic to the school (e.g., the students here just aren't very bright).
Specific versus pervasive	Optimists tend to explain adversity as a function of specific causes (e.g., new computer grading program we bought didn't meet our needs but another might); pessimists tend to explain adversity as a function of causes that are broad and pervasive (e.g., our record keeping system is useless).
Temporary versus permanent	Optimists tend to explain adversity as a function of causes that are temporary (e.g., we don't have enough money right now to buy the new computer grading program); pessimists tend to explain adversity as a function of causes that are permanent (e.g., we will never have the money to buy the computer software we need).

Source: Seligman, M. E. P. (1991). *Learned optimism.* New York: Knopf.

> Our principal is totally honest in his dealings with the faculty. He is direct with what he feels are our strengths and weaknesses and is always willing to help solve any problem that might arise . . . [This] keeps me open-minded in my dealings with my students . . . and others on the faculty. (p. 109)

The need for honesty is obvious. To sustain the outpouring of energy necessary for substantive change, teachers must have a sense that what they are told is accurate and that there are no important dynamics occurring about which they are not informed.

Consideration

This trait is sometimes referred to as a *people orientation* or a *concern for people*. Major leadership theorists have identified it as critical to effective leadership (Bass, 1990; Fullan, 1992; Hersey & Blanchard, 1977). Blase and Kirby (2000) note "Considerate principals were viewed as nondiscriminating; they show concern for all teachers. They express interest in their teachers' lives during both happy and sad events" (p.110). A quotation from one of the high school teachers in their study illustrates the impact of consideration:

> My principal was very understanding and flexible the times that I had to be absent due to hospitalization of family members. His cooperation and attempts to make my return to school smoother were above and beyond the call of duty. I feel that I've been treated with kindness and respect. I, in turn, tend to have a more compassionate attitude toward my students and their individual situations. (p.110)

As is the case with honesty, consideration helps build interpersonal relationships so necessary during the difficult times that seem to accompany substantive change.

Members of the leadership team should cultivate the dispositions of optimism, honesty, and consideration. In the final analysis, these characteristics might be as important as those that address the more technical aspects of school reform discussed in Chapter 17.

Epilogue

I end this book the way I began it. Public education stands at a point where it can enter *the best of times* even though to some it might appear that we are in *the worst of times*. In fact, perhaps the second phrase of Dickens's quote ". . . it was the age of wisdom, it was the age of foolishness" is even more appropriate. Even a cursory reading of the previous 17 chapters illustrates that I am highly optimistic about the guidance provided from 35 years of research. Following that guidance would be exceedingly wise; ignoring it would be exceedingly foolish. Whether we enter the *best of times* is dependent on whether we use the gifts research has provided wisely or foolishly.

Appendix:
Snapshot Survey of School Effectiveness Factors

	Question 1 To what extent do we engage in this behavior or address this issue?				Question 2 How much will a change in our practices on this item increase the academic achievement of our students?				Question 3 How much effort will it take to significantly change our practices regarding this issue?			
	Not at all			To a great extent	Not at all			To a great extent	Not much		A lot, but possible to do	Too much to do
IN MY SCHOOL . . .	1	2	3	4	1	2	3	4	1	2	3	4
Guaranteed and Viable Curriculum 1. The content considered essential for all students to learn versus the content considered supplemental has been identified and communicated to teachers.												
2. The amount of essential content that has been identified can be addressed in the instructional time available to teachers.												
3. The essential content is organized and sequenced in a way that students have ample opportunity to learn it.												
4. Someone checks to ensure that teachers address essential content.												

Snapshot Survey of School Effectiveness Factors (continued)	Question 1 To what extent do we engage in this behavior or address this issue?				Question 2 How much will a change in our practices on this item increase the academic achievement of our students?				Question 3 How much effort will it take to significantly change our practices regarding this issue?			
	Not at all			To a great extent	Not at all			To a great extent	Not much		A lot, but possible to do	Too much to do
IN MY SCHOOL . . .	1	2	3	4	1	2	3	4	1	2	3	4
5. The instructional time available to teachers is protected by minimizing interruptions and scheduled noninstructional activities.												
Challenging Goals and Effective Feedback 6. An assessment system is used that provides for timely feedback (e.g., at least every nine weeks) on specific knowledge and skills for individual students.												
7. Specific achievement goals are set for the school as a whole.												
8. Specific achievement goals are set for individual students.												
9. Performance on schoolwide and individual student goals is used to plan for future actions.												
Parent and Community Involvement 10. Effective vehicles are in place to communicate to parents and community.												
11. Effective vehicles are in place for parents and community to communicate to the school.												
12. Opportunities are provided for parents and community to be involved in the day-to-day operations of the school.												
13. Vehicles are in place for parents and community to be involved in the governance of the school.												
Safe and Orderly Environment 14. The physical environment and school routines have been structured to avoid chaos and promote good behavior.												
15. Clear rules and procedures pertaining to schoolwide behavior have been established.												

Snapshot Survey of School Effectiveness Factors (continued)	Question 1 To what extent do we engage in this behavior or address this issue?				Question 2 How much will a change in our practices on this item increase the academic achievement of our students?				Question 3 How much effort will it take to significantly change our practices regarding this issue?			
	Not at all			To a great extent	Not at all			To a great extent	Not much		A lot, but possible to do	Too much to do
IN MY SCHOOL . . .	1	2	3	4	1	2	3	4	1	2	3	4
16. Appropriate consequences for violations of schoolwide rules and procedures have been established and implemented.												
17. A program that teaches and reinforces student self-discipline and responsibility has been implemented.												
18. A system for early detection of students who are prone to violence and extreme behavior has been implemented.												
Collegiality and Professionalism 19. Norms for conduct that foster collegiality and professionalism among professional staff and administrators have been established.												
20. Governance structures that allow for teacher involvement in schoolwide decisions and policies have been established.												
21. Teachers are engaged in staff development activities that address specific content area issues and allow for "hands-on" trial and evaluation of specific techniques.												
Home Environment 22. Training and support are provided to parents to enhance their communication with their children, their supervision of their children, and their parenting style.												
Learned Intelligence and Background Knowledge 23. Students are involved in schoolwide programs that directly increase the number and quality of life experiences they have.												

Snapshot Survey of School Effectiveness Factors (continued)	Question 1 To what extent do we engage in this behavior or address this issue?				Question 2 How much will a change in our practices on this item increase the academic achievement of our students?				Question 3 How much effort will it take to significantly change our practices regarding this issue?			
	Not at all			To a great extent	Not at all			To a great extent	Not much		A lot, but possible to do	Too much to do
IN MY SCHOOL . . .	1	2	3	4	1	2	3	4	1	2	3	4
24. Students are involved in a schoolwide program of wide reading that emphasizes vocabulary development.												
25. Students are involved in a schoolwide program of direct instruction in vocabulary terms and phrases that are important to specific subject matter content.												
Student Motivation 26. Students are provided with feedback on their knowledge gain.												
27. Students are involved in simulation games and activities that are inherently engaging.												
28. Students are provided with opportunities to construct and work on long-term projects of their own design.												
29. Students are provided with training regarding the dynamics of motivation and how those dynamics affect them.												
	Very few, if any, do this			Almost everyone does this	Not at all			To a great extent	Not much		A lot, but possible to do	Too much to do
TEACHERS IN MY SCHOOL . . .	1	2	3	4	1	2	3	4	1	2	3	4
Instruction 30. Begin their instructional units by presenting students with clear learning goals.												
31. Begin their instructional units by asking students to identify personal learning goals that fit within the learning goals presented by the teacher.												

Snapshot Survey of School Effectiveness Factors (continued)	Question 1 To what extent do we engage in this behavior or address this issue?				Question 2 How much will a change in our current practices on this item increase the academic achievement of our students?				Question 3 How much effort will it take to significantly change our current practices regarding this issue?			
	Very few, if any, do this			Almost everyone does this	Not at all			To a great extent	Not much		A lot, but possible to do	Too much to do
TEACHERS IN MY SCHOOL …	1	2	3	4	1	2	3	4	1	2	3	4
32. Systematically provide students with specific feedback on the extent to which they are accomplishing the learning goals.												
33. Systematically ask students to keep track of their own performance on the learning goals.												
34. Systematically recognize students who are making observable progress toward the learning goals.												
35. Systematically emphasize the importance of effort with students.												
36. Organize students into groups based on their understanding of the content when appropriate.												
37. Organize students into cooperative groups when appropriate.												
38. Systematically provide specific feedback on the homework assigned to students.												
39. End their units by providing students with clear feedback on the learning goals.												
40. End their units by asking students to assess themselves relative to the learning goals.												
41. End their units by recognizing and celebrating progress on the learning goals.												
42. Prior to presenting new content, ask students questions that help them recall what they might already know about the content.												
43. Prior to presenting new content, provide students with direct links with previous knowledge or studies.												

Snapshot Survey of School Effectiveness Factors (continued)	Question 1 To what extent do we engage in this behavior or address this issue?				Question 2 How much will a change in our current practices on this item increase the academic achievement of our students?				Question 3 How much effort will it take to significantly change our current practices regarding this issue?			
	Very few, if any, do this			Almost everyone does this	Not at all			To a great extent	Not much		A lot, but possible to do	Too much to do
TEACHERS IN MY SCHOOL ...	1	2	3	4	1	2	3	4	1	2	3	4
44. Prior to presenting new content, provide ways for students to organize or think about the content (e.g., use advance organizers).												
45. Ask students to construct verbal or written summaries of new content.												
46. Ask students to take notes on new content.												
47. Ask students to represent new content in nonlinguistic ways (e.g., mental image, picture, pictograph, graphic organizer, physical model, enactment).												
48. Assign in-class and homework tasks that require students to practice important skills and procedures.												
49. Ask students to revise and correct errors in their notes as a way of reviewing and revising content.												
50. Ask students to revise and correct errors in their nonlinguistic representations as a way of reviewing and revising content.												
51. Prescribe in-class and homework assignments that require students to compare and classify content.												
52. Prescribe in-class and homework assignments that require students to construct metaphors and analogies.												
53. Prescribe in-class activities and homework assignments that require students to generate and test hypotheses regarding content.												

Snapshot Survey of School Effectiveness Factors (continued)	Question 1 To what extent do we engage in this behavior or address this issue?				Question 2 How much will a change in our current practices on this item increase the academic achievement of our students?				Question 3 How much effort will it take to significantly change our current practices regarding this issue?			
	Very few, if any, do this			Almost everyone does this	Not at all			To a great extent	Not much		A lot, but possible to do	Too much to do
TEACHERS IN MY SCHOOL …	1	2	3	4	1	2	3	4	1	2	3	4
Classroom Management 54. Have comprehensive and well-articulated rules and procedures for general classroom behavior, beginning and ending the period or day, transitions and interruptions, use of materials and equipment, group work, and seatwork.												
55. Use specific disciplinary strategies that reinforce appropriate behavior and provide consequences for inappropriate behavior.												
56. Use specific strategies that instill a sense of confidence in students that they are receiving proper guidance and direction.												
57. Use specific strategies that instill a sense of confidence in students that their concerns and wishes are being considered.												
58. Use different strategies with different types of students to provide them with a sense of acceptance by the teacher.												
59. Use specific techniques to keep aware of problems or potential problems in their classrooms.												
60. Respond to inappropriate behaviors quickly and assertively.												
61. Use specific techniques to maintain a healthy emotional objectivity when dealing with student misbehavior.												

Snapshot Survey of School Effectiveness Factors (continued)	Question 1 To what extent do we engage in this behavior or address this issue?				Question 2 How much will a change in our current practices on this item increase the academic achievement of our students?				Question 3 How much effort will it take to significantly change our current practices regarding this issue?			
	Very few, if any, do this			Almost everyone does this	Not at all			To a great extent	Not much		A lot, but possible to do	Too much to do
TEACHERS IN MY SCHOOL ...	1	2	3	4	1	2	3	4	1	2	3	4
Classroom Curriculum Design 62. When planning units of instruction, identify specific types of knowledge that are important for students to learn (e.g., important categories of knowledge, examples, sequences, comparisons, cause-and-effect relationships, correlational relationships, facts, incidents, episodes, terms, skills, processes).												
63. When planning units of instruction, ensure that students have multiple exposures to new content presented in a variety of forms (e.g., stories, descriptions) using a variety of media (e.g., read about the content, watch a demonstration, listen to a presentation).												
64. When planning units of instruction, make a clear distinction between skills and processes that are to be mastered versus skills and processes that are to be experienced but not mastered.												
65. When planning units of instruction, organize examples into categories or groups that demonstrate the essential features of the content.												
66. When planning units of instruction, ensure that students will be involved in complex projects that require them to address content in unique ways.												

ASCD has created the What Works in Schools online survey that includes an electronic version of this survey and an analysis of school and district results. Please contact ASCD at 800-933-2723 or go to www.whatworksinschools.org for details.

TECHNICAL NOTES

The following notes are intended to explain some of the more technical aspects of the research findings discussed in this book. These notes, however, are brief treatments of the topics addressed. For more detailed discussion, consult standard statistics textbooks, such as Cohen (1988); Cohen and Cohen (1975); Glass, McGaw, and Smith (1981); Glass, Willson, and Gottman (1975); and Hunter and Schmidt (1990).

Technical Note 1

One of the most common indices found in the research literature is the percent of variance explained (or *PV*). A basic assumption underlying the use of this index is that the percentage of variance explained by a predictor (or independent) variable (e.g., schooling) relative to a predicted (or dependent) variable (e.g., student achievement) represents the strength of relation between the two. Most commonly, a "set" of predictor variables is used.

For example, a given study might attempt to predict student achievement using (1) per pupil expenditures, (2) length of the school year, and (3) average years of experience per teacher. The predictor variables, considered as a set, would account for a proportion of total variance in the predicted variable. The process of determining the relationship between a predicted (dependent) variable and a predictor (independent) variable is commonly referred to as "regression analysis." The predicted variable is "regressed onto" the predictor variable. The index used to judge the influence of predictor variables is the ratio of variance accounted for by the predictor variables over the total variance of the predicted variable multiplied by 100.

$$PV = \frac{\text{percent of variance explained by predictor or independent variables}}{\text{percent of total variance in the predicted or dependent variable}} \times 100$$

An index closely related to *PV* is the correlation coefficient. When a single predictor or independent variable (e.g., socioeconomic status) is used with a predicted or dependent variable (e.g., student academic achievement), the relationship between the two can be expressed as *r*—the Pearson product-moment correlation. When multiple predictors (e.g., background knowledge, student motivation, socioeconomic status) are used with a predicted variable, the relationship between the predictor variables, considered as a set, and the predicted variable is expressed as *R*—the multiple correlation coefficient. In both cases, the percentage of variance accounted for (*PV*) in the predicted (dependent) variable by the predictor (independent) variables is computed by squaring the correlation coefficient (i.e., r^2 or R^2) and multiplying by 100. In short, there is a strong conceptual and mathematical relationship between *PV* and the univariate and multivariate correlation coefficients.

As common as is the use of r^2, R^2, and *PV*, they have been criticized as indicators of the relationship between predictor (independent) variables and the predicted (dependent) variable. Hunter and Schmidt (1990) explain

> The percent of variance accounted for is statistically correct, but substantively erroneous. It leads to severe underestimates of the practical and theoretical significance of relationships between variables. . . . The problem with all percent variance accounted for indices of effect size is that variables that account for small percentages of the variance often have very important effects on the dependent variable. (pp. 199–200)

Hunter and Schmidt use the correlation between aptitude and heredity reported by Jensen (1980) to illustrate this circumstance. This correlation is about 0.895, which implies that about 80 percent (0.895^2) of the variance in aptitude is a function of heredity and environment, leaving only 20 percent of the variance due to environment (*r* = 0.447). The relative influence of heredity on aptitude and environment on aptitude, then, is about 4 to 1 from the percentage of variance perspective. However, regression theory (Cohen & Cohen, 1975) tells us that the correlations between heredity and aptitude (*H*) and between environment and aptitude (*E*) (after the influence of heredity has been partialed out) are analogous to the regression weights in a linear equation predicting aptitude from heredity and environment when dependent and independent variables are expressed in standard score form. (For this illustration, we will assume that heredity and environment are independent). Using the quantities above, this equation would be as follows:

Predicted Aptitude = 0.895(*H*) + 0.447(*E*)

This equation states that an increase of one standard deviation in heredity will be accompanied by an increase of 0.895 standard deviation in aptitude. Similarly, an increase of one standard deviation in environment will be accompanied by an increase of 0.447 standard deviation in aptitude. This paints a very different picture of the relative influences of heredity and environment on aptitude. Here the ratio is 2 to 1 as opposed to 4 to 1 from the percentage of variance perspective.

Technical Note 2

The potentially misleading impressions given by percentage of variance explained has stimulated the use of the binomial effect size display (*BESD*). As described by Rosenthal and Rubin (1982), to employ the *BESD*, the predictor variable is thought of as being dichotomized into two distinct groups. In the *BESD* illustrations used in this book, the dichotomized independent variable is conceptualized as effective schools versus ineffective schools. Similarly, the predicted variable is dichotomized into success or failure on some criterion measure. In this book, the predicted variable is conceptualized as success or failure on some form of achievement test.

A common convention when using the *BESD* is to assume that the expectation for the predicted variable is a success rate of 0.50. To compute the *BESD*, the correlation coefficient is divided by 2 and then added to and subtracted from 0.50. For example, if the *r* between predictor and predicted is 0.50, then $0.50 \div 2 = 0.25$. The percentage of subjects in the experimental group that would be expected to "succeed" on the predicted variable is computed as $0.50 + 0.25 = 0.75$. The percentage of subjects in the experimental group that would be expected to "fail" on the criterion measure is $0.50 - 0.25 = 0.25$. The converse of these computations is used for the control group. Rosenthal and Rubin (1982) make the case for the use of *BESD* as a realistic representation of the size of the treatment effect when the outcome variable is continuous, provided that the groups are of equal size and variance.

Cohen dramatically illustrates the use of the *BESD* using an example from medicine.

This is depicted in the table below.

Binomial Effect Size Display with 1% of Variance (r = 0.10) Accounted For By Hypothetical Medical Treatment

Group	Outcome		
	% Alive	% Dead	Total
Treatment	55%	45%	100%
Control	45%	55%	100%

Note: Constructed from data in *Statistical Power for the Behavioral Sciences*, p. 534, by J. Cohen, 1988, Hillsdale, NJ: Erlbaum. "*r*" stands for the Pearson product-moment correlation coefficient.

The table exemplifies a situation in which the independent variable (i.e., membership in the experimental or control group) accounts for only one percent of the variance in the dependent variable (i.e., $r = 0.10$). The assumption here is that the independent variable is some sort of medical treatment that accounts for one percent of the variance in the outcome measure, which is being alive or dead. Yet, this one percent of explained variance translates into a 10 percentage point difference in terms of patients who are alive (or dead) based on group membership. As Cohen (1988) notes

> This means, for example, that a difference in percent alive between .45 and .55, which most people would consider important (*alive*, mind you!) yields $r = .10$, and "only 1% of the variance accounted for," an amount that operationally defines a "small" effect in my scheme. . . . "Death" tends to concentrate the mind. But this in turn reinforces the principle that the size of an effect can only be appraised in the context of the substantive

issues involved. An r^2 of .01 is indeed small in absolute terms, but when it represents a ten percentage point increase in survival, it may well be considered large. (p. 534)

This same point is further dramatized by Abelson (1985). After analyzing the effect of various physical skills on the batting averages of professional baseball players, he found that the percentage of variance accounted for by these skills was a minuscule 0.00317—not quite one-third of one percent ($r = 0.056$). Commenting on the implications for interpreting education research, Abelson notes

One should not necessarily be scornful of minuscule values for percentage of variance explained, provided there is statistical assurance that these values are significantly above zero, and that the degree of potential cumulation is substantial. (p. 133)

Finally, Cohen exhorts, "The next time you read 'only x% of the variance is accounted for,' remember Abelson's paradox" (p. 535).

Technical Note 3

To determine the impact on students of schools at the 99th percentile of the distribution, I am assuming that schools are distributed normally in terms of their effectiveness. I am also assuming that, on the average, schools account for 20 percent of the variance on student achievement which translates to $r = 0.447$. That is, the average correlation between the qualities of a school and student achievement is 0.447. Based on the research of Scheerens and Bosker (1997), I am assuming that the standard deviation of this distribution of correlations is 0.1068 (see Marzano, 2000a, pp. 57–58 for a discussion).

Schools at the 99th percentile would be 2.33 standard deviations above the mean. That is, the correlation between the qualities of schools at the 99th percentile and student achievement is 0.694 (.447 + 2.33 x 0.1068). Using the BESD, this implies that in these schools 84.7 percent of the students would pass a test on which half are expected to pass. Additionally, only 15.3 percent of the students would fail the test.

Technical Note 4

One of the most commonly used indices of the impact of an independent variable (e.g., the quality of a school) on a dependent variable (e.g., student academic achievement) is the effect size or *ES*. Actually, the generic term effect size applies to a variety of indices including *r*, *R*, and *PV*. However, as used in this book, *ES* means the standardized mean difference effect size. Glass (1976) first popularized this index, which is the difference between experimental and control means divided by an estimate of the population standard deviation—hence, the name standardized mean difference.

$$\text{standardized mean difference effect size} = \frac{\text{mean of experimental group} - \text{mean of control group}}{\text{estimate of population standard deviation}}$$

To illustrate the use of *ES*, assume that the achievement mean of a school with a given characteristic is 90 on a standardized test and the mean of a school that does not possess this characteristic is 80. Also assume that the population standard deviation is 10. The effect size would be

$$ES = \frac{90 - 80}{10} = 1.0$$

This effect size can be interpreted in the following way: the mean of the experimental group is 1.0 standard deviation larger than the mean of the control group. One might infer, then, that the characteristic possessed by the experimental school raises achievement test scores by one standard deviation. Thus, the effect size (*ES*) expresses the differences between means in standardized or "Z score" form. It is this characteristic that gives rise to another index commonly used in the research on school effects—percentile gain.

Percentile gain, or *Pgain*, is the expected gain (or loss) in percentile points of the average student in the experimental group compared to the average student in the control group. To illustrate, consider the same example. Given an effect size of 1.0, one can conclude that the average score in the experimental group is 34.134 percentile points higher than the average score in the control group. This is necessarily so since the *ES* translates the difference between experimental and control group means into Z score form. Distribution theory tells us that a Z score of 1.0 is at the 84.134 percentile point of the standard normal distribution. To compute the *Pgain*, then, *ES* is transformed into percentile points above or below the 50th percentile point on the standard normal distribution.

Technical Note 5

One of the most confusing aspects of the research on school effectiveness factors is the vastly different estimates of the percentage of variance accounted for by various factors. For example, I have reported in Chapter 1 that schools generally account for 20 percent of the variance in student achievement. Yet, studies by Ferguson (1991) and Ferguson and Ladd (1996) indicate that teacher qualifications alone account for 40 percent of the variance in student achievement. Darling-Hammond (2000) reports that teacher quality accounts for as much as 60 percent of the variance in student achievement. The reason for these discrepancies is that studies reporting that schools account for 20 percent of the variance (or less) in student achievement typically employ some type of design that attempts to explain the variance in achievement at the individual student level. Those studies that report much larger proportions of variance accounted for typically employ designs that attempt to explain the variance in achievement at the school, district, or even state levels. When school-, district-, or state-level averages are used as the dependent measures, the variances of these measures are, by definition, less than those for student-level data. Hence, estimates of variances accounted for are inflated.

Technical Note 6

The regression equation used to compute the values in Figure 8.3 (p. 74) was

predicted score = 0.895 x student background score + 0.365 x teacher score + 0.257 x school score

This equation was based on the assumption that a student background score accounts for 80 percent of the variance in student achievement, the teacher score accounts for 13.3 percent of the variance in student achievement, and the school score accounts for 6.7 percent of the variance in student achievement. These estimates were derived from Marzano (2000a). Student, teacher, and school scores were conceptualized as a scale with a range of 0 to 10. An ineffective teacher was assigned a score of 0, an average teacher was assigned a score of 5, and an effective teacher was assigned a score of 10. Likewise, an ineffective school was assigned a score of 0, an average school was assigned a score of 5, and an effective school was assigned a score of 10. Thus, scores of 0 and 10 represent extremes. In addition, these extreme scores were assigned Z scores of –3.00 (ineffective) and +3.00 (effective). The entire distribution of scores, then, was thought to span six standard deviations. Scores on the 0 to 10 scale were transformed to their Z score form and entered as values in the regression equation. Predicted scores were in Z score form. These were translated to percentiles to obtain the entries in Figure 8.3.

The two-year estimate for changes in percentile ranking depicted in Figure 8.3 are based on the following assumptions. Glass, McGaw, and Smith (1981) note that a typical one-year gain in learning is equivalent to one standard deviation on most standardized tests, particularly at the elementary school level. In terms of the prediction equation described, this would be the expected one-year gain for the student entering at the 50th percentile who is assigned to an average teacher in an average school. If no learning were to occur as a result of the teacher or the school (e.g., a teacher who has no effect on learning and a school that has no effect on learning), the student entering at a Z score level of 0 (i.e., the 50th percentile) would fall to a Z score level of –2.00 in two years. The regression equation predicts that the student who enters at a Z score level of 0 and is assigned to an ineffective teacher in an ineffective school would drop to a Z score level of –1.87. Given Glass, McGaw, and Smith's estimate of an increase of 1.00 standard deviations per year, it is reasonable to assume that a decrease of 1.87 standard deviations would take about two years. Assuming that the rate of increase in Z score standing is the same as the rate of decrease, one can estimate the same two-year time frame for the student in the highly effective school with the highly effective teacher.

REFERENCES

Abelson, R. P. (1985). A variance explained paradox: When a little is a lot. *Psychological Bulletin, 97,* 166–169.

Ackerman, P. L. (1996). A theory of adult intellectual development: Process, personality, interests, and knowledge. *Intelligence, 22,* 227–257.

Airasian, P. W. (1994). *Classroom assessment* (2nd ed.). New York: McGraw Hill.

Albert, L. (1989). *Cooperative discipline.* Circle Pines, MN: American Guidance Service.

Alderman, G. L., & Nix, M. (1997). Teachers' intervention preferences related to explanations for behavior problems, severity of the problem, and teacher experience. *Behavioral Disorders, 22,* 87–95.

Alexander, P. A., & Judy, J. E. (1988). The interaction of domain-specific and strategic knowledge in academic performance. *Review of Educational Research, 58*(4), 375–404.

Alexander, P. A., Kulikowich, J. M., & Schulze, S. K. (1994). How subject-matter knowledge affects recall and interest. *American Educational Research Journal, 31*(2), 313–337.

American Institute for Research. (1999). *An educator's guide to schoolwide reform.* Arlington: VA: Educational Research Service.

Anastasi, A. (1982). *Psychological testing* (5th ed.). New York: Macmillan.

Anderson, C. S. (1982). The search for school climate: A review of the research. *Review of Educational Research, 52,* 368–420.

Anderson, J. (1990). *Cognitive psychology and its implications.* New York: W. H. Freeman and Company.

Anderson, J. R. (1982). Acquisition of cognitive skills. *Psychological Review, 89,* 369–406.

Anderson, J. R. (1983). *The architecture of cognition.* Cambridge, MA: Harvard University Press.

Anderson, J. R. (1995). *Learning and memory: An integrated approach.* New York: John Wiley & Sons.

Anderson, J. R., Greeno, J. G., Reder, L. M., & Simon, H. A. (2000). Perspectives on learning, thinking and activity. *Educational Researcher, 29*(4), 11–13.

Anderson, J. R., Reder, L. M., & Simon, H. A. (1995). *Applications and misapplications of cognitive psychology to mathematics education.* Unpublished paper, Carnegie Mellon University, Department of Psychology, Pittsburgh, PA. Available: http://act.psy.cmu.edu/personal/ja/misapplied.html

Anderson, J. R., Reder, L. M., & Simon, H. A. (1996). Situated learning and education. *Educational Researcher, 25*(4), 5–11.

Anderson, R. C. (1994). Role of reader's schema in comprehension, learning and memory. In R. B. Ruddell, M. R. Ruddell, & H. Singer (Eds.), *Theoretical models and processes of reading* (4th ed., pp. 469–482). Newark, DE: International Reading Association.

Andrews, G. R., & Debus, R. L. (1978). Persistence and the causal perception of failure: Modifying cognitive attributions. *Journal of Educational Psychology, 70,* 154–166.

Andrews, J. W., Blackmon, C. R., & Mackey, J. A. (1980). Preservice performance and the National Teacher Examinations. *Phi Delta Kappan, 61*(5), 358–359.

Antunez, B. (2000). *When everybody is involved: Parents and communities in school reform.* National Center for Bilingual Education [Online]. Available: http://www.ncbe.gwu.edu/ncbepubs/tasynthesis/framing/6parents.htm

Armour-Thomas, E., Clay, C., Domanico, R., Bruno, K., & Allen, B. (1989). An outlier study of elementary and middle schools in New York City: Final report. NY: New York City Board of Education.

Ashton, P., & Crocker, L. (1987, May-June). Systematic study of planned variations: The essential focus of teacher education reform. *Journal of Teacher Education, 38,* 2–8.

Atkinson, J. W. (1957). Motivational determinants of risk-taking behavior. *Psychological Review, 64,* 359–372.

Atkinson, J. W. (1964). *An introduction to motivation.* Princeton, NJ: Van Nostrand.

Atkinson, J. W. (1987). Michigan studies of fear failure. In F. Halisch & J. Kuhl (Eds.), *Motivation, intention and volition* (pp. 47–60). Berlin: Springer.

Atkinson, J. W., & Raynor, J. O. (1974). *Motivation and achievement.* New York: Wiley.

Bamburg, J., & Andrews, R. (1990). School goals, principals and achievement. *School Effectiveness and School Improvement, 2,* 175–191.

Bandura, A. (1997). *Self-efficacy: The exercise of control.* New York: W. H. Freeman and Co.

Bangert-Downs, R. L., Kulik, C. C., Kulik, J. A., & Morgan, M. (1991). The instructional effects of feedback in test-like events. *Review of Educational Research, 61*(2), 213–238.

Barr, A. S. (1958). Characteristics of successful teachers. *Phi Delta Kappan, 39,* 282–284.

Barrell, J. (2001). Designing the invitational environment. In A. Costa (Ed.), *Developing minds: A resource book for teaching thinking* (3rd ed., pp. 106–110). Alexandria, VA: Association for Supervision and Curriculum Development.

Barth, P., Haycock, K., Jackson, H., Mora, K., Ruiz, P., Robinson, S., & Wilkins, A. (1999). *Dispelling the myth: High poverty schools exceeding expectations.* Washington, DC: The Education Trust.

Bass, B. M. (1990). *Bass and Stogdill's handbook of leadership: Theory, research, and managerial applications* (3rd ed.). New York: Free Press.

Baumrind, D. (1978). Parent disciplinary patterns and social competence in children. *Youth and Society, 9,* 239–276.

Baumrind, D. (1991). Parenting styles and adolescent development. In J. Brooks-Gunn, R. Lerner & A. C. Peterson (Eds.), *The Encyclopedia of Adolescence* (pp. 746–758). New York: Garland.

Bear, G. G. (1998). School discipline in the United States: Prevention, correction, and long-term social development. *School Psychology Review, 27*(1), 14–32.

Beck, I., & McKeown, M. (1991). Conditions of vocabulary acquisition. In R. Barr, M. Kamil, P. Mosenthal, & P. D. Pearson (Eds.), *Handbook of reading research* (Vol. 2, pp. 789–814). New York: Longman.

Bennett, W. J. (1986). *What works: Research about teaching and learning.* Washington, DC: U.S. Department of Education.

Bennett, W. J. (1992). *The de-valuing of America: The fight for our culture and our children.* New York: Summit Books.

Berliner, D. C. (1986). In pursuit of the expert pedagogue. *Educational Researcher, 15*(7), 5–13.

Berliner, D. C., & Biddle, B. J. (1995). *The manufactured crisis: Myths, frauds, and the attack on America's public schools.* Reading, MA: Addison-Wesley.

Berliner, D. C., & Tikunoff, W. J. (1976). The California beginning teacher study. *Journal of Teacher Education, 27,* 24–30.

Berman, S. (2001). Thinking in context: Teaching for open-mindedness and critical understanding. In A. L. Costa (Ed.), *Developing minds: A resource book for teaching thinking* (pp. 11–17). Alexandria, VA: Association for Supervision and Curriculum Development.

Bierman, K. L., Miller, C. L., & Stabb, S. D. (1987). Improving the social behavior and peer acceptance of rejected boys: Effects of social skill training with instructions and prohibitions. *Journal of Consulting and Clinical Psychology, 55,* 194–200.

Billings, W. H., & Enger, J. M. (1995, November 8–10). *Perceptions of Missouri high school principals regarding the effectiveness of in-school suspension as a disciplinary procedure.* Paper presented at the annual meeting of the Mid-south Educational Research Association, Biloxi, MS. (ERIC Document Reproduction Service No. ED392169)

Bittle, R. G. (1975). Improving parent-teacher communication through recorded telephone messages. *Journal of Educational Research, 69*(3), 87–95.

Black, P., & Wiliam, D. (1998). Assessment and classroom learning. *Assessment in Education, 5*(1), 7–74.

Blase, J., & Blase, J. (1998). *Handbook of instructional leadership: How really good principals promote teaching and learning.* Thousand Oaks, CA: Corwin Press.

Blase, J., & Blase, J. (2001). *Empowering teachers: What successful principals do* (2nd ed.). Thousand Oaks, CA: Corwin Press.

Blase, J., & Kirby, P. C. (2000). *Bringing out the best in teachers: What effective principals do* (2nd ed.). Thousand Oaks, CA: Corwin Press.

Bloom, B. S. (1976). *Human characteristics and school learning.* New York: McGraw-Hill.

Bloom, B. S. (1984). The 2 Sigma problem: The search for methods of instruction as effective as one-to-one tutoring. *Educational Researcher, 13*(6), 4–16.

Blum, R. E., Butler, J. A., & Olson, N. L. (1987). Leadership for excellence: Research-based training for principals. *Educational Leadership, 45*(1), 25–29.

Blumberg, A., & Greenfield, W. (1986). *The effective principal: Perspectives on school leadership* (2nd ed.). Boston: Allyn & Bacon.

Boersma, F. J., & Chapman, J. W. (1982). Teachers' and mothers' academic achievement expectations for learning disabled children. *Journal of School Psychology, 2,* 216–225.

Boocock, S. S. (1972). *An introduction to the sociology of learning.* Boston: Houghton-Mifflin.

Bosker, R. J. (1992). *The stability and consistency of school effects in primary education.* Enschede, The Netherlands: University of Twente.

Bosker, R. J., & Witziers, B. (1995, January). *School effects, problems, solutions and a meta-analysis.* Paper presented at the International Congress for School Effectiveness and School Improvement, Leeuwarden, The Netherlands.

Bosker, R. J., & Witziers, B. (1996, April). *The magnitude of school effects. Or: Does it really matter which school a student attends?* Paper presented at the annual meeting of the American Educational Research Association, New York.

Bossert, S., Dwyer, D., Rowan, B., & Lee, G. (1982). The instructional management role of the principal. *Educational Administration Quarterly, 18,* 34–64.

Boulanger, D. F. (1981). Ability and science learning. *Journal of Research in Science Teaching, 18*(2), 113–121.

Bracey, G. W. (1997). *Setting the record straight: Responses to misconceptions about public education in the United States.* Alexandria, VA: Association for Supervision and Curriculum Development.

Bradshaw, J., & Amundson, K. J. (1985). *Homework: Helping students achieve.* (Report No. ISBN-087652-1030). Arlington, VA: American Association of School Administrators. (ERIC Document Reproduction Service No. ED266526)

Brandt, R. (1987). On leadership and student achievement: A conversation with Richard Andrews. *Educational Leadership, 45*(1), 9–17.

Brandt, R. (1998). *Powerful learning.* Alexandria, VA: Association for Supervision and Curriculum Development.

Brekelmans, M., Wubbels, T., & Creton, H. A. (1990). A study of student perceptions of physics teacher behavior. *Journal of Research in Science Teaching, 27,* 335–350.

Brewer, D. J., & Stacz, C. (1996). *Enhancing opportunity to learn measures in NCES data.* Santa Monica, CA: RAND.

Brewster, C., & Fager, J. (1998). *Student mentoring.* Portland, OR: Northwest Regional Educational Laboratory.

Brodie, F. M. (1974). *Thomas Jefferson: An intimate history.* New York: Bantam.

Brookover, W. B., Beady, C., Flood, P., Schweitzer, J., & Wisenbaker, J. (1979). *School social systems and student achievement: Schools can make a difference.* New York: Praeger.

Brookover, W. B., & Schneider, J. M. (1975). Academic environments and elementary school achievement. *Journal of Research and Development in Education 9* (1), 82–91.

Brookover, W. B., Schweitzer, J. G., Schneider, J. M., Beady, C. H., Flood, P. K., & Wisenbaker, J. M. (1978). Elementary school social climate and school achievement. *American Research Journal, 15,* 301–318.

Brooks, D. M., & Hawke, G. (1985, April). *Effective and ineffective session opening teacher activity and task structures.* Paper presented at the annual meeting of the American Educational Research Association, Chicago.

Brooks, J. G., & Brooks, M. G. (1999). *In search of understanding: The case for the constructivist classroom.* Alexandria, VA: Association for Supervision and Curriculum Development.

Brooks, J. G., & Brooks, M. G. (2001). Becoming a constructivist teacher. In A. L. Costa (Ed.), *Developing minds: A resource book for teaching thinking* (3rd ed., pp. 150–157). Alexandria, VA: Association for Supervision and Curriculum Development.

Brophy, J. E. (1996). *Teaching problem students.* New York: Guilford.

Brophy, J. E., & McCaslin, M. (1992). Teachers' reports of how they perceive and cope with problem students. *Elementary School Journal, 93,* 3–68.

Brown, C. A., Smith, M. S., & Stein, M. K. (1995, April). *Linking teacher support to enhanced classroom instruction.* Paper presented at the annual meeting of the American Educational Research Association, New York.

Brown, J. S., Collins, A., & Dugild, P. (1989). Situated cognition and the culture of learning. *Educational Researcher, 18*(1), 34–41.

Bruer, J. T. (1993). *Schools for thought: A science of learning in the classroom.* Cambridge, MA: MIT Press.

Bruer, J. T. (1997). Education and the brain: A bridge too far. *Educational Researcher, 26*(8), 4–16.

Bucknam, R. B. (1976). The impact of EBCE: An evaluator's viewpoint. *Illinois Career Education Journal, 33*(3), 32–36.

Burstein, L. (Ed.). (1992). *The IEA study of mathematics III: Student growth and classroom processes.* New York: Pergamon Press.

Byrk, A. S., & Raudenbush, S. W. (1992). *Hierarchical linear models.* New York: Sage.

Byrne, C. J. (1983). *Teacher knowledge and teacher effectiveness: A literature review, theoretical analysis and discussion of research strategy.* Paper presented at the meeting of the Northwestern Educational Research Association, Ellenville, NY.

Cahen, S., & Davis, D. (1987). A between-grade levels approach to the investigation of the absolute effects of schooling on achievement. *American Educational Research Journal, 24,* 1–2.

Caine, R. N., & Caine, G. (1991). *Making connections: Teaching and the human brain.* Alexandria, VA: Association for Supervision and Curriculum Development.

Caine, R. N., & Caine, G. (1997). *Education on the edge of possibility.* Alexandria, VA: Association for Supervision and Curriculum Development.

Caldwell, B. (1992). The principal as leader of the self-managing school. *Journal of Educational Administration, 30,* 6–19.

Callahan, C. M., & Rivera, F. P. (1992). Urban high school youth and handguns: A school-based survey. *Journal of the American Medical Association, 206,* 3,038–3,042.

Campbell, J. (1986). *Winston Churchill's afternoon nap.* New York: Simon & Schuster.

Canter, L., & Canter, M. (1976). *Assertive discipline: A take-charge approach for today's educators.* Seal Beach, CA: Canter & Associates.

Canter, L., & Canter, M. (1992). *Assertive discipline: Positive behavior management for today's classroom.* Santa Monica, CA: Canter & Associates.

Carkhuff, R. R. (1987). *The art of helping VI.* Amherst, MA: Human Resource Development Press.

Carnine, D. (1992). Introduction. In D. Carnine & E. J. Kameenui (Eds.), *Higher order thinking: Designing curriculum for mainstream students* (pp. 1–22). Austin, TX: Pro-ed.

Carnine, D., & Kameenui, E. J. (Eds.). (1992). *Higher order thinking: Designing curriculum for mainstream students.* Austin, TX: Pro-ed.

Carr, E. G., & Durand, V. M. (1985). Reducing behavior problems through functional communication training. *Journal of Applied Behavior Analysis, 18,* 111–126.

Carroll, J. B. (1963). A model of school learning. *Teachers College Record, 64,* 723–733.

Carroll, J., Davies, P., & Richman, B. (1971). *The American Heritage word frequency book.* Boston: Houghton Mifflin.

Caswell, H. L., & Campbell, D. S. (1935). *Curriculum development.* New York: American Book Company.

Cattell, R. B. (1987). *Intelligence: Its structure, growth and action* (Rev. ed.). Amsterdam: North Holland Press. (Original work published 1971)

Center for Community Education. (1989). *A model for rural schools to involve parents in the education of their children.* Bozeman, MT: Montana State University. (ERIC Document Reproduction Service No. ED329395)

Chall, J.S. (1987). Two vocabularies for reading: Recognition and meaning. In M.G. McKeown & M.E. Curtis (Eds.) *The nature of vocabulary acquisition.* (pp. 7–17). Hillsdale, NJ: Erlbaum.

Chapin, M., & Dyck, D. G. (1976). Persistence in children's reading behavior as a function of N length and attribution retraining. *Journal of Abnormal Psychology, 85,* 511–515.

Charters, W. W., Jr. (1963). The social background of teaching. In N. L. Gage (Ed.), *Handbook of research on teaching* (pp. 270–294). Chicago: Rand McNally.

Chase, W. G., & Simon, H. A. (1973). Perception on chess. *Cognitive Psychology, 4,* 55–81.

Chavkin, N. F., & Williams, D. L., Jr. (1985). *Parent involvement in education project. Executive summary of the final report.* Austin, TX: Southwest Educational Development Lab. (ERIC Document Reproduction Service No. ED266874)

Cheng, Y. (1994). Principal's leadership as a critical factor for school performance: Evidence from multi-levels of primary schools. *School Effectiveness and School Improvement, 5,* 299–317.

Christenson, S. L., Rounds, T., & Gorney, D. (1992). Family factors and student achievement: An avenue to increase students' success. *School Psychology Quarterly, 7*(3), 178–206.

Chubb, J. E., & Moe, T. M. (1990). *Politics, markets, and America's schools.* Washington, DC: The Brookings Institute.

Chung, G., & Paul, R. (1996). *School-wide discipline policies: In-school suspension in one middle school.* Charlottesville, VA: University of Virginia. (ERIC Document Reproduction Service No. ED420105)

Cizek, G. J. (2001). Conjectures on the rise and call of standard setting: An introduction to context and practice. In G. J. Cizek (Ed.), *Setting performance standards: Concepts, methods, and perspectives* (pp. 3–18). Mahwah, NJ: Erlbaum.

Clements, B. S., & Evertson, C. M. (1982). *Orchestrating small group instruction in elementary school classrooms* (Report No. 6053). Austin, TX: The Research and Development Center for Teacher Education.

Clinton, G. (2002). Setting up a school-based mentoring program. *The Prevention Researcher, 9*(1), 4–7.

Cobb, P. Yackel, E., & Wood, T. (1992). A constructivist alternative to the representational view of mind in mathematics education. *Journal of Research in Mathematics Education, 23*, 2–33.

Cobb, P., Wood T., Yackel, E., Nicholls, J., Wheatly, G., Trigatti, B., & Perlwitz, M. (1991). Assessment of a problem-centered second grade mathematics project. *Journal for Research in Mathematics Education, 22*, 3–29.

Cohen, D. K., & Hill, H. (1997, April). *Instructional policy and classroom performance: The mathematics reform in California.* Paper presented at the annual meeting of the American Educational Research Association, Chicago.

Cohen, E., & Miller, R. (1980). Coordination and control of instruction in schools. *Pacific Sociological Review, 4*, 446–473.

Cohen, J. (1987). Parents as educational models and definers. *Journal of Marriage and the Family, 49*, 339–349.

Cohen, J. (1988). *Statistical power for the behavioral sciences.* Hillsdale, NJ: Erlbaum.

Cohen, J., & Cohen, P. (1975). *Applied multiple regression/correlation analysis for the behavioral sciences.* New York: John Wiley & Sons.

Coldron, J., & Boulton, P. (1996). What do parents mean when they talk about discipline in relation to their children's school? *British Journal of Sociology of Education, 17*(1), 53–64.

Coldron, J., & Bouton, P. (1991). Happiness as a criterion of parents' choice of school. *Journal of Education Policy, 6*, 169–178.

Coleman, J. S., Campbell, E. Q., Hobson, C. J., McPartland, J., Mood, A. M., Weinfield, F. D., & York, R. L. (1966). *Equality of educational opportunity.* Washington, DC: U. S. Government Printing Office.

Collins, A., Brown, J. S., & Newmann, S. (1989). Cognitive apprenticeship: Teaching students the craft of reading, writing, and mathematics. In L. B. Resnick (Ed.), *Knowing, learning, and instruction: Essays in honor of Robert Glaser* (pp. 453–494). Hillsdale, NJ: Erlbaum.

Colvin, G., Kameenui, E., & Sugai, G. (1993). Reconceptualizing behavior management and schoolwide discipline in general education. *Education and Treatment of Children, 16*, 361–381.

Combs, A. W. (1982). *A personal approach to teaching: Beliefs that make a difference.* Boston: Allyn & Bacon.

Comer, J. P. (1984). Home-school relationships as they affect the academic success of children. *Education and Urban Society, 16*(3), 323–337.

Comer, J. P. (1988). Educating poor minority children. *Scientific American, 259*(5), 42–48.

Comer, J. P., Haynes, N. M., Joyner, E. T., & Ben-Avie, M. (Eds.). 1996). *Rallying the whole village.* New York: Teachers College Press.

Conant, E. H. (1973). *Teacher and paraprofessional work productivity.* Lexington, MA: D. C. Heath.

Conley, S., & Bacharach, S. (1990). From site management to participatory school-site management. *Phi Delta Kappan, 17*(7), 539–544.

Cooper, H. (1989). Synthesis of research on homework. *Educational Leadership, 47*, 85–91.

Cormier, S. M., & Hagman, J. D. (Eds.). (1987). *Transfer of learning: Contemporary research and application.* New York: Academic Press.

Costa, A. L. (1984). A reaction to Hunter's "Knowing Teaching and Supervising." In P. L. Hosford (Ed.), *Using what we know about teaching* (pp. 196–203). Alexandria, VA: Association for Supervision and Curriculum Development.

Cotton, K. (1995). *Effective schooling practices: A research synthesis. 1995 update.* School Improvement Research Series. Portland, OR: Northwest Regional Educational Laboratory.

Covington, M. V. (1984). The motive for self-worth. In R. Ames & C. Ames (Eds.), *Research on motivation in education* (Vol. 1, pp. 77–113). New York: Academic Press.

Covington, M. V. (1985). The role of self-processes in applied social psychology. *Journal of the Theory of Social Behavior, 15*, 355–389.

Covington, M. V. (1987). Achievement motivation, self-attributions and exceptionality. In J. D. Day & J. G. Borkowski (Eds.), *Intelligence and exceptionality* (pp. 173–213). Norwood, NJ: Ablex.

Covington, M. V. (1992). *Making the grade: A self-worth perspective on motivation and school reform.* New York: Cambridge University Press.

Covington, M. V., & Beery, R. G. (1976). *Self-worth and school learning.* New York: Holt, Rinehart & Winston.

Covington, M. V., Omelich, C. L., & Schwarzer, R. (1986). Anxiety, aspirations, and self-concept in the achievement process. A longitudinal model with latent variables. *Motivation and Emotion, 10*, 71–88.

Creemers, B. P. M. (1994). *The effective classroom.* London: Cassell.

Csikszentmihalyi, M. (1990). *Flow: The psychology of optimal experience.* New York: Harper & Row.

Cuban, L. (1990). Performing again, again, and again. *Educational Researcher, 19*(1), 3–13.

Cuban, L. (1992). How the curriculum is shaped. In P. W. Jackson (Ed.), *Handbook of research in curriculum* (pp. 216–247). New York: Macmillan.

Darling-Hammond, L. (1997). *Doing what matters most: Investing in quality teaching.* NY: National Commission on Teaching and America's Future.

Darling-Hammond, L. (1997b). *The right to learn: A blueprint for creating schools that work.* San Francisco: Jossey-Bass.

Darling-Hammond, L. (2000). Teacher quality and student achievement: A review of state policy evidence. *Education Policy Analysis Archives, 8*(1), 1–50. Available: http://epaa.asu.edu/epaa/v8nl

De Charms, R. (1972). Personal causation training in the schools. *Journal of Applied Social Psychology, 2*, 95–113.

deGroot, A. D. (1946). Thought and choice in chess. The Hague: Mouton.

Deal, T. E., & Kennedy, A. A. (1983). Culture and school performance. *Educational Leadership, 40*(5), 14–15.

Deal, T. E, & Peterson, K. D. (1990). *The principal's role in shaping school culture.* Washington, DC: U.S. Department of Education, Office of Educational Research and Improvement.

Deci, E. L., & Ryan, R. M. (1980). The empirical exploration of intrinsic motivational processes. In L. Berkowitz (Ed.), *Advances in experimental social psychology* (Vol. 13, pp. 39–80). New York: Academic Press.

Deci, E. L., & Ryan, R. M. (1985). *Intrinsic motivation and self-determination in human behavior.* New York: Plenum.

Deitz, S. M., & Repp, A. C. (1973). Decreasing classroom misbehavior through the use of DRL schedules and reinforcement. *Journal of Applied Behavior Analysis, 6*, 457–463.

Dickman, M. H., & Stanford-Blair, N. (2002). *Connecting leadership to the brain.* Thousand Oaks, CA: Corwin Press.

Dochy, F., Segers, M., & Buehl, M. M. (1999). The relationship between assessment practices and outcomes of studies: The case of research on prior knowledge. *Review of Educational Research, 69*(2), 145–186.

Dow, P. (1991). *Schoolhouse politics: Lessons from the Sputnik era.* Cambridge, MA: Harvard University Press.

Downing, J. H. (1996). *Establishing a proactive discipline plan in elementary physical education.* Unpublished document, no location given. (ERIC Document Reproduction Service No. ED413291).

Doyle, W. (1986). Classroom organization and management. In M. C. Wittrock (Ed.), *Handbook of research on teaching* (3rd ed., pp. 392–431). New York: Macmillan.

Doyle, W. (1990). Classroom management techniques. In O. C. Moles (Ed.), *Student discipline strategies: Research and practice* (pp. 113–129). Albany, NY: State University of New York Press.

Doyle, W. (1992). Curriculum and pedagogy. In P.W. Jackson (Ed.) *Handbook of research in curriculum* (pp. 486–516). New York: Macmillan.

Drabman, R., & Spitalnik, R. (1973). Social isolation as a punishment procedure: A controlled study. *Journal of Experimental Child Psychology, 5,* 236–249.

Dreikurs, R. (1968). *Psychology in the classroom* (2nd ed.). New York: Harper & Row.

Dreikurs, R., Grunwald, B., & Pepper, F. (1982). *Maintaining sanity in the classroom: Classroom management techniques* (2nd ed.). New York: Harper & Row.

Druckman, D., & Bjork, R. A. (Eds.). (1994). *Learning, remembering, believing: Enhancing human performance.* Washington, DC: National Academy Press.

Duke, D. (1982). Leadership functions and instructional effectiveness. *NASSP Bulletin, 66,* 5–9.

Duke, D. L. (1979). Editor's preface. In D. L. Duke (Ed.), *Classroom management* (78th Yearbook of the National Society for the Study of Education, Part 2, pp. i–xxi). Chicago: University of Chicago Press.

Duke, D., & Canady. L. (1991). *School policy.* New York: McGraw Hill.

Dunne, R. J., & Harris, L. G. (1997). Organizational dimensions of climate and the impact on school achievement. *Journal of Instructional Psychology, 25*(2), 100–114.

Dweck, C. S. (1975). The role of expectations and attributions in the alleviation of learned helplessness. *Journal of Personality and Social Psychology, 31,* 674–685.

Dwyer, D. (1986). Understanding the principal's contribution to instruction. *Peabody Journal of Education, 63,* 3–18.

Eberts, R., & Stone, J. (1988). Student achievement in public schools: Do principals make a difference? *Economics of Education Review, 7,* 291–299.

Eckholm, M. (1992). Evaluating the effects of comprehensive school leadership education in Sweden. *Education and Urban Society, 24,* 365–385.

Edmonds, R. R. (1979a). *A discussion of the literature and issues related to effective schooling.* Cambridge, MA: Center for Urban Studies, Harvard Graduate School of Education.

Edmonds, R. R. (1979b, October). Effective schools for the urban poor. *Educational Leadership, 37,* 15–27.

Edmonds, R. R. (1979c). Some schools work and more can. *Social Policy, 9,* 28–32.

Edmonds, R. R. (1981a). Making public schools effective. *Social Policy, 12*(2).

Edmonds, R. R. (1981b). *A report on the research project, "Search for effective schools..." and certain of the designs for school improvement that are associated with the project.* Unpublished report prepared for NIE. East Lansing, MI: The Institute for Research on Teaching, College of Education, Michigan State University.

Elberts, R. W., & Stone, J. A. (1988). Student achievement in public schools: Do principals make a difference? *Economic Education Review, 1,* 291–299.

Elias, M. J., & Clabby, J. F. (1989). *Social decision making skills: A curriculum guide for the elementary grades.* Gaithersburg, MD: Aspen.

Elias, M. J., & Tobias, S. E. (1996). *Social problem solving: Interventions in the schools.* New York: Guilford.

Elley, W. B. (1989). Vocabulary acquisition from listening to stories. *Reading Research Quarterly, 24,* 174–187.

Elliott, S. N., Witt, J. C., Galvin, G. A., & Peterson, R. (1984). Acceptability of positive and reductive behavioral interventions: Factors that influence teachers' decisions. *Journal of School Psychology, 22,* 353–360.

Ellis, A. (1977). The basic clinical theory of rational-emotive therapy. In A. Ellis & R. Grieger (Eds.), *Handbook of rationale-emotive therapy.* New York: Springer.

Emmer, E. T., & Evertson, C. M. (1981). Synthesis of research on classroom management. *Educational Leadership, 38,* 342–347.

Emmer, E. T., Evertson, C. M., & Anderson, L. M. (1980). Effective classroom management at the beginning of the school year. *The Elementary School Journal, 80,* 219–231.

Emmer, E. T., Evertson, C. M., Sanford, J. P., Clements, B. S., & Worsham, M. E. (1984). *Classroom management for secondary teachers.* Englewood Cliffs, NJ: Prentice-Hall.

Emmons, C. L., Efimba, M. O., & Hagopian, G. (1998). A school transformed: The case of Norman S. Weir. *Journal of Education for Students Placed at Risk, 3*(1), 39–51.

Engle, S. H., & Ochoa, A. S. (1988). *Education for democratic citizenship: Decision making in the social studies.* New York: Teachers College Press.

English, F. W. (2000). *Deciding what to teach and test: Developing, aligning, and auditing the curriculum.* Thousand Oaks, CA: Corwin Press.

Epstein, J. L. (1991). Effects on student achievement of teachers' practices of parent involvement. In S. B. Silvern (Ed.), *Advances in reading/language research: Vol. 5. Literacy through family, community, and school interaction* (pp. 261–276). Greenwich, CT: JAI Press.

Epstein, J. L., & Becker, H. J. (1982). Teacher practices of parent involvement. *Elementary School Journal, 83,* 103–113.

Evertson, C. M. (1982). Differences in instructional activities in higher- and lower-achieving junior high English and math classes. *The Elementary School Journal, 82,* 329–350.

Evertson, C. M., & Emmer, E. T. (1982). Effective management at the beginning of the school year in junior high classes. *Journal of Educational Psychology, 74,* 485–498.

Evertson, C. M., Emmer, E. T., Clements, B. S., Sanford, J. P., & Worsham, M. E. (1984). *Classroom management for elementary teachers.* Englewood Cliffs, NJ: Prentice-Hall.

Evertson, C. M., Sanford, J. P, & Emmer, E. T. (1981). Effects of class heterogeneity in junior high school. *American Educational Research Journal, 18,* 219–232.

Fan, X., & Chen, M. (2001). Parental involvement and students' academic achievement: A meta-analysis. *Educational Psychology Review, 13*(1), 1–22.

Farr, R., Tulley, M., & Rayford, L. (1984). *Local district adoption practices in non-adoption states.* Unpublished manuscript. Bloomington, IN: School of Education, University of Indiana.

Fehrman, P. G., Keith, T. Z., & Reimers, T. M. (1987). Home influence on school learning: Direct and indirect effects of parental involvement on high school grades. *Journal of Educational Research, 80,* 330–337.

Feiman-Nemser, S., & Floden, R. E. (1986). The culture of teaching. In M. C. Wittrock, (Ed.), *Handbook of research on teaching* (3rd ed, pp. 505–526). New York: Macmillan.

Feldman, R. A., Caplinger, T. E., & Wodarski, J. S. (1983). *The St. Louis conundrum: The effective treatment of antisocial youths*. Englewood Cliffs, NJ: Prentice-Hall.

Ferguson, P., & Womack, S. T. (1993). The impact of subject matter and education coursework on teaching performance. *Journal of Teacher Education, 44*(1), 55–63.

Ferguson, R. F. (1991, Summer). Paying for public education: New evidence on how and why money matters. *Harvard Journal on Legislation, 28*(2), 465–498.

Ferguson, R. F., & Ladd, H. F. (1996). How and why money matters: An analysis of Alabama schools. In H. Ladd (Ed.), *Holding schools accountable* (pp. 265–298). Washington, DC: Brookings Institute.

Filipczak, J., Lordeman, A., & Friedman, R. M. (1977, April). *Parental involvement in the schools: Toward what end?* Paper presented at the annual meeting of the American Educational Research Association, New York.

Finn, C. E., Jr. (1991). *We must take charge: Our schools and our future*. New York: The Free Press.

Finn, C. E., Jr. (1998, March 25). Why America has the world's dimmest bright kids. *Wall Street Journal*, p. A22.

Fisher, C. W., Filby, N., Marliave, R. S., Cahen, L. S., Dishaw, M. M., Moore, J. E., & Berliner, D. C. (Eds.). (1978). *Teaching behaviours, academic learning time and student achievement*. San Francisco: Far West Laboratory of Educational Research and Development.

Fisher, D., Henderson, D., & Fraser, G. (1995). Interpersonal behavior in senior high school biology classes. *Research in Science Education, 25*(2), 125–133.

Fitts, P. M., & Posner, M. I. (1967). *Human performance*. Belmont, CA: Brooks Cole.

Flavell, J. H. (1971). Stage-related properties of cognitive development. *Cognitive Psychology, 2*, 421–453.

Florian, J. (1999). *Teacher survey of standards-based instruction: Addressing time*. Aurora, CO: Mid-continent Research for Education and Learning.

Foxx, R. M. (1978). An overview of overcorrection. *Journal of Pediatric Psychology, 3*, 97–101.

Fraser, B. J. (1986). Two decades on perceptions of classroom environment. In B. J. Fraser (Ed.), *The study of learning environments* (pp. 1–33). Salem, OR: Assessment Research.

Fraser, B. J., Walberg, H. J., Welch, W. W., & Hattie, J. A. (1987). Synthesis of educational productivity research [Special issue]. *International Journal of Educational Research, 11*(2), 145–252.

Freeman, B. (1994). Power motivation and youth: An analysis of troubled students and student leaders. *Journal of Counseling and Development, 72*(6), 661–671.

Friedkin, N. E., & Slater, M. R. (1994). School leadership and performance: A social network approach. *Sociology of Education, 67*, 139–157.

Fullan, M. (1982). *The meaning of educational change*. New York: Teachers College Press.

Fullan, M. G. (1993). *Change forces: Probing the depths of educational reform*. New York: Falmer Press.

Fullan, M., & Hargreaves, A. (1996). *What's worth fighting for in your school?* New York: Teachers College Press.

Gaddy, B. B., Hall, T. W., & Marzano, R. J. (1996). *School wars: Resolving our conflicts over religion and values*. San Francisco: Jossey-Bass Publishers.

Garet, M., Porter, A. C., Desimone, L., Birman, B. F., & Yoon, K. S. (2001). What makes professional development effective? Results from a national sample of teachers. *American Educational Research Journal, 38*(4), 115–145.

Gazzaniga, M. S. (1992). *Nature's mind: The biological roots of thinking, emotions, sexuality, language and intelligence*. New York: Basic Books.

Geisler-Brenstein, E., & Schmeck, R. R. (1996). The revised inventory of learning processes: A multifaceted perspective on individual differences in learning. In M. Birenbaum & F. J. R. C. Cochy (Eds.), *Alternatives in assessment of achievements, learning processes, and prior knowledge* (pp. 284–317). Boston: Kluwer.

Gigliotti, R. J., & Brookover, W. B. (1975). The learning environment: A comparison of high and low achieving elementary schools. *Urban Education, 10*, 245–261.

Glasman, N., & Binianimov, I. (1981). Input-output analyses of schools. *Review of Educational Research, 51*, 509–539.

Glass, G. V. (1976). Primary, secondary, and meta-analyses of research. *Educational Researcher, 5*, 3–8.

Glass, G. V., McGaw, B., & Smith, M. L. (1981). *Meta-analysis in social research*. Beverly Hills, CA: Sage Publication.

Glass, G. V., Willson, V. L., & Gottman, J. M. (1975). *Design and analysis of time-series experiments*. Boulder, CO: Colorado Associated University Press.

Glasser, W. (1969). *Schools without failure*. New York: Harper and Row.

Glasser, W. (1986). *Control theory in the classroom*. New York: Harper and Row.

Glasser, W. (1990). *The quality school: Managing students without coercion*. New York: Harper and Row.

Glickman, C. D. (1993). *Renewing American schools: A guide for school-based action*. San Francisco: Jossey-Bass.

Glickman, C. D. (1998). *Education and democracy: The premise of American schools*. San Francisco: Jossey-Bass.

Goldstein, A. P., Sprafkin, R. P., Gershaw, J. N., & Klein, P. (1980). *Skillstreaming the adolescent*. Champaign, IL: Research Press.

Goldstein, H. (1997). Methods of school effectiveness research. *School Effectiveness and School Improvement, 8*(4), 369–395.

Gonder, P. O. (1981). Exchange school and community resources. In D. Davies (Ed.), *Communities and their schools*. New York: McGraw-Hill.

Gonzalez, R-A. M., & Blanco, N. C. (1991). Parents and children: Academic values and school achievement. *International Journal of Educational Research, 15*, 163–169.

Good, T. L. (1982). How teachers' expectations affect results. *American Education, 18*(10), 25–32.

Good, T. L., & Brophy, J. E. (1986). School effects. In M. C. Wittrock (Ed.), *Handbook of research on teaching* (3rd ed., pp. 570–602). New York: Macmillan.

Good, T. L., & Brophy, J. E. (1994). *Looking in classrooms* (6th ed.). New York: Harper Collins.

Good, T., & Brophy, J. (1995). *Contemporary educational psychology* (5th ed.). White Plains, NY: Longman.

Goodson, B. D., & Hess, R. D. (1975). *Parents as teachers of young children: An evaluative review of some contemporary concepts and programs*. Washington, DC: U.S. Department of Health, Education and Welfare, Office of Education.

Gordon, T. (1970). *Parent effectiveness training*. New York: Wyden.

Gordon, T. (1974). *Teacher effectiveness training*. New York: Wyden.

Gottfredson, D. C., Hybl, L. G., Gottfredson, G. D., & Castaneda, R. P. (1986). School climate assessment instruments: A review. In H. Freiberg, A. Driscoll, & S. Knight (Eds.), *School climate* (pp. 49–81). Bloomington, IN: Phi Delta Kappa Center on Evaluation, Development, and Research.

Gottfredson, G. D. (1987). American education–American delinquency. *Today's Delinquent*, 6, 5–70.

Graue, M. E., Weinstein, T., & Walberg, H. J. (1983, April). *School-based home instruction and learning: A quantitative synthesis.* Paper presented at the annual meeting of the American Educational Research Association, Montreal, Canada.

Graves, M. F., & Slater, W. H. (1987, April). *Development of reading vocabularies on rural disadvantaged students, intercity disadvantaged students and middle class suburban students.* Paper presented at the AERA conference, Washington, DC.

Grayson, D. A., & Martin, M. D. (1985). *Gender expectations and student achievement: Participant manual.* Downey, CA: Los Angeles County Office of Education.

Green, J., & Barnes, D. (1993). *Discipline in secondary schools: How administrators deal with student misconduct.* Muncie, IN: Teachers College, Ball State University. (ERIC Document Reproduction Service No. ED357507)

Griffith, J. (2000). School climate on group evaluation and group consensus: Student and parent perceptions of the elementary school environment. *The Elementary School Journal*, 101(1), 35–61.

Grogger, J. (1997). Local violence and educational attainment. *The Journal of Human Resources*, 32(4), 659–682.

Grossman, J. B., & Johnson, A. (2002). Assessing the effectiveness of mentoring programs. *The Prevention Researcher*, 9(1), 8–11.

Gullatt, D. E., & Lemoine, D. A. (1997). Truancy: What's a principal to do? *American Secondary Education*, 16(1), 7–12.

Guskey, T. R. (2000). *Evaluating professional development.* Thousand Oaks, CA: Corwin Press.

Guzzetti, B. J., Snyder, T. E., & Glass, G. V. (1993). Promoting conceptual change in science: A comparative meta-analysis of instructional interventions from reading education and science education. *Reading Research Quarterly*, 28(2), 117–155.

Hall, G. E., & Hord, S. M. (1987). *Change in schools: Facilitating the process.* Albany, NY: State University of New York Press.

Hall, G. E., & Loucks, S. F. (1978). A developmental model for determining whether the treatment is actually implemented. *American Educational Research Journal*, 14(3), 263–270.

Hall, G. E., Loucks, S. F., Rutherford, W. L., & Newlove, B. W. (1975). Levels of use of the innovation: A framework for analyzing innovation adoption. *Journal of Teacher Education*, 26(1), 52–56.

Haller, E. P., Child, D. A., & Walberg, H. J. (1988). Can comprehension be taught? A quantitative synthesis of "metacognitive studies." *Educational Researcher*, 17(9), 5–8.

Hallinger, P., & Murphy, J. (1985). Assessing the instructional leadership behavior of principals. *The Elementary School Journal*, 82(2), 217–248.

Hallinger, P., & Murphy, J. (1986). The social context of effective schools. *American Journal of Education*, 94, 328–355.

Hallinger, P., & Murphy, J. F. (1987). Assessing and developing instructional leadership. *Educational Leadership*, 45(1), 54–61.

Hallinger, P., Bickman, L., & Davis, K. (1996). School context, principal leadership, and student reading achievement. *The Elementary School Journal*, 96(5), 527–549.

Hambleton, R. K. (2001). Setting performance standards on educational assessments and criteria for evaluating the process. In G. J. Cizek (Ed.), *Setting performance standards: Concepts, methods, and perspectives* (pp. 89–116). Mahwah, NJ: Erlbaum.

Haney, W., Madaus, G., & Kreitzer, A. (1987). Charms talismanic: Testing teachers for the improvement of American education. In E. Z. Rothkopf (Ed.), *Review of research in education: Vol. 14* (pp. 169–238). Washington, DC: American Educational Research Association.

Harnischfeger, A., & Wiley, D. (1978). *Conceptual and policy issues in elementary school teaching: Learning.* Paper presented at the Annual Meeting of the American Educational Research Association, Toronto.

Harris, A., & Jacobson, M. (1972). *Basic elementary reading vocabulary.* New York: Macmillan.

Harris, K. R. (1985). Definitional, parametric, and procedural considerations in timeout interventions and research. *Exceptional Children*, 51, 279–288.

Hart, L. A. (1983). *Human brain and human learning.* New York: Longman.

Harter, S. (1980). The perceived competence scale for children. *Child Development*, 51, 218–235.

Harter, S. (1999). *The construction of the self: A developmental perspective.* New York: The Guilford Press.

Hattie, J. A. (1992). Measuring the effects of schooling. *Australian Journal of Education*, 36(1), 5–13.

Haycock, K. (1998). Good teaching matters. . . . a lot. *Thinking K–16*, 3(2), 1–14.

Heck, R. (1993). School context, principal leadership, and achievement: The case of secondary schools in Singapore. *Urban Review*, 25, 151–166.

Heck, R. H., & Marcoulides, G. A. (1990). Examining contextual differences in the development of instructional leadership and school achievement. *The Urban Review*, 22(4), 247–265.

Herman, J. L., Klein, D. C. D., & Abedi, J. (2000). Assessing students' opportunity to learn: Teacher and student perspectives. *Educational Measurement: Issues and Practice*, 19(4), 16–24.

Hersey, P., & Blanchard, K. (1977). *Management of organizational behavior: Utilizing human resources.* Englewood Cliffs, NJ: Prentice-Hall.

Hess, R. D., Holloway, S. D., Dickson, W. P., & Price, G. G. (1984). Maternal variables as predictors of children's school readiness and later achievement in vocabulary and mathematics in sixth grade. *Child Development*, 55, 1902–1912.

Heurnstein, R. J., & Murray, C. (1994). *The bell curve: Intelligence and class structure in American life.* New York: The Free Press.

Hicks, D. (1993). Narrative discourse and classroom learning: An essay response to Eagan's "Narrative of learning: A voyage of implications." *Linguistics and Education*, 5, 127–148.

Hirsch, E. D., Jr. (1987). *Cultural literacy: What every American needs to know.* Boston: Houghton Mifflin.

Hirsch, E. D., Jr. (1996). *The schools we need and why we don't have them.* New York: Doubleday.

Ho Sui-Chu, E., & Willms, J. D. (1996). Effects of parental involvement on eighth-grade achievement. *Sociology of Education*, 69, 126–141.

Holt, S. B., & O'Tuel, F. S. (1989). The effect of Sustained Silent Reading and Writing on achievement and attitudes of seventh and eighth grade students reading two years below grade level. *Reading Improvement*, 26(4), 290–297.

Hopkins, D., & Ainscow, M. (1993). *Making sense of school improvement: An interim account of the IQEA project.* Paper presented at the ESRC Seminar Series on School Effectiveness and School Improvement. Sheffield.

Hord, S. M., Rutherford, W. L., Huling-Austin, L., & Hall, G. E. (1987). *Taking charge of change.* Alexandria, VA: Association for Supervision and Curriculum Development.

Hoy, W., Tarter, C. J., & Kottkamp, B. (1991). *Open schools, healthy schools.* Newbury Park, CA: Sage.

Hunt, L. C. (1970). Six steps to the individualized reading program (IRP). *Elementary English, 48,* 27–32.

Hunter, J. E., & Schmidt, F. L. (1990). *Methods of meta-analysis: Correcting error and bias in research findings.* Newbury Park, CA: Sage.

Hunter, M. (1969). *Teach more—faster!* El Segundo, CA: TIP Publications.

Hunter, M. (1984). Knowing, teaching, and supervising. In P. Hosford (Ed.), *Using what we know about teaching* (pp. 169–192). Alexandria, VA: Association for Supervision and Curriculum Development.

Husen, T. (Ed.). (1967a). *International study of achievement in mathematics* (Vol. 1). New York: John Wiley & Sons.

Husen, T. (Ed.). (1967b). *International study of achievement in mathematics* (Vol. 2). New York: John Wiley & Sons.

Irvin, L. K., & Lundervold, D. A. (1988). Social validation of decelerative (punishment) procedures by special educators of severely handicapped students. *Research in Developmental Disabilities, 9,* 331–350.

Jencks, C., Smith, M. S., Ackland, H., Bane, M. J., Cohen, D., Grintlis, H., Heynes, B., & Michelson, S. (1972). *Inequality: A reassessment of the effects of family and schooling in America.* New York: Basic Books.

Jenkins, J. R., Stein, M. L., & Wysocki, K. (1984). Learning vocabulary through reading. *American Educational Research Journal, 21*(4), 767–787.

Jensen, A. R. (1980). *Bias in mental testing.* New York: The Free Press.

Johnson, D. W., & Johnson, R. T. (1979). Cooperation, competition and individualization. In H. J. Walberg (Ed.), *Educational environments and effects* (pp. 101–119). Berkeley, CA: McCutchan.

Johnson, F. L., Brookover, W. B., & Farrell, W. C. (1989, April). *The effects of principals', teachers', and students' perceptions of parents' role. Interest and expectation for their children's education on student academic achievement.* Paper presented at the American Educational Research Association Annual Meeting, San Francisco, CA.

Joyce, B., Wolf, J., & Calhoun, E. (1993). *The self-renewing schools.* Alexandria, VA: Association for Supervision and Curriculum Development.

Kameenui, E. J. (1992). Toward a scientific pedagogy of learning disabilities. In D. Carnine & E. J. Kameenui (Eds.), *Higher order thinking: Designing curriculum for mainstream students* (pp. 247–267). Austin, TX: Pro-ed.

Karweit, N. L. (1983). *Time on task: A research review.* Baltimore: Johns Hopkins University Press.

Kauffman, J. M., & Wong, K. L. (1991). Effective teachers of students with behavioral disorders: Are generic teaching skills enough? *Behavioral Disorders, 16,* 225–237.

Kaufman, K. F., & O'Leary, K. D. (1972). Reward, cost, and self-evaluation procedures for disruptive adolescents in a psychiatric hospital at school. *Journal of Applied Behavior Analysis, 5,* 293–309.

Keith, T. R. (1987). Homework. In A. Thomas & J. Grimes (Eds.), *Children's needs: Psychological perspectives* (pp. 275–282). Washington, DC: The National Association of School Psychologists.

Kendall, J. (2000). Topics: A roadmap to standards. *NASSP Bulletin, 84*(620), 37–44.

Kendall, J. S., & Marzano, R. J. (2000). *Content knowledge: A compendium of standards and benchmarks for K–12 education* (3rd ed.). Alexandria, VA: Association for Supervision and Curriculum Development.

Kerman, S., Kimball, T., & Martin, M. (1980). *Teacher expectations and student achievement.* Bloomington, IN: Phi Delta Kappan.

Kinder, D., & Bursuck, W. (1992). The research for a unified social studies curriculum: Does history really repeat itself? In D. Carnine & E. J. Kameenui (Eds,), *Higher order thinking: Designing curriculum for mainstreamed students* (pp. 23–38). Austin, TX: Pro-ed.

Kingery, P. M., McCoy-Simandle, L. & Clayton, R. (1997). Risk factors for adolescent violence: The importance of vulnerability. *School Psychology International, 18,* 49–60.

Kinneavy, J. L. (1991). Rhetoric. In J. Flood, J. M. Jensen, D. Lapp, & J. R. Squire (Eds.), *Handbook of research on teaching the English language arts.* New York: Macmillan.

Kintsch, W. (1974). *The representation of meaning in memory.* Hillsdale, NJ: Lawrence Erlbaum.

Kintsch, W. (1979). On modeling comprehension. *Educational Psychologist, 1,* 3–14.

Klausner, S. Z. (1965). *The quest for self-control.* New York: Free Press.

Knight, P. (1992). How I use portfolios in mathematics. *Educational Leadership, 49*(8), 71–72.

Kohn, A. (1993). *Punished by rewards: The trouble with gold stars, incentive plans, A's, praise and other bribes.* Boston: Houghton Mifflin.

Kohn, A. (1996). *Beyond discipline: From compliance to community.* Alexandria, VA: Association for Supervision and Curriculum Development.

Kohn, A. (2000). *The case against standardized testing: Raising the scores, ruining the schools.* Portsmouth, NH: Heinemann.

Kolers, P. A. (1976). Reading a year later. *Journal of Experimental Psychology: Human Learning and Memory, 2,* 554–565.

Kolers, P. A. (1979). A pattern analyzing basis of recognition. In L. S. Cermak and F. I. M. Craik (Eds.), *Levels of processing in human memory.* Hillsdale, NJ: Lawrence Erlbaum.

Kounin, J. S. (1970). *Discipline and group management in classrooms.* New York: Holt, Rinehart & Winston.

Kounin, J. S. (1983). *Classrooms: Individual or behavior settings? Micrographs in teaching and learning.* (General Series No. 1). Bloomington, IN: Indiana University, School of Education. (ERIC Document Reproduction Service No. 240 070)

Kube, B., & Ratigan, G. (1992). Putting the attendance policy to the test. *The Clearing House, 65*(3), 348–350.

Kumar, D. D. (1991). A meta-analysis of the relationship between science instruction and student engagement. *Education Review, 43*(1), 49–66.

LaBerge, D., & Samuels, S. J. (1974). Toward a theory of automatic information processing in reading comprehension. *Cognitive Psychology, 6,* 293–323.

Larson, J. (1998). Managing student aggression in high schools: Implications for practice. *Psychology in the Schools, 35*(3), 283–295.

Leal, R. (1994). Conflicting views of discipline in San Antonio schools. *Education and Urban Society, 27*(1), 35–44.

Leary, T. (1957). *An interpersonal diagnosis of personality*. New York: Ronald Press Company.

LeDoux, J. E. (1994, June). Emotion, memory, and brain. *Scientific American, 270*(6), 50–57.

LeDoux, J. E. (1996). *The emotional brain: The mysterious underpinnings of emotional life*. New York: Simon & Schuster.

Leinhardt, G., & Greens, J. G. (1986). The cognitive skill of teaching. *Journal of Educational Psychology, 78*, 75–95.

Leler, H. (1983). Parent education and involvement in relation to the schools and to parents of school-aged children. In R. Hoskins & D. Adamson (Eds.), *Parent education and public policy* (pp. 141–180). Norwood, NJ: Ablex.

Lepper, M. R., Keavney, M., & Drake, M. (1996). Intrinsic motivation and extrinsic rewards: A commentary on Cameron and Pierce's meta-analysis. *Review of Educational Research, 66*, 5–32.

Lesh, R., & Zowejeski, J. S. (1992). Problem solving. In T. R. Post (Ed.), *Teaching mathematics in grades K–8: Research-based methods* (pp. 47–88). Needham Heights, MA: Allyn & Bacon.

Levine, D. U, & Lezotte, L. W. (1990). *Unusually effective schools: A review and analysis of research and practice*. Madison, WI: National Center for Effective Schools Research and Development.

Levine, J. R. (1992, April). *The effects of different attendance policies on student attendance and achievement*. Paper presented at the annual meeting of the Eastern Psychological Association, Boston, MA. (ERIC Document Reproduction Service No. ED348762)

Levy, J., Wubbels, T., Brekelmans, M., & Morganfield, B. (1997). Language and cultural factors in students' perceptions of teacher communication style. *International Journal of Intercultural Relationships, 21*, 29–56.

Lindsley, O. R. (1972). From Skinner to precision teaching. In J. B. Jordan & L. S. Robbins (Eds.), *Let's try doing something else kind of thing*. Arlington, VA: Council on Exceptional Children.

Lipham, J. (1981). *Effective principal, effective school*. Reston, VA: American Association of School Principals.

Lipsey, M. W., & Wilson, D. B. (1993). The efficacy of psychological, educational, and behavioral treatment: Confirmation from meta-analysis. *American Psychologist, 48*(12), 1181–1209.

Litow, L., & Pumroy, D. K. (1975). A brief review of classroom group-oriented contingencies. *Journal of Applied Behavior Analysis, 8*, 341–347.

Little, J. W. (1990). The persistence of privacy: Autonomy and initiative in teachers' professional relations. *Teachers College Record, 91*(4), 509–536.

Little, J. W. (1993). Teachers' professional development in a climate of educational reform. *Educational Evaluation and Policy Analysis, 15*(2), 129–151.

Lobitz, W. C. (1974). A simple stimulus cue for controlling disruptive classroom behavior. *Journal of Abnormal Child Psychology, 2*, 143–152.

Lortie, D. (1975). *School teacher. A sociological study*. Chicago, IL: Univeristy of Chicago Press.

Losen, S. M., & Diament, B. (1978). *Parent conferences in the schools*. Boston: Allyn & Bacon.

Loucks, S. F. (1975). *A study of the relationship between teacher level of use of the innovation of individualized instruction and student achievement*. Unpublished doctoral dissertation, University of Texas at Austin.

Lowry, R., Sleet, D., Duncan, C., Powell, K., & Kolbe, L. (1995). Adolescents at risk for violence. *Educational Psychology Review, 7*(1), 7–39.

Luyten, H. (1994). *School effects: Stability and malleability*. Enschide The Netherlands: University of Twente.

Madaus, G. F., Airasian, P. W., & Kellaghan, T. (1980). *School effectiveness: A reassessment of the evidence*. New York: McGraw-Hill.

Madaus, G. F., Kellaghan, T., Rakow, E. A., & King, D. (1979). The sensitivity of measures of school effectiveness. *Harvard Educational Review, 49*(2), 207–230.

Madsen, C. H., Jr., Becker, W. C., & Thomas, D. R. (1968). Rules, praise, and ignoring: Elements of elementary and classroom control. *Journal of Applied Behavior Analysis, 1*, 139–150.

Maeroff, G. I. (1988). Blueprint for empowering teachers. *Phi Delta Kappan, 69*(7), 473–477.

Malone, T. W. (1981a). Toward a theory of intrinsically motivating instruction. *Cognitive Science, 4*, 333–369.

Malone, T. W. (1981b, April). *What makes things fun to learn? A study of intrinsically motivating computer games*. Paper presented at the American Education Research Association Annual Meeting, Los Angeles, CA.

Marjoribanks, K. (1988). Perceptions of family environments, educational and occupational outcomes: Social-status differences. *Perceptual and Motor Skills, 66*, 3–9.

Markus, H., & Ruvulo, A. (1990). Possible selves. Personalized representations of goals. In L. Pervin (Ed.), *Goal concepts in psychology* (pp. 211–241). Hillsdale, NJ: Lawrence Erlbaum.

Martens, B. K., & Meller, P. J. (1990). The application of behavioral principles to educational settings. In T. B. Gutkin & C. R. Reynolds (Eds.), *Handbook of school psychology* (pp. 612–634). New York: Wiley.

Martini, M. (1995). Features of home environments associated with children's school success. *Early Child Development and Care, 111*, 49–68.

Marzano, R. J. (1998a). *A theory-based meta-analysis of research on instruction*. Aurora, CO: Mid-continent Research for Education and Learning. (ERIC Document Reproduction Service No. ED 427 087)

Marzano, R. J. (1998b). Unpublished data on time necessary to teach standards. Aurora, CO: Mid-continent Regional Educational Laboratory.

Marzano, R. J. (1992). *A different kind of classroom: Teaching with dimensions of learning*. Alexandria, VA: Association for Supervision and Curriculum Development.

Marzano, R. J. (2000a). *A new era of school reform: Going where the research takes us*. Aurora, CO: Mid-continent Research for Education and Learning. (ERIC Document Reproduction Service No. ED454255)

Marzano, R. J. (2000b). *Transforming classroom grading*. Alexandria, VA: Association for Supervision and Curriculum Development.

Marzano, R. J. (2002). *Identifying the primary instructional concepts in mathematics: A linguistic approach*. Englewood, CO: Marzano & Associates.

Marzano, R. J., Gaddy, B. B., & Dean, C. (2000). *What works in classroom instruction?* Aurora, CO: Mid-continent Research for Education and Learning.

Marzano, R. J., & Kendall, J. S. (1996). *A comprehensive guide to designing standards-based districts, schools, and classrooms*. Alexandria, VA: Association for Supervision and Curriculum Development.

Marzano, R. J., Kendall, J. S., & Gaddy, B. B. (1999). *Essential Knowledge: The debate over what American students should know*. Aurora, CO Mid-continent Regional Educational Laboratory.

Marzano, R. J., & Marzano, J. S. (in preparation). *Classroom management that works*.

Marzano, R. J., Pickering, D. J., Arredondo, D. E., Blackburn, G. J., Brandt, R. S., Moffett, C. A., Paynter, D. E., Pollock, J. E., & Whisler, J. S. (1997). *Dimensions of learning trainer's manual (2nd ed.)*, Alexandria, VA: Association for Supervision and Curriculum Development.

Marzano, R. J., Pickering, D. J., & Pollock, J. E. (2001). *Classroom instruction that works: Research-based strategies for increasing student achievement*. Alexandria, VA: Association for Supervision and Curriculum Development.

Marzano, R. J., & Riley, A. (1984). Unpublished data. Aurora, CO: Mid-continent Regional Educational Laboratory.

Maslow, A. (1968). *Toward a psychology of being*. New York: Harper.

Maslow, A. (1971). *The farther reaches of human nature*. New York: Viking.

Mayer, D. P., Mullens, J. E., Moore, M. T., & Ralph, J. (2000). *Monitoring school quality: An indicator's report*. Washington, DC: U.S. Department of Education: National Center for Education Statistics.

Mayer, V. J., & Lewis, D. K. (1979). An evaluation of the use of a time-series single-subject design. *Journal of Research in Science Teaching, 16*, 137–144.

McClelland, D. C. (1965). Toward a theory of motive acquisition. *American Psychologist, 20*, 321–333.

McCombs, B. L., & Whisler, J. S. (1997). *The learner-centered classroom and school*. San Francisco: Jossey-Bass.

McDill, E., Rigsby, L., & Meyers, E. (1969). Educational climates of high schools: Their effects and sources. *American Journal of Sociology, 74*, 567–586.

McKeown, M. G., & Curtis, M. E. (Eds.). (1987). *The nature of vocabulary acquisition*. Hillsdale, NJ: Erlbaum.

McMillan, J. H. (1997). *Classroom assessment: Principles and practices for effective instruction*. Needham Heights, MA: Allyn & Bacon.

McMillan, J. H. (2000). *Basic assessment concepts for teachers and administrators*. Thousand Oaks, CA: Corwin Press.

Medway, F. (1979). Causal attributions for school-related problems: Teacher perceptions and teacher feedback. *Journal of Educational Psychology, 71*, 809–818.

Meichenbaum, D. (1977). *Cognitive behavior modification*. New York: Plenum Press.

Melaragno, R. J., Keesling, J. W., Lyons, M. F., Robbins, A. E., & Smith, A. G. (1981). *Parents and federal education programs: Vol. 1. The nature, causes, and consequences of parental involvement*. Santa Monica, CA: Systems Development Corp.

Miller, A., Ferguson, E., & Simpson, R. (1998). The perceived effectiveness of rewards and sanctions in primary schools: Adding in the parental perspective. *Educational Psychology, 18*(1), 55–64.

Miller, L. (1994, September 7). Violence, discipline, top public's school concerns, poll finds. *Education Week*, p. 7.

Miller, S., & Sayre, K. (1986, April). *Case studies of affluent effective schools*. Paper presented at the annual meeting of the American Educational Research Association, San Francisco.

Monk, D. H. (1994). Subject matter preparation of secondary mathematics and science teachers and student achievement. *Economics of Education Review, 13*(2), 125–145.

Morrow, L. M., Pressley, M., Smith, J. K., & Smith, M. (1997). The effect of a literature-based program integrated into literacy and science instruction. *Reading Research Quarterly, 32*, 54–76.

Mortimore, P., Sammons, P., Stoll, L., Lewis, D., & Ecob, R. (1988). *School matters: The junior years*. Somerset: Open Books.

Murnane, R. J. (1985, June). *Do effective teachers have common characteristics: Interpreting the quantitative research evidence*. Paper presented at the National Research Council Conference on Teacher Quality in Science and Mathematics, Washington, DC.

Murphy, J., & Hallinger, P. (1989). Equity as access to learning: Curricular and instructional differences. *Journal of Curriculum Studies, 21*, 129–149.

Murphy, J., & Hallinger, P. (1992). The principalship in an era of transformation. *Journal of Educational Administration, 30*, 77–88.

Nagy, N. M., Campenni, C. E., & Shaw, J. N. (2000). *A survey of Sustained Silent Reading practices in seventh-grade classrooms* [Online]. Available: http://readingonline.org

Nagy, W. E., & Anderson, R. C. (1984). How many words are there in printed school English? *Reading Research Quarterly, 19*(3), 304–330.

Nagy, W. E., & Herman, P. A. (1984). *Limitations of vocabulary instruction* (Tech. Rep. No. 326). Urbana, IL: University of Illinois, Center for the Study of Reading. (ERIC Document Reproduction Service No. ED248498)

Nagy, W. E., & Herman, P. A. (1987). Breadth and depth of vocabulary knowledge: Implications for acquisition and instruction. In M. C. McKeown & M. E. Curtis (Eds.), *The nature of vocabulary instruction* (pp. 19–36). Hillsdale, NJ: Erlbaum.

National Center for Educational Statistics (2002). *CCD Quick Facts*. http://nces.ed.gov/ccd/quickfacts.html

National Commission on Excellence in Education (1983). *A nation at risk: The imperative for educational reform*. Washington, DC: Government Printing Office.

National Commission on Teaching and America's Future (1998). *What matters most: Teaching for America's future*. New York: Author.

National Council of Teachers of Mathematics (2000). *Principles and standards for school mathematics*. Reston, VA: Author.

National Education Association. (1982). *Productive relationships: Parent-school-teacher*. Washington, DC: Author.

National Education Commission on Time and Learning (1994). *Prisoners of time*. Washington, DC: U. S. Department of Education.

National Education Goals Panel. (1994, August). *Data volume for the national education goals report, Vol. 1: National data*. Washington, DC: Author.

National Institute of Child Health and Human Development (2000). Report of the National Reading Panel. *Teaching children to read: An evidence-based assessment of the scientific research literature on reading and its implications for reading instruction* [Online]. Available: http://www.nichd.nih.gov/publications/nrp/smallbook.htm

National Research Council (1999). *Uncommon measures: Equivalence and linkage among educational tests*. Washington, DC: Author.

Nelson, J. R. (1996). Designing schools to meet the needs of students who exhibit disruptive behavior. *Journal of Emotional and Behavioral Disorders, 4*(3), 147–161.

Nelson, J. R., Martella, R., & Galand, B. (1998). The effects of teaching school expectations and establishing a consistent consequence on formal office disciplinary actions. *Journal of Emotional and Behavioral Disorders, 6*(3), 153–161.

Nelson, R., & Carr, B. A. (1999). *Think Time™ strategy for schools: Bringing order to the classroom (2nd ed)*. Longmont, CO: Sopris West.

Neufeld, J., & Freeman, D. (1992, November). *Teachers' perceptions of the principal's role in facilitating teacher improvement within the ASU-Tempe PDS*. Paper presented at the annual meeting of the Arizona Educational Research Organization, Phoenix, AZ.

Neuman, S. B. (1980). Television: Its effects on reading and school achievement. *The Reading Teacher, 33*, 801–805.

Nisbett, R. E., & Wilson, T. D. (1977). Telling more than we can know: Verbal reports on mental processes. *Psychological Review, 84*, 231–259.

Noguera, P. A. (1995). Preventing and producing violence: A critical analysis of responses to school violence. *Harvard Educational Review, 65*(2), 189–212.

Nuthall, G. (1999). The way students learn: Acquiring knowledge from an integrated science and social studies unit. *The Elementary School Journal, 99*(4), 303–341.

Nuthall, G., & Alton-Lee, A. (1993). Predicting learning from student experience of teaching: A theory of student knowledge construction in classrooms. *American Educational Research Journal, 30*(4), 799–840.

Nuthall, G., & Alton-Lee, A. (1995). Assessing classroom learning: How students use their knowledge and experience to answer classroom achievement test questions in science and social studies. *American Educational Research Journal, 32*(1), 185–223.

O'Leary, K. D., Becker, W. C., Evans, M. B., & Saudargas, R. A. (1969). A token reinforcement program in a public school: A replication and systematic analysis. *Journal of Applied Behavior Analysis, 2*, 3–13.

Oakes, J. (1989). Detracking schools: Early lessons from the field. *Phi Delta Kappan, 73*, 448–454.

Oliva, P. F. (1982). *Developing the curriculum.* Boston: Little Brown.

Olmsted, P. P. (1983). *Long-term effects of Parent Education Follow Through program participation.* Chapel Hill: University of North Carolina, School of Education.

Onikama, D. L., Hammond, O. W., & Koki, S. (1998). *Family involvement in education: A synthesis of research for Pacific educators.* Honolulu, HI: Pacific Regional Educational Laboratory.

Owens, R. G. (1987). *Organizational behavior in education* (3rd ed.). Englewood Cliffs, NJ: Prentice-Hall.

Paik, H. (1995). *Television viewing and mathematics achievement.* Paper presented at the annual meeting of the International Communication Association. (ERIC Document Reproduction Service No. ED384940)

Paivio, A. (1990). *Mental representations: A dual coding approach.* New York: Oxford University Press.

Parent Teacher Association. (1997). *PTA Guide to the National Standards for Parent/Family Involvement Programs* [Online]. Available: http://www.pta.org/programs/stnrdgd.htm [1998, April].

Park, C. (1976). The Bay City experiment. . . as seen by the director. *Journal of Teacher Education, 7*, 5–8.

Parker, F. C., & McCoy, J. F. (1977). School-based intervention for the modification of excessive absenteeism. *Psychology in the Schools, 14*, 84–88.

Patrick, J. (1992). *Training: Research and practice.* San Diego, CA: Academic Press.

Paulson, S. E. (1994a). Parenting style and parental involvement: Relations with adolescent achievement. *Mid-Western Educational Researcher, 7*, 6–11.

Paulson, S. E. (1994b). Relations of parenting style and parental involvement with ninth-grade students' achievement. *Journal of Early Adolescence, 14*, 250–267.

Peng, S. S., & Wright, D. (1994). Explanation of academic achievement of Asian American students. *Journal of Educational Research, 87*, 346–352.

Peterson, K. (1994). *Building collaborative cultures. Seeking ways to reshape urban schools.* North Central Regional Educational Laboratory. Available: http://www.ncrel.org/sdrs/areas/issues/educators/leadership/le0pet.htm

Piaget, J. (1971). *Genetic epistemology* (E. Duckworth, Trans.). New York: Norton.

Pilgreen, J. L. (2000). *The SSR handbook: How to organize and manage a sustained silent reading program.* Portsmouth, NH: Boynton/Cook Publishers.

Pilgreen, J., & Krashen, S. (1993, Fall). Sustained Silent Reading with English as a Second Language high school students: Impact on reading comprehension, reading frequency, and reading enjoyment. *School Library Media Quarterly*, 21–23.

Pinker, S. (1997). *How the mind works.* New York: W. W. Norton & Company.

Popham, W. J. (2001). *The truth about testing: An educator's call to action.* Alexandria, VA: Association for Supervision and Curriculum Development.

Powell, G. (1980, December). *A meta-analysis of the effects of "imposed" and "induced" imagery upon word recall.* Paper presented at the annual meeting of the National Reading Conference, San Diego, CA. (ERIC Document Reproduction Service No. ED199644)

Pressley, M. (1998). *Reading instruction that works: The case for balanced teaching.* New York: Guilford.

Purkey, S. C., & Smith, M. S. (1982). *Effective schools: A review.* Madison, WI: Wisconsin Center for Educational Research, School of Education, University of Wisconsin at Madison.

Purkey, S. C., & Smith, M. S. (1983). Effective schools: A review. *The Elementary School Journal, 83*(4), 427–452.

Radencich, M. C., & Schumm, J. S. (1988). *How to help your child with homework.* Minneapolis, MN: Free Spirit Publishing, Inc.

Raudenbush, S. W., & Byrk, A. S. (1988). Methodological advances in analyzing the effects of schools and classrooms on student learning. In E. Z. Rothkopf (Ed.), *Review of research in education: Vol. 15* (pp. 423–475). Washington, DC: American Educational Research Association.

Raudenbush, S. W., & Willms, J. D. (1995). The estimation of school effects. *Journal of Educational and Behavioral Statistics, 20*(4), 307–335.

Reeves, D. B. (2002). *Holistic accountability: Serving students, schools, and community.* Thousand Oaks, CA: Corwin Press.

Reigeluth, C. M., & Stein, F. S. (1983). The elaboration theme of instruction. In C. M. Reigeluth (Ed.), *Instruction-design theories and models: An overview of their current status* (pp. 335–381). Hillsdale, NJ: Erlbaum.

Reilly, J. M. (1992). *Mentorship: The essential guide for school and business.* Dayton, OH: Ohio Psychology Press.

Reimers, T. M., Wacker, D. P., & Koeppl, G. (1987). Acceptability of behavioral interventions: A review of the literature. *School Psychology Review, 16*, 212–227.

Resnick, L. B. (1987). Learning in school and out. *Educational Researcher, 16*(9), 13–20.

Restak, R. M. (1994). *The modular brain.* New York: Touchstone.

Reuter, G. S. (1963). *The length of the school day.* Chicago: American Federation of Teachers.

Reynolds, D., & Teddlie, C. (2000). The process of school effectiveness. In C. Teddlie & D. Reynolds (Eds.), *The international handbook of school effectiveness research* (pp. 134–159). New York: The Falmer Press.

Reynolds, D., & Teddlie, C. (with Hopkins, D., & Stringfield, S.). (2000). Linking school effectiveness and school improvement. In C. Teddlie & D. Reynolds (Eds.), *The international handbook of school effectiveness research* (pp. 206–231). New York: Falmer Press.

Rickover, H. G. (1959). *Education and freedom.* New York: E. P. Dutton.

Robbins, C., & Ehri, L. C. (1994). Reading storybooks to kindergartners helps them learn new vocabulary words. *Journal of Educational Psychology, 86*, 54–64.

Robitaille, D. (Ed.). (1993). *Curriculum frameworks for mathematics and science.* Vancouver, Canada: Pacific Educational Press.

Rogosa, D. R., Brandt, D., & Zimowsky, M. (1982). A growth curve approach to the measurement of change. *Psychological Bulletin, 90*, 726–748.

Rolfhus, E. L., & Ackerman, P. L. (1999). Assessing individual differences in knowledge: Knowledge, intelligence, and related traits. *Journal of Educational Psychology, 91*(3), 511–526.

Rosenau, J. S. (1998). *Familial influences on academic risk in high school: A multi-ethnic study.* (Doctoral dissertation, Temple University, 1998). (UMI No. 9911056)

Rosenholtz, S. J. (1989). *Teachers' workplace: The social organization of schools.* New York: Teachers College Press.

Rosenhouse, J., Feitelson, D., Kita, B., & Goldstein, Z. (1997). Interactive reading aloud to Israeli first graders: Its contribution to literacy development. *Reading Research Quarterly, 32,* 168–183.

Rosenshine, B. (1983). Teaching functions in instructional programs. *Elementary School Journal, 83*(4), 335–351.

Rosenthal, R., & Jacobson, L. (1968). *Pygmalion in the classroom: Teacher expectation and pupils' intellectual development.* New York: Holt, Rinehart & Winston.

Rosenthal, R., & Rubin, D. B. (1982). A simple general purpose display of magnitude of experimental effect. *Journal of Educational Psychology, 74*(2), 166–169.

Rothblum, E. D., Solomon, L. J., & Murakami, J. (1986). Affective, cognitive and behavioral differences between high and low procrastinators. *Journal of Counseling Psychology, 33,* 387–394.

Rothmann, R. (1988). Student proficiency in math is "dismal," NAEP indicates. *Education Week, I,* 23–26.

Rotter, J. C., & Robinson, E. H., III. (1982). *Parent-teacher conferencing.* Washington, DC: National Education Association.

Rovee-Collier, C. (1995). Time windows in cognitive development. *Developmental Psychology, 31*(2), 147–169.

Rowe, K. J., & Hill, P. W. (1994). *Multilevel modeling in school effectiveness research: How many levels.* Paper presented at the International Congress for School Effectiveness and Improvement, Melbourne, Australia.

Rowe, K. J., Hill, P. W., & Holmes-Smith, P. (1995). Methodological issues in educational performance and school effectiveness research: A discussion with worked examples. *Australian Journal of Education, 39*(3), 217–248.

Rowe, M. (1974). Wait-time and rewards as instructional variables, their influence on language, logic and fate control. Part 1 Wait-time. *Journal of Research in Science Teaching, 11,* 81–94.

Rumelhart, D. E., & Norman, D. A. (1981). Accretion, tuning and restructuring: Three modes of learning. In J. W. Colton & R. Klatzky (Eds.), *Semantic factors in cognition.* Hillsdale, NJ: Lawrence Erlbaum.

Rutter, M., Maughan, B., Mortimore, P., Ouston, J., & Smith, A. (1979). *Fifteen thousand hours: Secondary schools and their effects on children.* Cambridge, MA: Harvard University Press.

Sadker, M., & Sadker, D. (1994). *Failing at fairness: How America's schools cheat girls.* New York: Macmillan.

Sammons, P. (1999). *School effectiveness: Coming of age in the twenty-first century.* Lisse: Swets and Zeitlinger.

Sammons, P., Hillman, J., & Mortimore, P. (1995). *Key characteristics of effective schools: A review of school effectiveness research.* London: Office of Standards in Education and Institute of Education.

Sanders, W. L., & Horn, S. P. (1994). The Tennessee value-added assessment system (TVAAS): Mixed-model methodology in educational assessment. *Journal of Personnel Evaluation in Education, 8,* 299–311.

Sanford, J. P., Emmer, E. T., & Clements, B. S. (1983). Improving classroom management. *Educational Leadership, 40,* 56–61.

Sautter, R. C. (1995). Standing up to violence. *Phi Delta Kappan.* [Special Report], k1–k12.

Saylor, J. G., & Alexander, W. M. (1974). *Planning curriculum for schools.* New York: Holt, Rinehart & Winston.

Schalock, D. (1979). Research on teacher selection. In D. C. Berliner (Ed.), *Review of research in education, Vol. 7.* Washington, DC: American Educational Research Association.

Schank, R. C. (1990). *Tell me a story: A new look at real and artificial memory.* New York: Charles Scribner & Sons.

Scheerens, J. (1992). *Effective schooling: Research, theory and practice.* London: Cassell.

Scheerens, J., & Bosker, R. (1997). *The foundations of educational effectiveness.* New York: Elsevier.

Schiefele, U., & Krapp, A. (1996). Topics of interest and free recall of expository text. *Learning and Individual Differences, 8*(2), 141–160.

Schiefele, U., Krapp, A., & Winteler, A. (1992). Interest as a predictor of academic achievement: A meta-analysis of research. In K. A. Renninger, S. Hidi, & A. Krapp (Eds.), *The role of interest in learning and development* (pp. 183–212). Hillsdale, NJ: Erlbaum.

Schlechty, P. C. (1990). *Schools for the 21st century.* San Francisco: Jossey-Bass.

Schmidt, W. H., McKnight, C. C., & Raizen, S. A. (1996). *Splintered vision: An investigation of U.S. science and mathematics education: Executive summary.* Lansing, MI: U.S. National Research Center for the Third International Mathematics and Science Study, Michigan State University.

Schmoker, M. (1999). *Results: The key to continuous school improvement* (2nd ed.). Alexandria, VA: Association for Supervision and Curriculum Development.

Schmoker, M. (2001). *The results fieldbook: Practical strategies from dramatically improved schools.* Alexandria, VA: Association for Supervision and Curriculum Development.

Scott-Jones, D. (1984). Family influences on cognitive development and school achievement. *Review of Research in Education, 11,* 259–304.

Seligman, M. E. P. (1975). *Helplessness: On depression, development, and death.* San Francisco: Freeman.

Seligman, M. E. P. (1991). *Learned optimism.* New York: Knopf.

Seligman, M. E. P., Maier, S. F., & Geer, J. (1968). The alleviation of learned helplessness in the dog. *Journal of Abnormal Psychology, 73,* 256–262.

Seligman, M. E. P., Maier, S. F., & Solomon, R. L. (1971). Unpredictable and uncontrollable aversive events. In F. R. Brush (Ed.), *Aversive conditioning and learning.* New York: Academic Press.

Sergiovanni, T. J. (1992). *Moral leadership: Getting to the heart of school improvement.* San Francisco: Jossey-Bass.

Sewall, A. M., & Chamberlin, G. D. (1997). *Safety or discipline: The real issue in public schools.* Unpublished paper, University of Arkansas at Little Rock. (ERIC Document Reproduction Service No. ED417–470)

Sheats, D., & Dunkleberger, G. E. (1979). A determination of the principal's effect in school-initiated home contacts concerning attendance of elementary school students. *Journal of Educational Research, 72*(6), 310–312.

Sheets, R. (1994, February). *Student voice: Factors that cause teacher/student confrontations in a pluralistic classroom.* Paper presented at the Annual Conference of the National Association of Minority Education, Seattle, WA. (ERIC Document Reproduction Service No. ED371089)

Shiffrin, R. M., & Schneider, W. (1977). Controlled and automatic human information processing: II. Perceptual learning, automatic attending, and a general theory. *Psychological Review, 84,* 127–190.

Shure, M. B. (1992). *I can problem solve: An interpersonal cognitive problem-solving program: Intermediate elementary grades.* Champaign, IL: Research Press.

Simon, H. A. (1980). Problem solving and education. In D. T. Tuma & F. Reif (Eds.), *Problem solving and education: Issues in teaching and learning.* Hillsdale, NJ: Erlbaum.

Sipe, C. L. (1999). Mentoring adolescents: What we have learned. In J. Baldwin Grossman (Ed.), *Contemporary issues in mentoring.* Philadelphia: Public/Private Ventures.

Snow, R. E., & Lohman, D. F. (1989). Implications of cognitive psychology for educational measurement. In R. Linn (Ed.), *Educational measurement* (3rd ed., pp. 263–331). London: Collier Macmillan Publishers.

Snyder, C. R. (1984, September). Excuses, excuses: They sometimes actually work to relieve the burden of blame. *Psychology Today, 18,* 50–55.

Soar, R. S., & Soar, R. M. (1979). Emotional climate and management. In P. L. Peterson & H. J. Walberg (Eds.), *Research on teaching: Concepts, findings, and implications* (pp. 97–119). Berkeley, CA: McCutchan.

Soar, R. S., Medley, D. M., & Coker, H. (1983). Teacher evaluation: A critique of currently used methods. *Phi Delta Kappan, 65*(4), 239–246.

Solomon, L. J., & Rothblum, E. D. (1984). Academic procrastination: Frequency and cognitive-behavioral correlates. *Journal of Counseling Psychology, 31,* 503–509.

Sousa, D. (2001). *How the brain learns* (2nd ed.). Thousand Oaks, CA: Corwin Press.

Stage, S. A., & Quiroz, D. R. (1997). A meta-analysis of interventions to decrease disruptive classroom behavior in public education settings. *School Psychology Review, 26*(3), 333–368.

Stahl, S. A., & Fairbanks, M. M. (1986). The effects of vocabulary instruction: A model-based meta-analysis. *Review of Educational Research, 56*(1), 72–110.

Stallworth, N. T., & Williams, D. L., Jr. (1982). *Executive summary of the final report: A survey of parents regarding parent involvement in the schools.* Austin, TX: Southwest Educational Development Laboratory.

Steinkamp, M. W., & Maehr, M. L., (1983). Affect, ability, and science achievement: A quantitative synthesis of correlational research. *Review of Educational Research, 53* (3), 369–396.

Stevenson, H. W., & Lee, S. (1990). Contexts of achievement: A study of American, Chinese, and Japanese children. *Monographs of the Society for Research in Child Development, 55,* 1–106.

Stevenson, H. W., & Stigler, J. W. (1992). *The learning gap: Why our schools are failing and what we can learn from Japanese and Chinese education.* New York: Simon & Schuster.

Stigler, J. W., & Hiebert, J. (1999). *The teaching gap: Best ideas from the world's teachers for improving education in the classroom.* New York: The Free Press.

Stodolsky, S. S. (1989). Is teaching really by the book? In P. W. Jackson & S. Haroutunian-Gordon (Eds.), *Eighty-ninth yearbook of the National Society for the Study of Education, Part I* (pp. 159–184). Chicago: University of Chicago Press.

Stringfield, S., & Teddlie, C. (1989). The first three phases of the Louisiana school effectiveness study. In B. P. M. Creemers, T. Peters, & D. Reynolds (Eds.), *School effectiveness and school improvement: Proceedings of the Second International Congress, Rotterdam* (pp. 281–294). Lisse: Swets & Zeitlinger.

Sugai, G., & Colvin, G. (1996). Debriefing: A proactive addition to negative consequences for problem behavior. *Education and Treatment of Children, 20,* 209–221.

Swick, K. (1991). *A rural teacher-parent partnership for the enhancement of school success: An executive summary.* (ERIC Document Reproduction Service No. ED336205)

Sylwester, R. (1995). *A celebration of neurons: An educator's guide to the human brain.* Alexandria, VA: Association for Supervision and Curriculum Development.

Sylwester, R. (2000). *A biological brain in a cultural classroom: Applying biological research to classroom management.* Thousand Oaks, CA: Corwin Press.

Sylwester, R., & Margulies, N. (1998). *Discover your brain.* Tucson, AZ: Zephyr Press.

Tamir, P. (1996). Science assessment. In M. Birenbaum & F. J. R. C. Dochy (Eds.), *Alternatives in assessment of achievements, learning processes, and prior knowledge* (pp. 93–129). Boston: Kluwer.

Tangri, S., & Moles, O. (1987). Parents and the community. In V. Richardson-Koehler (Ed.), *Educators' handbook: A research perspective* (2nd ed., pp. 519–550). New York: Longman.

Teddlie, C., & Reynolds, D. (Eds.). (2000). *The international handbook of school effectiveness research.* New York: The Falmer Press.

Teddlie, C., & Stringfield, S. (1993). *Schools do make a difference: Lessons learned from a 10-year study of school effects.* New York: Teachers College Press.

Teddlie, C., Reynolds, D., & Sammons, P. (2000). The methodology and scientific properties of school effectiveness research. In C. Teddlie & D. Reynolds (Eds.), *The international handbook of school effectiveness research* (pp. 55–133). New York: Falmer Press.

Teddlie, C., Stringfield, S, & Reynolds, D. (2000). Context issues within school effectiveness research. In C. Teddlie & D. Reynolds, *The international handbook of school effectiveness research* (pp. 160–185). New York: The Falmer Press.

Teddlie, C., Stringfield, S., Wimpelberg, R., & Kirby, P. (1989). Contextual differences in models for effective schooling in the USA. In B. P. M. Creemers, T. Peters, & D. Reynolds (Eds.), *School effectiveness and school improvement: Proceedings of the Second International Congress,* pp. 34–59. Rotterdam: Swets & Zeitlinger.

Thomas, M. D. (n.d). *Volunteerism in public education.* Salt Lake City, UT: Salt Lake School District.

Tobias, S. (1994). Interest, prior knowledge and learning. *Review of Educational Research, 64*(1), 37–54.

Tobin, T. J., & Sugai, G. M. (1999). Using sixth-grade school records to predict school violence, chronic discipline problems, and high school outcomes. *Journal of Emotional and Behavioral Disorders, 7*(1), 40–53.

Tollefson, N., & Chen, J. (1988). Consequences of teachers' attributions for student failure. *Teaching and Teacher Education, 4,* 259–265.

Toulmin, S., Rieke, R., & Janik, A. (1981). *An introduction to reasoning.* New York: Macmillan.

Tyack, D. (1974). *The one best system: A history of American urban education.* Cambridge, MA: Harvard University Press.

Tyack, D., & Tobin, W. (1994). The "grammar" of schooling: Why has it been so hard to change? *American Educational Research Journal, 31,* 453–479.

U.S. Department of Education, National Center for Education Statistics. (1998). *Pursuing excellence: A study of U.S. twelfth-grade mathematics and science achievement in international context.* Washington, DC: U. S. Government Printing Office.

van der Werf, G. (1997). Differences in school and instruction characteristics between high-, average-, and low-effective schools. *School Effectiveness and School Improvement, 8*(4), 430–448.

van Dijk, T. A. (1977). *Text and context.* London: Longman.

van Dijk, T. A. (1980). *Macrostructures.* Hillsdale, NJ: Erlbaum.

van Dijk, T. A., & Kintsch, W. (1983). *Strategies of discourse comprehension.* Hillsdale, NJ: Lawrence Erlbaum.

Van Houten, R., Nau, P. A., Mackenzie-Keating, S. E., Sameoto, D., & Colavecchia, B. (1982). An analysis of some variables influencing the effectiveness of reprimands. *Journal of Applied Behavior Analysis, 15,* 65–83.

van Tartwijk, J. (1993). *Sketches of teacher behavior.* Utrecht The Netherlands: WCC.

van Tartwijk, J., Fisher, D., Fraser, B., & Wubbels, T. (1994). *The interpersonal significance of molecular behavior of science teachers in lab lessons: A Dutch perspective.* Paper presented at the 1994 NARST Annual Meeting, Anaheim, CA. (ERIC Document Reproduction Service No. ED368579)

Venesky, R. L. (1992). Textbooks in school and society. In P. W. Jackson (Ed.), *Handbook of research in curriculum* (pp. 438–461). New York: Macmillan.

Vernon, P. E. (1965). Personality factors in teacher trainee selection. *British Journal of Educational Psychology, 35,* 140–149.

Villani, C. J. (1996). *The interaction of leadership and climate in four suburban schools: Limits and possibilities.* Doctoral dissertation, Fordham University, New York, NY. (UMI No. 9729612)

Voekl, K. E. (1993). Academic achievement and expectations among African-American students. *Journal of Research and Development in Education, 27,* 42–55.

Wahba, N. A., & Bridwell, L. G. (1976). Maslow reconsidered: A review of research on the need of hierarchy theory. *Organizational Behavior and Human Performance, 15,* 212–240.

Walberg, H. J. (1980). *A psychological theory of educational productivity.* Washington, DC: National Institute of Education. (ERIC Document Reproduction Service No. ED206042)

Walberg, H. J. (1984). Improving the productivity of America's schools. *Educational Leadership,* 19–27.

Walberg, H. J. (1997). Uncompetitive American schools: Causes and cures. In *Brookings papers on educational policy.* Washington, DC: The Brookings Institute.

Walberg, H. J. (1999). Productive teaching. In H. C. Waxman & H. J. Walberg (Eds.), *New directions for teaching practice and research,* 75–104. Berkeley, CA: McCutchen Publishing Corporation.

Walberg, H. J., & Waxman, H. C. (1983). Teaching, learning, and the management of instruction. In D. C. Smith (Ed.), *Essential knowledge for beginning educators,* pp. 34–59, Washington, DC: American Association of Colleges for Teacher Education.

Walker, H. M., Colvin, G., & Ramsey, E. (1995). *Antisocial behavior in school: Strategies and best practices.* Pacific Grove, CA: Brooks/Cole.

Wang, M. C., Haertel, G. D., & Walberg, H. J. (1993). Toward a knowledge base for school learning. *Review of Educational Research, 63*(3), 249–294.

Ward, C. M. (1998). Student discipline and alleviating criminal behavior in the inner city. *The Urban Review, 30*(1), 29–49.

Watson, T. S., Sterling, H. E., & McDade, A. (1997). Demythifying behavioral consultation. *School Psychology Review, 26,* 467–474.

Weglinsky, H. (2000). *How teachers matter: Bringing the classroom back into discussions of teacher quality.* Princeton, NJ: Educational Testing Service.

Weiner, B. (1972). *Theories of motivation: From mechanism to cognition.* Chicago: Markham.

Weiner, B. (1974). *Achievement motivation and attribution theory.* Morristown, NJ: General Learning Press.

Weiner, B., Frieze, L., Kukla, A., Reed, L., Rest, S., & Rosenbaum, R. (1971). Perceiving the causes of success and failure. In E. E. Jones, D. E. Kanouse, H. H. Kelley, R. E. Nisbett, S. Valins, & B. Weiner (Eds.), *Attribution: Perceiving the causes of behavior* (pp. 95–121). Morristown, NJ: General Learning Press.

Weissberg, R. P., Jackson, A., & Shriver, T. (1993). Promoting positive social development and health practices in young urban adolescents. In M. J. Elias (Ed.), *Social decision making and life skills development: Guidelines for middle school educators* (pp. 45–78). Gaithersburg, MD: Aspen.

Welch, F. (1974). Relationships between income and schooling. In F. N. Kerlinger (Ed.), *Review of research in education.* Ithaca, NY: Peacock.

White, K. R. (1982). The relationship between socioeconomic status and academic achievement. *Psychological Bulletin, 91*(3), 461–481.

Whitener, E. M. (1989). A meta-analytic review of the effect on learning of the interaction between prior achievement and instructional support. *Review of Educational Research, 59*(1), 65–86.

Wiley, D., & Yoon, B. (1995). Teacher reports of opportunity to learn: Analyses of the 1993 California learning assessment system. *Educational Evaluation and Policy Analysis, 17*(3), 355–370.

Wilkins, J. L. M. (1997). *Modeling correlates of problem-solving skills: Effects of opportunity-to-learn on the attainment of higher-order thinking skills in mathematics.* Unpublished doctoral dissertation, University of Illinois at Urbana-Champaign. (UMI No. 9732288)

Willett, J. B. (1985). *Investigating systematic individual difference in academic growth.* Unpublished doctoral dissertation, Stanford University, Palo Alto, CA.

Willett, J. B. (1988). Questions and answers in the measurement of change. *Review of Research in Education* (Vol. 15, pp. 345–422). Washington, DC: American Educational Research Association.

Williams, P. A., Haertel, E. H., Haertel, G. D., & Walberg, H. J. (1982). The impact of leisure-time television on school learning. *American Educational Research Journal, 19,* 19–50.

Willingham, W. W., Pollack, J. M., & Lewis, C. (2002). Grades and test scores: Accounting for observed differences. *Journal of Educational Measurement, 39,* (1), 1–37.

Willms, J. D. (1992). *Monitoring school performance: A guide for educators.* Washington, DC: The Falmer Press.

Wilson, T. D., & Linville, P. W. (1985). Improving the performance of college freshmen with attributional techniques. *Journal of Personal and Social Psychology, 49,* 287–293.

Wilson, V. L. & Putnam, R. R. (1982). A meta-analysis of pretest sensitization effects on experimental design. *American Educational Research Journal, 19*(2), 249–258.

Winborn, J. D. (1992, November). *A study of the effectiveness of a Saturday school in reducing suspension, expulsion, and corporal punishment.* Paper presented at the annual meeting of the Mid-south Educational Research Association, Knoxville, TN. (ERIC Document Reproduction Service No. ED355663)

Wise, K. C., & Okey, J. R. (1983). A meta-analysis of the effects of various science teaching strategies on achievement. *Journal of Research in Science Teaching, 20*(5), 415–425.

Witziers, B., & Bosker, R. J. (1997, January). *A meta-analysis on the effects of presumed school effectiveness enhancing factors*. Paper presented at ICSEI, Memphis, TN.

Wlodkowski, R. J. (1982). *Discipline: The great false hope*. Milwaukee, WI: The University of Wisconsin-Milwaukee. (ERIC Document Reproduction Service No. 224782)

Wolfe, P. (2001). *Brain matters: Translating research into classroom practice*. Alexandria, VA: Association for Supervision and Curriculum Development.

Wright, S. P., Horn, S. P., & Sanders, W. L. (1997). Teacher and classroom context effects on student achievement. Implications for teacher evaluation. *Journal of Personnel Evaluation in Education, 11*, 57–67.

Wubbels, T., Brekelmans, M., van Tartwijk, J., & Admiral, W. (1999). Interpersonal relationships between teachers and students in the classroom. In H. C. Waxman & H. J. Walberg (Eds.), *New directions for teaching practice and research* (pp. 151–170). Berkeley, CA: McCutchan.

Wubbels, T., & Levy, J. (1993). *Do you know what you look like? Interpersonal relationships in education*. London: The Falmer Press.

Wyatt, W. J., & Hawkins, R. P. (1987). Rate of teachers' verbal approval and disapproval: Relationship to grade level, classroom activity, student behavior, and teacher characteristics. *Behavior Modification, 11*, 27–51.

Yap, K. O., & Enoki, D. Y. (1995). In search of the elusive magic bullet: Parental involvement and student outcomes. *School Community Journal, 5*, 97–106.

Yoon, B., Burstein, L., & Gold, K. (undated). *Assessing the content validity of teachers' reports of content coverage and its relationship to student achievement* (CSE Rep. No. 328). Los Angeles: Center for Research in Evaluating Standards and Student Testing, University of California, Los Angeles.

Zabel, M. K. (1986, November). Timeout use with behaviorally disordered students. *Behavioral Disorders*, 15–21.

Zoeller, C., Mahoney, G., & Weiner, B. (1983). Effects of attribution training on the assembly task performance of mentally retarded adults. *American Journal of Mental Deficiency, 88*, 109–112.

INDEX

Page references for figures are indicated with an *f* after the page number.

ABOUT THE AUTHOR

Robert J. Marzano is a Senior Scholar at Mid-Continent Research for Education and Learning in Aurora, Colorado; an Associate Professor at Cardinal Stritch University in Milwaukee, Wisconsin; Vice President of Pathfinder Education, Inc.; and a private consultant operating out of Centennial, Colorado. He is responsible for translating research and theory into classroom practice. His most recent book, *A Handbook for Classroom Instruction That Works* (Marzano, Norford, Paynter, Pickering, & Gaddy, 2001; ASCD), is a practical handbook for using the groundwork and theory found in *Classroom Instruction That Works: Research Strategies for Increasing Student Achievement* (Marzano, Pickering, & Pollock, 2001; ASCD). In addition, Marzano headed a team of authors who developed *Dimensions of Learning* (ASCD), and is the senior author of *Tactics for Thinking* (ASCD). Other notable publications address standards as described in the two books *Essential Knowledge: The Debate Over What American Students Should Know* (Marzano, Kendall, & Gaddy, 1999; ASCD/McREL) and *A Comprehensive Guide to Designing Standards-Based Districts, Schools, and Classrooms* (Marzano & Kendall, 1996; ASCD/McREL). Marzano has also recently completed books entitled *Transforming Classroom Grading* (2000, ASCD) and *Designing a New Taxonomy of Educational Objectives* (2000, Corwin Press). He has developed programs and practices used in K–12 classrooms that translate current research and theory in cognition into instructional methods.

Marzano received his B.A. in English from Iona College in New York; an M.Ed. in Reading/Language Arts from Seattle University, Seattle, Washington; and a Ph.D. in Curriculum and Instruction from the University of Washington, Seattle. Marzano was a Senior Fellow with McREL from 1981 until 2001; before that he was a tenured associate professor at the University of Colorado at Denver, and a high school English teacher and department chair.

An internationally known trainer and speaker, Marzano has authored 19 books and more than 150 articles and chapters in books on such topics as reading and writing instruction, thinking skills, school effectiveness, restructuring, assessment, cognition, and standards implementation.

He may be contacted at 7127 S. Danube Court, Centennial, CO 80016. Phone: 303-796-7683. E-mail: robertjmarzano@aol.com.

RELATED ASCD RESOURCES:
INSTRUCTIONAL STRATEGIES

ASCD stock numbers are in parentheses.

Audiotapes

Instructional Approaches of Superior Teachers (#299202) by Lloyd Campbell

Planning Units Around Essential Understanding & Questions (#298294) by Lynn Erickson

Putting Best Practices to Work on Behalf of Improving Student Learning (#298132) by Kathleen Fitzpatrick

Teaching for the 21st Century (#297247) by Linda Darling-Hammond

Using Dimensions of Learning as a Tool to Increase Student Success (#200120) by James Riedl and Lucinda Riedl

Online Professional Development

Go to ASCD's Home Page (http://www.ascd.org) and click on Training Opportunities:

ASCD Online Tutorials on Standards, Differentiating Instruction, and the Brain and Learning

ASCD Professional Development Online Courses in Differentiating Instruction, Leadership, and the Brain and Learning

Print Products

Becoming a Better Teacher: Eight Innovations That Work (#100043) by Giselle Martin-Kniep

The Differentiated Classroom: Responding to the Needs of All Learners (#199040) by Carol Ann Tomlinson

Dimensions of Learning Teacher's Manual, 2nd Edition (#197133) by Robert J. Marzano, Debra Pickering, and others

Educating Everybody's Children: Diverse Teaching Strategies for Diverse Learners (#195024) edited by Robert Cole

Enhancing Professional Practice: A Framework for Teaching (#196074) by Charlotte Danielson

A Field Guide to Using Visual Tools (#100023) by David Hyerle

A Different Kind of Classroom: Teaching with Dimensions of Learning (#61192107) by Robert J. Marzano

A Handbook for Classroom Instruction that Works (#101041) by Robert J. Marzano, Jennifer S. Norford, Diane E. Paynter, Debra J. Pickering, and Barbara B. Gaddy

Research You Can Use to Improve Results (#399238) by Kathleen Cotton

Tools for Learning: A Guide for Teaching Study Skills (#61190086) by M. D. Gall, Joyce P. Gall, Dennis R. Jacobsen, and Terry L. Bullock

Understanding by Design (#198199) by Grant Wiggins and Jay McTighe

The Understanding by Design Handbook (#199030) by Jay McTighe and Grant Wiggins

Visual Tools for Constructing Knowledge (#196072) by David Hyerle

Videotapes

Helping Students Acquire and Integrate Knowledge Series (5 videos) (#496065) by Robert Marzano

How to Improve Your Questioning Techniques (#499047), Tape 5 of the "How To" Series

How to Use Graphic Organizers to Promote Student Thinking (#499048), Tape 6 of the "How To" Series

Concept Definition Map (#499262), Tape 5 of The Lesson Collection Video Series: Reading Strategies

Library of Teaching Strategies Part I & II (#614178)

What Works in Schools (3 videos) (#403047)

For additional resources, visit us on the World Wide Web (http://www.ascd.org), send an e-mail message to member@ascd.org, call the ASCD Service Center (800-933-ASCD or 703-578-9600, then press 2), send a fax to 703-575-5400, or write to Information Services, ASCD, 1703 N. Beauregard St., Alexandria, VA 22311-1714 USA.